God the Problem

God the Problem

Gordon D. Kaufman

Harvard University Press, Cambridge, Massachusetts,

For
David and Gretchen
Anne and Edmund

whose generation
may decide
the future of "God"

To believe in God is to long for His existence and, further, it is to act as if He existed; it is to live by this longing and to make it the inner spring of our action.

Unamuno

Contents

Preface   xi

Part I. Introduction

1
The Problem of God   3

2
Christian Theology and the Scientific Study of Religion   17

Part II. God

3
Transcendence without Mythology   41

4
Two Models of Transcendence   72

5
God as Symbol   82

Part III. God and the World

6
On the Meaning of "Act of God"   119

7
Revelation and Cultural History   148

8
God and Evil   171

Part IV. Belief and Unbelief

9
Secular, Religious, and Theistic World-Views   203

10
The Foundations of Belief   226

11
The Secular Utility of "God-Talk"   257

Index   273

Preface

The present volume consists of essays written over a number of years and addressed to particular occasions or problems; it is not, therefore, a strictly continuous argument, and it does not purport to discuss in full all the issues that it raises or addresses. (The sequence of chapters does, however, present—I believe—an orderly and logical development of ideas.) Any reader will discover gaps that remain unfilled and will discern some inconsistencies, or at least tensions, between some of the earlier essays and those written later, as the position I was attempting to formulate became clearer to me. In many respects these are experimental essays, and the contentions set forth in them must be regarded as tentative and subject to revision.

Nevertheless, I think that the position expressed herein is a fundamentally coherent one and that the central model with which I have tried to work—the notion of God as *agent,* as one who *acts*—represents a reasonable way to interpret the principal themes and conceptions inherited from Western religious traditions. This is, of course, not the only way to understand the conception of God that has grown up in the West; many alternative patterns have been proposed. But I am prepared to argue both that this conception is closer than others to the core meaning carried in ordinary Western languages and that it (or something like it) is in fact indispensable if we are to make sense of the central claims of Christian or Jewish faith.[1]

[1] Although the notion of God as agent seems presupposed by

For the most part these essays are concerned with formal critical problems connected with the notion of God as agent; they are far from containing a full exposition of the Christian doctrine of God. If the reader is interested in the latter, he should supplement the present volume with my *Systematic Theology: A Historicist Perspective* (New York: Scribner's 1968). A large portion of that work is devoted to the doctrine of God and especially to its christological or revelational foundations. The essays in the present volume move in the opposite direction: they attempt to show how the concept of God is grounded in ordinary human experience. Since experience is the other principal root of all theological notions, and just as essential as revelation if those notions are to be intelligible (see *Systematic Theology*, Chapter 4), this change of direction or focus should not be interpreted as meaning I am retracting the claims of the earlier volume, but rather that I am here attempting to fill in in some detail certain indispensable features of the conception of God there left, at best, in barest outline.

Four of the essays found in this volume have previously been published, at least in part; the other seven have been presented as lectures or papers in different forms and on various occasions. Five of these latter (Chapters 2, 5, 7, 8, and 10) were the basis of the Andrew C. Zenos Lectures, delivered at McCormick Theological Seminary in Chicago, November 4–6, 1970.

Two of the previously published essays (Chapters 3 and 6) have not been revised substantively. I would no longer formulate the problems of those essays quite as I originally did, but their fundamental contentions still seem to me substantially correct. I have, therefore, left their texts unchanged (except for minor editorial changes) and have contented myself with

---

most contemporary theologians—Paul Tillich is the single outstanding exception, and he is not fully consistent on this point—Austin Farrer has been almost alone in trying to specify carefully and consistently just what this might be understood to mean. (See esp. *Finite and Infinite* [Westminster: Dacre Press, 1943], and *Faith and Speculation* [London: A. and C. Clark, 1967].)

augmenting the footnotes when it seemed desirable to add or qualify some point. Such additions have been marked with brackets. Chapter 4 is considerably shorter than the earlier version and otherwise revised; some portions which I now regard as mistaken, or at least misleading, have been eliminated. Chapter 1 consists of a major portion of an earlier article, supplemented with considerable new material.

The most important matter, with regard to the development or modification of my position, to which I should call attention here, can perhaps best be indicated by reference to an analysis by Michael McLain of three of these articles (Chapters 3, 4, and 6).[2] McLain points out that the personalistic model on the basis of which I try to develop conceptions of transcendence and God depends on an understanding of the self as in principle private or hidden in certain crucial respects. Such a view, he contends, is "residually Cartesian" in that it separates the mind or subjectivity of the self too sharply from the body and in fact tends to identify the "true" self only with the inner subject. McLain correctly points out, however, that contemporary philosophical analyses of our language about persons (he discusses P. F. Strawson's work in particular) show that a bifurcation of this sort is not tenable, for we ascribe both physical and mental characteristics both to ourselves and to other selves, and we regularly use our person-language objectively (that is, with reference to others) as well as subjectively (with reference to states of our own consciousness). Indeed, the peculiar characteristic of this language is precisely its double (objective/subjective) reference. To reduce or ignore either dimension is to misuse the language and to involve ourselves in logical absurdities. Such procedures fail to recognize that when we speak of persons it is neither just with "minds" (idealism) or "bodies" (behaviorism) with which we have to deal but rather with a unique sort of unified reality, an "embodied subject."

I want to make clear here that I concur completely with

[2] See "On Theological Models," *Harvard Theological Review*, 62:155–187 (1969). I have also benefited from personal correspondence with McLain on the issues he raises.

McLain in his principal critical point that neither a dualistic nor a one-sidedly subjectivistic conception of the self is tenable. I also admit that some of the formulations in my earlier articles (particularly the one reprinted as Chapter 4) lend themselves to interpretation of the subjective as the "real" self —as well they might since at one time I held to such a view (though not, I would hope, in quite the extreme form McLain attributes to me). In recent years I have realized, however, that it is the concept of *agent* (rather than of subject) that is of crucial importance here, and the only agents whom we know are embodied physical persons, who act in and through physical motions and movements and who speak by means of physical noises; this position was already evident in my writing, I would have thought, with the publication of the third article (Chapter 6) which McLain analyzes, for there I am concerned almost exclusively with agent and act.[3] I am quite prepared, therefore, to disavow the one-sidedly subjectivistic implications of my earlier forms of expression and to accept the main lines of the description of agency, and the knowledge of agents, which McLain sets out.

However, from this I do not draw McLain's conclusion, that my earlier discussions of transcendence and of the revelatory character of the knowledge of God are to be called seriously into question. On the contrary, precisely the points I had made in the relatively crude subject/object language criticized by McLain can and must be made, it seems to me, on the basis of the contemporary philosophical analysis of agency and action. McLain seems to think that because I emphasize that knowledge of others comes more through their "revealing" themselves to us than through simple "observation" of them (see, for example, Chapter 4, below), I am committed to regarding the physical movements of others as simply adventitiously related to their inner subjectivity, indeed, as essentially similar to those of nonhuman objects. But, he points out, contemporary philosophical analysis has made eminently clear that we

[3] McLain does note a change in my position (*ibid.*, pp. 185–186), but he seems to attribute it to a careless slip rather than growing sophistication.

simply do not "treat our observations of the states and behavior of persons as identical in kind with our ordinary observation of physical things and processes . . . We persistently view human behavior as expressive of, and imbued with, thoughts, feelings, and intentions, and we are right in doing so . . ."[4] McLain's point here is precisely the one I was also trying (though not too successfully) to express. We make a sharp distinction between persons and things, between agents whose action is informed by intention, and mere physical objects. The physical movements and noises made by other persons are regarded by us as not "merely physical," but as intentional and often communicative, that is, as informed by purposiveness and meaning. What I have referred to in these essays as "revelation" is precisely this exposure to us of such underlying intentionality and purposiveness, but we grasp this in processes distinct from, and much more complex than, the "mere observation" through which we learn about ordinary physical things. Although we often can in some sense "perceive" another's purpose in his action ("Now I see what he's trying to do!"), this is precisely because we look for intention and meaning in what another person does and says, and we may find just that *revealed* in his action and speech. Moreover, as McLain concedes, it is only "because I have knowledge from the 'inside,' so to speak, of my 'active center' that I can grasp what it means to act, and, correspondingly, that I can distinguish between an occurrence and an action"[5] in the behavior either of others or myself.

I could hardly have made the central point better or more explicitly. Our understanding of the predicates we ascribe to selves—intention, memory, pain, and the like—has an indispensable ground in our own "inward" experience. "Pain," for example, as anyone who has felt it knows well, does not refer merely to externally observable pain-behavior (however much that serves as our criterion for applying this word to others): it refers above all to something we *feel* or *experience* or *have* as conscious subjects, and it is for this reason alone (and not

4 *Ibid.*, pp. 166–167.
5 *Ibid.*, p. 168.

because of the way we externally observe our bodies to be behaving) that we can and do say, "I am in pain." It is precisely because of this inwardly experienced dimension of meaning, moreover, that I know what I am ascribing to another when, on seeing his facial grimace and hearing his outcries, I say, "He is in pain." It is also true, of course, as Ludwig Wittgenstein, Strawson, and others have made clear, and as McLain emphasizes, that it would not be possible to ascribe such predicates to myself, unless there were also other subjects to which I could equally well apply them; self- and other-ascription grow up together and are logically interdependent. However, inasmuch as we do not have the same grounds for ascription of such predicates in these two cases, each having its own appropriate criteria, it is clear that this very double-ascription itself implies that we necessarily take the behavior of others to have an "inward side" (not directly open to us) as well as the "outside" which we can observe: the body of the other is taken "as manifesting the person whose body it is," not simply "as a physical object."[6]

Thus, the self has a kind of privacy or subjectivity that is not directly open to others' observation, and that makes possible deceiving others, if one chooses, by deliberately acting and speaking in a way they will interpret mistakenly. It would be misleading, of course, to suggest a kind of parallelism or duality between "inner" and "outer," as though they were two distinct kinds of reality existing side by side. In many (perhaps most) of our actions and experiences, to make this distinction at all would be artificial and misleading. Even where it seems appropriate and necessary to distinguish between external behavior and inner states there is doubtless a connection between them, and that no merely adventitious one: certain standard sorts of action regularly express certain intentions. It is only because of such intrinsic connections that we can act at all (Otherwise how would we ever know just what action to perform in order to realize a particular intention?) or can discern the purposes and goals underlying the actions of others. But

[6] Virgil Aldrich, "Reflections on Ayer's *The Concept of a Person*," *Journal of Philosophy*, 62:124 (1965).

with a fully developed self or agent the connection between inner and outer is not rigidly fixed or unbreakable. When necessary or desirable the ego can retreat into subjectivity and decide which of its intentions will be expressed in actions or words and which will be concealed or disguised. It can, moreover, determine whether to express these intentions only in (physical) action or to communicate them more explicitly in speech.

Though speaking is itself an action "perceived" by the other, it is expressly intended to communicate intentions or meanings openly and clearly, whereas most other actions, though also the expression of intention, do not ordinarily have this additional function. When another speaks we hardly hear the noises he makes, for we are "listening to what he is saying," that is, to the structure of *meaning* (not the pattern of sound waves) he is communicating; we may see his body, but it is *he* (the active self) to whom we are attending. Doubtless the meaning could not be communicated without the noise (or some other physical vehicle), and the self is not separable from the body that it informs. But in neither case are the two terms simply to be identified (as McLain sometimes seems to suggest)—we do distinguish the dead from the living, and gibberish from speech—and the two are certainly not perceptible in the same sense or the same way.

McLain is quite right in insisting that the two sides of the self cannot be logically conceived as separable from or fully independent of each other. But precisely because there are these *two*—inner subjectivity as well as a bodily or observable side—the self has a certain privacy and in its innermost recesses even a measure of inaccessibility, apart from its own deliberate acts of communication.[7]

It is on the basis of these facts that I contend it is appropriate

[7] For an excellent analysis of this matter in terms of the logic or grammar of our language dealing with knowledge of (other) selves, see Stanley Cavell, "Knowing and Acknowledging," in *Must We Mean What We Say?* (New York: Scribner's, 1969). See also A. J. Ayer, "Privacy," in *Studies in the Philosophy of Thought and Action,* ed. P. F. Strawson (London: Oxford University Press, 1968).

to speak of selves as "transcending" (though not separable from) what are physically perceivable as their bodies, and to regard knowledge of them in this aspect as given through a kind of "revealing" or "unveiling" of that which would otherwise be hidden from our direct view. Doubtless revelation of the intentions informing our actions frequently occurs directly and simply in and through the actions themselves (which, as we sometimes say, often "speak louder than words"). But much of our activity is not fully transparent: in such cases, if the intentions informing it are to be known by others, we have to act deliberately to reveal them, through speech or other means of communication. It is on the basis of this model of the hiddenness and transcendence intrinsic to selfhood and the consequent revelatory character of our knowledge of other selves that, as I argue, a meaningful doctrine of God as agent can be constructed.

I cannot discuss here the many other excellent points of criticism raised by McLain (but see note 22 in Chapter 6), nor his own constructive proposals. With the qualifications suggested in the preceding paragraphs, I commend his article to the interested reader as a thoughtful and careful critique of certain positions taken—or, as I would prefer to think, unintentionally implied—in this volume.

One more word of introduction may be in order. All the essays included here are directly concerned with the meaning of talk about God, with understanding how God is related to the world, with the significance and foundations of belief in God, or with defining the human task of thinking about God— theology. Theology, however, is much broader in its implications and inclusive in its subject matter than the phrase "thinking about God" might at first suggest. Accordingly, the essay devoted to a description of theology itself (Chapter 2) defines and introduces a field of much wider scope and more general character than is represented in the other chapters, focused as they are on various aspects of the problem of God more narrowly conceived. Despite its broader conception, I have felt it appropriate to include this paper here, both because it introduces and describes the mode of thinking carried out in the other chapters and also because it reminds the reader that theology is not confined to thinking about God in any narrow sense, but involves a full-blown interpretation of man and the world as well.

I am grateful to The Christian Century Foundation for giving me permission to republish a portion of my article, "Theological Historicism as an Experiment in Thought," which appeared in *The Christian Century*, 83:268–271 (March 2, 1966); to Harper and Row for permission to republish a portion of my paper, "Two Models of Transcendence: An Inquiry into the Problem of Theological Meaning," which first appeared in *The Heritage of Christian Thought: Essays in Honor of Robert L. Calhoun*, ed. R. E. Cushman and E. Grislis (copyright 1965 by Robert Earl Cushman and Egil Grislis); and to the *Harvard Theological Review* for permission to republish two of my articles, "On the Meaning of 'God': Transcendence without Mythology," and "On the Meaning of 'Act of God'" (copyright 1966 [and 1968] by the President and Fellows of Harvard College).

I want to express my gratitude to the John Simon Guggenheim Memorial Foundation of New York for a research grant during the academic year 1969–1970. I hardly see how I could have completed this book without the time thus made available to me.

I am very grateful to the faculty of McCormick Theological Seminary in Chicago for inviting me to deliver the Andrew C. Zenos Lectures, November 4–6, 1970. The graciousness of President Marshall Scott, and of my faculty host, Professor Robert Evans, was much appreciated, and the responsiveness of the audience to the lectures encouraged me to proceed toward their publication in the considerably expanded form in which they appear here.

There are many others to whom thanks are due, but I can here mention only a few: Mrs. Arthur Kooman, for faithfully typing and retyping manuscript copy; George Rupp and Mark Taylor for careful, critical reading of the manuscript, and some useful suggestions for changes; my wife Dorothy and my children, for various kinds of assistance with proofreading, checking references, and the like; and not least, the many students at Harvard Divinity School who have suffered through these ideas in various stages of their development, for their unhesitating willingness to criticize freely, thus helping me to come to clearer and more adequate formulations.

G.D.K.
Cambridge, Massachusetts
July, 1971

Part I. Introduction

1

The Problem of God[*]

The years between 1920 and 1940 were a time of theological reawakening, in which the significance and weightiness of the Christian tradition and vocabulary were rediscovered. This was accordingly a time of great constructiveness, given vitality by the sense that the deeper meaning of Christian faith, after almost having been lost, was once again being appropriated.

The problem that Karl Barth and others saw so clearly was twofold. On one hand Western man's confidence in himself and his own cultural achievements had grown to the point where he supposed he could solve his major problems; the need to rely on his Creator and Redeemer, as spoken of in Christian faith, was increasingly being forgotten. On the other hand World War I and the other twentieth-century crises seemed to signalize the very breakdown of Western culture, showing that the only truly adequate rock for human existence and salvation was this almost forgotten God. Accordingly, the human condition was perceived and analyzed in existentialistic categories of despair, anxiety, and guilt, with salvation by the God and Father of Jesus Christ loudly proclaimed as the only solution to the human problem. In the decades of the 1920's through the 1940's, with Western civilization tottering and memories of the "faith of our fathers" still alive, this view persuaded many. Even—perhaps especially—after World War II had ended and the atomic age with all its terrors and new

---

* The opening sections of this essay originally appeared in an article on "Theological Historicism as an Experiment in Thought," in *The Christian Century*, 83:268–271 (March 2, 1966).

anxieties had been ushered in, the call for a radical act of faith in a (more or less) traditionally defined and validated God was convincing. Thus for a period of thirty or forty years it was possible and appropriate to engage in large-scale and exciting theological reconstruction which had ultimate roots and justification in "revelation alone" (the somewhat honorific way of referring to the Protestant Christian tradition).

I

I do not wish to criticize the work or depreciate the significance of the men of this period. We have all learned much from them, most notably how to think theologically. And without that the tasks of the present generation could be neither apprehended nor carried through. But the historical situation has changed and with it the theological task. The great critical questions posed by liberalism and humanism about cultural relativity, the relation of Christianity to the other world religions, "mythological" versus "scientific" thinking and so forth —questions that were more or less ignored or overlooked during the neo-orthodox period—have come into view once again and are demanding attention. Most notable of all in this respect is the central conception on which the whole theological program rests, the problem of "God." What do we mean by "God"? Can this notion be made intelligible at all to "modern man" or does it depend on outgrown mythological patterns of thought? Which of a variety of alternative interpretations of the term are to be preferred? What criteria can be offered for determining a (or the) valid or correct view?

These of course are not new questions; in many respects they are as old as theology itself. But they were not at the center of discussion during the neo-orthodox period. The recent crises in Western culture had marked out a particular task for that period—the reappropriation of the Christian theological vocabulary and conceptuality—and this could hardly have been accomplished if much energy had been expended in scrutinizing and questioning the ultimate assumptions of that vocabulary and tradition. Radical questioning had already gone so far that many thought it doubtful that the Christian perspective was worth serious attention at all any more, and it was only the shaking of the very foundations of Western culture, combined with the boldest and baldest kind of forthright assertion of the significance of the Christian interpretation of the human condition, that succeeded in giving Christian faith another hearing. We of the present generation cannot thank the Barths and Niebuhrs and Tillichs enough for their achievement in this respect, and it would indeed be ungrateful of us to quibble over their failure to continue and to answer the radical questioning of presuppositions that was characteristic of the immediately previous generations. If they had attended to such issues it is doubtful they could have performed the task which was theirs.

Though the cultural crisis that helped give neo-orthodoxy its hearing is by no means past, we have learned to live with it pretty well and are beginning to hope once again that man can sufficiently control his destiny to manage both the bomb and the population explosion. It is hardly so obvious now that our salvation is to be found in Jesus Christ and him alone: in our day such phrases, repeated too often, have the ring of empty jargon. This does not mean that the theological revival was to no avail. On the contrary, precisely because of that revival the present generation, having been schooled by neo-orthodoxy, is in a position to face these social and cultural issues with, we hope, somewhat more theological sophistication than was possible earlier. Despite frequent announcements of the "death of God," the outcome of this new confrontation is quite unpredictable, and there is, I think, the possibility of genuine theological creativity. But at the moment the situation is very indeterminate, with leading alternatives far from clear. *like in slave trade?*

Adding to the fluidity of the situation is the recent movement in the philosophical community away from the dogmatism and constrictions of logical positivism to the openness and catholicity of interest characteristic of the "ordinary language" students of the later Wittgenstein. The newer methods of linguistic analysis are making it possible to grasp with deeper insight and understanding the philosophical significance of such terms as "person," "action," "purpose," "freedom," "mind," "will," and so forth—concepts absolutely crucial to theology, but which had earlier been subjected to a positivistic skeptical reduction rendering them highly problematical. It is promising indeed that precisely at the moment when theologians are finding it necessary to reexamine critically the religious vocabulary, and especially its central and most problematic term—"God"—there are appearing philosophical methods of linguistic study and analysis that make it possible to sort out and clarify misleading usages and to grasp and explore the most subtle nuances. There is good reason to hope that coming years will see clarification of many of the puzzles and paradoxes of much recent theology which accepted too uncritically the ponderous and often misleading metaphysical presuppositions and linguistic confusions of German (philosophical and theological) idealism and existentialism. If so, theology may yet become the tool of careful, critical, and clear thought.

Certainly it would be foolish in this sort of situation to proceed with one's theological work as though the foundations were absolutely firm and unshakable, one's only task being the straightforward explication of the Christian faith. Perhaps the past generation could work that way; ours cannot. Our task is precisely that of more carefully exploring these foundations, determining what among them is safe and secure, what shaky and to be cut away. For this kind of work it is necessary to be open toward the manifold ways of doing theology and understanding Christian faith, which are increasingly appearing on the scene—here tolerance of and indeed rejoicing in theological pluralism is called for—while at the same time one takes upon himself the risk of exploring some of the uncertain byways. Such researches may be regarded as "experiments in thought," to use Kierkegaard's phrase, that is, attempts to ferret out what is contained in an idea or a concept or a perspective in order better to understand its meaning and implications. When one takes up this experimental stance toward his theological work he does not commit himself absolutely to the position he is exploring, as some of the existentialists used to hold necessary. The commitment here is more tentative:

one devotes himself sufficiently to a point of view to give perhaps a good many years of his life to determining what is contained or implied in it, while simultaneously recognizing that
there are other ways of doing theology, other "experiments"
being carried on that are worth observing and learning from
and that may ultimately turn up conclusions requiring the
abandonment of one's own position. A theologian with such a
pluralistic and experimental orientation will rejoice precisely
in the diversity and openness of the current theological scene
because of his conviction that it is only through the strife of
perspectives and systems that some new truth, beyond all the
currently struggling partial insights, may be won. *sometimes belated*

II

The central problem of theological discourse, not shared
with any other "language game," is the meaning of the term
"God." "God" raises special problems of meaning because it is
a noun which by definition refers to a reality transcendent of,
and thus not locatable within, experience. A new convert may
wish to refer the "warm feeling" in his heart to God, but God
is hardly to be identified with this emotion; the biblicist may
regard the Bible as God's Word; the moralist may believe God
speaks through men's consciences; the churchman may believe
God is present among his people—but each of these would
agree that God himself transcends the locus referred to. As the
Creator or Source of all that is, God is not to be identified with
any particular finite reality; as the proper object of ultimate
loyalty or faith, God is to be distinguished from every proxi-
mate or penultimate value or being. But if absolutely nothing
within our experience can be directly identified as that to
which the term "God" properly refers, what meaning does or
can the word have?

For the Judaeo-Christian tradition God has been the primary
and fundamental reality with reference to which all of life—
indeed all of creation—was oriented and understood. To our
modern empirical, secular, and pragmatic temper, however, it
has seemed increasingly dubious, ever since the Enlighten-

ment, whether it is either reasonable or necessary to believe in such a transcendent Reality: human life can be adequately understood as an emergent from evolving nature, and the meaning of human existence can be found in the cultural values produced by man's creative genius and the social interaction of which love is the profoundest form. Is not talk about God simply a vestige of earlier stages of man's historical development which, however appropriate and necessary in its own time, is no longer relevant or useful in ours?

A number of theological responses to this challenge have been, and doubtless will be, made. These range from acquiescence in the contentions about the "death of God" and trying to reconceive Christian faith without him (for example, Feuerbach in the nineteenth century and the so-called radical theologians of the twentieth), through the attempt to reinterpret the notion of God so as to make it largely a symbol for "depths" of human cultural—particularly "religious"—meaning and value rather than the name of a transcendent quasi-personal being (Schleiermacher and Tillich), to the bald and bold reassertion of God's majesty as itself (dialectically) exemplified precisely by his very absence from our experience (Barth). Many others have been content simply to stop concerning themselves about God and his will and to conduct their lives largely in secular humanistic terms.

I do not propose in this book to discuss all these positions;[1] nor shall I seek to "answer" their various shortcomings directly. What I am attempting is to explore in some detail the logic of the concept of God (or the grammar of the word "God," if you

[1] Fortunately that task has already been well performed by Langdon Gilkey in his recent book, *Naming the Whirlwind: The Renewal of God-Language* (Indianapolis: Bobbs-Merrill, 1969). I might note in passing that, although there is much in Gilkey's constructive answer to these problems with which I concur, his position is fundamentally different from mine. Instead of attempting to ground talk about God directly on itself or in its own terms, so to speak, he seeks to found it on what he takes to be man's inherently religious nature (essentially the Schleiermacher-Tillich position), which he attempts to show betrays itself even in our secular existence. This suggests that his position is basically "religious" (in the sense of Chapter 9 of the present volume) rather than "theistic."

prefer—though I cannot claim to be doing linguistic analysis in the technical sense) in order to make clear to myself—and I hope to others—just what we are trying to say when we speak of God.[2] In these explorations, though I also share in the profound cultural and philosophical confusions and doubts about such talk, I have attempted chiefly to see what can be said positively or affirmatively. This is not because I am trying to present a defense against widespread criticism and attack, but because I am convinced we must get clear what is in the term before we can intelligently evaluate its continued meaning and use. In these essays, therefore, I have sought to uncover something of the existential or experiential bases of talk about God and have also attempted to discern what uses or significance (and possible validity) such talk could reasonably be said to have. I have been particularly concerned to see how our world and our experience would (do) look if God is taken seriously, and in this light I have approached the question why men might (do) continue to find talk about him meaningful and important, and, indeed, profess belief in him.

III

It cannot, of course, be claimed that all the important issues facing a contemporary reconception of God are discussed herein. God is problematical to men in many different senses

[2] This does not mean that I shall present here a full philosophical analysis of the cognitive status of "God-talk," in view of the challenge that it is cognitively "meaningless." That task has recently been performed in exhaustive fashion by Raeburne S. Heimbeck in *Theology and Meaning: A Critique of Metatheological Scepticism* (London: George Allen and Unwin, 1969). Heimbeck shows that use of the so-called verifiability criterion to demonstrate the cognitive meaninglessness of talk about God derives from "the confusion of the problem of identifying God *in experience* with the problem of identifying God *in thought*" (p. 108), and that in fact "Cognitive significance is a precondition, a presupposition, of checkability" (p. 75) rather than the reverse. If Heimbeck's careful logical and semantic analysis is substantially correct, as I am persuaded it is at least on these points, what is now demanded is thoughtful and imaginative *theo*logical analysis and reconception in face of the increasingly problematic status of traditional interpretations of God. Just that is attempted in the present volume.

and ways, and it would not be possible to deal with them all in the compass of a few essays. It is important to note how various are the issues involved, for much of the contemporary discussion of the problem of God is misleading or unclear owing to confusions among these quite different sorts of problems.

(1) Most common, perhaps, in contemporary theological and philosophical circles, is discussion of the way in which God is a problem semantically or linguistically. Is there any reality at all to which the word "God" refers, or is this simply and purely a creation of the human imagination? Certainly the traditional conceptions of God as *a* being "up there" in the heavens, who rules the world, are no longer credible, indeed, appear to be almost childish fairy tales to many of us. Since seemingly no clear experiential evidence can be cited either for or against that to which the word "God" allegedly refers, the question has repeatedly been raised whether all talk about him is not in the strict sense cognitively meaningless.

(2) There is the conceptual or metaphysical question of how we are to conceive God in view of his supposed transcendence of experience and the world. *What* is God? What sort of reality or being is he? In terms of what images or models is he to be interpreted so we can make clear to ourselves just what we are talking—or trying to talk—about, when we speak of God? What more can be said than that he is simply unknowable mystery, the ultimate X? What positive content does or can the concept of God have?

And how is the relation of this X to the world, and to the natural and historical events occurring within the world, to be conceived? An older theology thought of these relations in terms of such categories as creation, providential governance or sustenance of the world, and miracle. But it is questionable whether we are able to make these conceptions intelligible to ourselves any longer, in view of the way we have come to conceive natural and historical order under the influence of modern scientific, philosophical, and historical studies.

(3) Related to these linguistic and conceptual problems, serious methodological problems arise for the discipline of

theology. Since we do not know just how, or as what, to conceive God, how are we to approach the problem of thinking about him? On what basis can criteria for sorting out more from less valid or adequate ways to conceive him be specified, and how are methodologies for thinking about him to be developed? With other philosophical or social problems, however difficult and confused they may be, there usually is a way to begin attacking them, but how does one get a good grip on the problem of thinking clearly about God? *Ask for More disclosure?*

One should not suppose that the problems about God that *PrE* I have been mentioning are simply the product of contemporary skepticism or unbelief. They belong to the very notion of *Schism?* God itself as faith apprehends it. For faith has always claimed that God's goodness and glory are far too great for the human mind to grasp, that man's proper attitude vis-à-vis God is therefore awe, worship, adoration. But how does one stand in awe of something without having some conception of it? Can men really worship and adore what is a mere empty X to them? Can they pray to a—_____? The more that faith wishes to emphasize God's greatness and glory and transcendence—which are, after all, all ideas about God—the more urgent becomes the question of how God is to be conceived.

(4) Moving on from these difficult conceptual issues, we turn to the (more traditional) epistemological question. If there is a God, how is he known? through so-called religious experience? on the basis of inferences made from ordinary experience and our scientific knowledge of nature? on the authority of the Bible, or tradition or church? through his revelation of himself? What is to be made of the "arguments for the existence of God"? What is meant by "God's revelation," and how is it to be recognized? Is theological knowledge partly "natural," partly "revealed"? If so, how are these related to each other? A great complex of very difficult epistemological issues belongs to the problem of God.

(5) Somewhat tangential to this series of problems is the question of how the Western concept of God is to be related to the conceptions of ultimate reality in non-Western cultures

and religions. Earlier generations could, perhaps, interpret such traditions in terms of categories like "idolatry" or "paganism," but the increasingly problematic status of Christian faith, on the one hand, and the growing appreciation of the meaningfulness and significance of other perspectives, on the other, has rendered such simplistic approaches indefensible. It is no longer to be expected that other cultures will—or should—simply be "converted" to Christian or generally Western notions and attitudes. Is it time for the concept of God to be transformed and regenerated by the introduction of subtle Eastern conceptions of divine reality, or by robustly primitive, notions of divine power(s)? Should it be dispensed with altogether in some new syncretism of religious traditions that will emerge with the coming world culture? Or, on the contrary, is it justifiable to maintain that the central emphasis on transcendent agency that the term "God" has long expressed should be preserved and developed and even highlighted precisely now with this unprecedented emergence of an increasingly universal civilization and culture?

(6) Within devout circles of faith more existential, less theoretical, features of the problems associated with God and his transcendence are usually focused upon (and these are sometimes confused—often for polemical purposes—with some of the issues we have been noticing). Thus, for the believer God's "hiddenness" may become a serious problem. Why does God so often fail to make his presence known to men, even when they cry to him desperately? Why does he conceal himself even from the most faithful and devout? If God is so great and good and real, why is prayer often so empty, and spiritual discipline and dedication seemingly so fruitless and unsatisfying?

Oh, that I knew where I might find him,
    that I might come even to his seat! . . .
Behold, I go forward, but he is not there;
    and backward, but I cannot perceive him;
on the left hand I seek him, but I cannot behold him;
    I turn to the right hand, but I cannot see him (Job 23:3, 8–9).

This sense of the distance and inaccessibility of God may be magnified to desperate proportions by a personal sense of guilt: Is it my own hateful, sinful self, and that alone, that blocks my vision of the Holy One? Is it simply that I am perversely turning away from him whom my heart seeks, not he hiding himself from me?

(7) Closely related to this hiddenness or inaccessibility of God, so fearful to faith, is the whole nest of problems that the experience of evil raises for the conception of and belief in God. In face of death camps, hydrogen bombs, and napalm, of unbearably painful and destructive diseases, of impersonal calamities and unmerited suffering, how can one say that the Ruler of the world is good, loving, merciful, as he is traditionally claimed to be? Is there any justification for applying such appellations to God? If there is a God at all, would not our experience of evil argue that he must be a terrible demon, an offense to mankind and all toward which it aspires, one to be despised, rather than a loving and merciful Father and Redeemer? The peculiarly overwhelming evils of the twentieth century have brought home this dimension of the problem of God with renewed force. + Isaiah 45:7, Jeremiah 25:27?

(8) The very concept of God raises serious problems for man's sense of moral autonomy and responsibility. As Nietzsche, Sartre, and others have seen, if there is a God (in anything like the traditional sense), we men are not morally self-determining: we must conform ourselves, willy-nilly, to the divine will; we may not do whatever we choose. Men's actions, and even their ethical intuitions and consciences, are subject to a higher norm not of their own creation and not under human control. Human welfare, even the well-being of humanity as a whole, cannot, then, be the final criterion of right and wrong, good and evil, for us: there is an ultimate "teleological suspension of the ethical" (Kierkegaard) as all human standards, values, and insights are called into question, and this threatens the very fabric of human life.

May it not be the case, moreover, that the very act of believing in God is in itself morally dubious? May this not be largely an attempt to avoid taking full responsibility for ourselves and our lives by creating in fantasy a "heavenly father" into whose care we can place ourselves when the facts of life become too unpleasant? Is faith perhaps to be understood as but another of the many ways in which men seek to "escape from freedom" (Fromm)?

(9) There are a number of technical problems raised by the concept of God, for example, the special paradoxes faced by Christian theology when it tries to think of God as three persons in one substance, or as incarnate in Jesus Christ; the difficulties that arise from attempting to reconcile the anthropomorphisms of the biblical portrait of God with philosophical demands for absoluteness and unconditionedness; the difficult problems of formulating with clarity and consistency God's attributes, such as omniscience or eternity; and the like.

(10) Finally, I must mention one more sense in which God is a problem, at least to some. Despite his highly problematical status, despite all the difficulties connected with the notion of God and with belief in him, despite widespread claims that "God is dead," many of us do not seem ready, or able, to give him up, to let him go, to forget him. No matter how outmodel he seems, and how much we would like to write him off, we find that we must struggle with him whether we like it or not. He has been too powerful in our history—the most profound symbol in our culture—just to die easily. And so, perhaps precisely because he is so elusive, so dubious, so problematical, he remains a serious issue for us, for our lives and culture, for our world.

These different senses in which God is a problem are all significant and important. They cannot be reduced to each other, and they dare not be confused with each other if we are to make any headway at all in understanding this symbol and its power and significance. In the present volume I have not been able to deal with all these different senses of the problem of God. I have thought it worthwhile, however, to distinguish them briefly in this way so that we can sense something of the many-sided complexity of the issues with which we shall be grappling, and will not be so likely to suppose that clarification or illumination of this or that point has settled all the difficult questions.

IV

In the essays in this volume I attempt to explore various dimensions of the concept of God with the help of the model of *agency:* God is taken to be one who *acts*—to create the world and everything in it, to govern the world in accord with his sovereign purposes and respond to and interact with his creatures, to bring the world and all beings in it to the completion and fulfillment that he originally posited for them. It must be admitted that this notion of God as an agent who acts on and in the world is in many respects highly problematical. It seems to imply that God is to be distinguished sharply from the world (the context of all our experience), that he somehow "transcends" it, is "above" or "beyond" it. Although such ideas are certainly consistent with, and probably in certain respects indispensable to, the traditional Judaeo-Christian notion of God, they have, as we have already noted, seemed increasingly dubious to many modern thinkers. Hegel lays down a particularly powerful argument to the effect that the notion of God's transcendence, or radical otherness from and independence of all finite being, rests on a serious misunderstanding and is in fact logically incoherent. God must (logically) either be conceived as a dimension, feature, or quality of that all-inclusive totality which we call the "world," or, alternatively, he may himself be understood as the all-inclusive whole within which we, and all other finite beings, "live and move and have our being" (Acts 17:28). Many great successors of Hegel, from Feuerbach down to some of the most recent philosophical analysts of theological language, have appropriated and expanded upon this central contention that the notion of God as radically transcendent is logically incoherent.

I regard it as far from certain that they are not fundamentally correct in their claims, though I have not fully made up my mind on this matter. In any case in the present essays I have attempted to set out and articulate notions of divine transcendence and agency that make possible retention of a conception of God as one who acts upon and interacts with his creatures. Whether my efforts here have met with any success, in view of the very serious problems facing all such proposals, only the critical response and analysis addressed to them will make clear.

2

Christian Theology and the Scientific Study of Religion

In considering the problem of the relation of Christian theology to the scientific or descriptive study of religion,[1] it is important to clarify immediately a certain incongruity or imbalance between the two principal matters to be discussed. I do not refer to the claim that "scientific study" is supposedly "objective" and "impartial" while theology is "subjective" and "confessional." Nor do I refer to the fact that scientific work is public and open to confirmation or rejection by any qualified observers, while theology is relative to the interests of a particular historical community and can be accepted—even understood—only by members of that community. I mean rather to indicate another distinction between these terms, more important than those just mentioned, but not always noted: they are of a completely different logical order or order of generality.

Christian theology purports to give an interpretation of man, the world, and God; that is, it presents an anthropology, a cosmology, and a theology, an overall interpretation of man and his environment and the ultimate reality with which man has to do. In this sense it is all-inclusive, giving a framework of interpretation within which all else that is said about man and his world ought in some way to fit. It sets out a perspective intended to illumine the whole of life, a perspective within

[1] In this paper I shall use "scientific study of religion," "phenomenological study of religion," and "descriptive study of religion" interchangeably.

which all the absurdities, fragments, meaningful experiences, and difficulties can be grasped and profoundly understood. The scientific or phenomenological study of religion, in contrast, makes no such pretentious claims. At most it purports to interpret the meaning, significance, and value of a particular segment of human culture, the religious sector. But it may claim even less: setting aside any efforts to assess directly the "significance" of religious phenomena, or to rank them in some order of importance or value, it may claim merely to set out the "facts" about man's religiousness, to describe man's religious institutions, practices, and beliefs as objectively as possible, leaving evaluation to others. In such a program it may not be felt necessary even to work within a general theory of the nature of human culture or an explicit understanding of the nature of man, to say nothing of raising questions about cosmology or the ultimate reality with which man has to do. The scientific study of religion is a modest effort to see what man, in his religious aspect, has done and is doing, and that is all. As such, it must be supplemented by studies of man in his political, economic, scientific, aesthetic, and other dimensions, in order to develop a rounded theory of human nature and experience. By itself at most it could be said to illumine one side of man's being.

How are two intellectual enterprises with such widely different objectives and claims to be compared, or even closely related, to each other? Surely those who have assumed that theology is simply the "science of religion," or that the descriptive study of religious phenomena will have some direct, even determinative, import for theological work, have made a serious logical category-error. We are working with different orders of generality here, with disciplines that have sharply differing objectives and necessarily divergent methods, and the question of their relationship to each other, and their reciprocal effects, will be complex and difficult. How shall we proceed?

Christian theology is an attempt to give an overarching interpretation of man and his world from a particular ("religious") point of view; the scientific study of religion is an attempt to grasp and interpret religious phenomena (including the construction of theologies) from a neutral or objective point of view. One attempts to portray and interpret the whole within which man finds himself from a particular perspective alleged to illumine that whole in a definitive way; the other attempts to set out and interpret just such particular perspectives by a general method applicable (with appropriate adjustments) to all phenomena and experience. Each approach has its own particularity and definiteness as well as a certain generality and universality. But in the one case—theology—the particularity is of perspective and method, and the generality is of subject matter; in the other case, there is a particularity of subject matter but a generality of method and an attempted neutrality in point of view.

This suggests that these disciplines will be appropriately related to each other not by any kind of subsumption of one under the other, but rather in more dialectical terms. The sociology and psychology of religion should help to identify and clarify the peculiarities of the perspective within which the theologian is operating; they should make possible comparison of this perspective with others and perhaps make clear its limitations as well as its peculiar strengths. In this way, through throwing light on *who he is* and on the peculiarities of what he is doing, the descriptive study of religion should be of importance and aid to the theologian, and this deeper self-knowledge and self-understanding may have profound effects on the way he does theology as well as on his theological conclusions. On the other hand, theological work, concerned as it is with man in his wholeness and man in relation to the ultimate reality with which he has to do, should alert the phenomenologist to questions about himself as a human being (and thus as a scientist) and about the broader human context and meaning of his work, which he might otherwise overlook; this deeper self-knowledge and self-understanding may in turn have profound effects on his phenomenological investigations and on his scientific conclusions, as well as on his interpretation of the meaning or significance of his work.

With this introduction in mind, I would like now to sketch

an interpretation of the methods and objectives of Christian theology, with some attention to the way these are affected by scientific studies of religion. I leave it for specialists in the scientific study of religion to reflect in detail on the significance of theology for their own work.

I

During the recent neo-orthodox period of Christian theology much was made of the importance of "an independent theological method" (Barth). This meant that theology must not take the norms or criteria by which it conducts its work and evaluates its conclusions from some other intellectual discipline, for example, the philosophy of religion, but must develop its own criteria and norms independently and on its own basis. At stake here was not only the perfectly legitimate desire that the theologian should be his own boss and not the slave of some other discipline: every sort of intellectual inquiry must claim the right and authority to develop its own methods for dealing appropriately with its peculiar subject matter. With theology, a much more far-reaching claim was being made; Christian faith, it was said, is rooted in the recognition and acknowledgment of God's definitive act of revealing himself to man in Jesus Christ; and Christian theology is reflection on and interpretation of that faith and the revelation in which it is rooted. This means that theology, in a way unique among man's intellectual activities, is founded upon an awareness of, and is responsible to, *God's truth* as he himself has made it known. For this reason, the theologian may not rest content with the criteria and methods appropriate to other intellectual disciplines—however much he must also utilize those norms— and he certainly may not appropriate such criteria uncritically for his own work, simply subjecting what is derived from God's revelation to critical scrutiny on such a basis. On the contrary, since it is *God* with whom the theologian qua theologian has to do, and since God has himself acted to make himself known, it is obvious that the ultimate court of appeal for all theological work will have to be God's revelation: all criteria for theological work must be drawn from that event, or, if that is not always possible, they must be critically reexamined and reformulated in the light of that event.

Were theology to accept methods or criteria from some discipline other than itself, it would be denying in its procedures what it claims to be explicating as subject matter, namely the finality of God's self-revelation. Instead of accepting God's revelation as the ultimate standard in terms of which all human conceptions—relative, limited, confused, and prejudiced as they are—must be judged, one would be judging that revelation itself by precisely such inadequate human standards. Thus, the absoluteness of God's own truth, which he had graciously revealed as a corrective to human error and sin, itself becomes subordinated to them. In this way theology, instead of being the interpretation and explication of Christian faith, becomes the instrument of its denial. The only way to avoid this inversion of what it sets out to do and be is for theology steadfastly to insist on developing its own norms, criteria, and methods in direct faithfulness to God's revelation, without regard to the criteria or conclusions of other sciences or philosophies. In a special and unique sense Christian theology must have a method independent of all man's other intellectual activities.

Obviously no one could carry through such a program with complete success, and no one, I suppose—certainly not Karl Barth—believed himself to have done so: men's intellectual activities cannot in this way be completely isolated from each other. But that was not the point. The notion of an independent theological method was an ideal the theologian was to keep before himself continuously, and in terms of which he would judge and criticize his work, seeking always to purify it to a yet higher degree. Thus, presumably, he would at least be moving in the right direction, though he never actually attained his goal. Such an understanding of theology, of course, did not encourage the exploration of, and certainly not the incorporation of, scientific or phenomenological materials into one's theological work. On the contrary, the really alert and self-conscious theologian attempted, as far as possible, to develop his position entirely from within, through a spinning out of the implications and meaning of what he took to be God's revelation, in this way developing an interpretation of man, the world in which man finds himself, and the God to whom man owes ultimate allegiance. Moreover, no matter how unintelligible or absurd the theologian's interpretations might seem to those outside the "theological circle" (to use Paul Tillich's phrase), his stance was internally completely coherent. To have such a watertight position at a time when the theological ark seemed to all external appearances to be a very leaky vessel only enhanced the approach further in the eyes of its advocates.

Today few if any would advocate an independent method for theology in this sense. Two of the leaks in the old boat proved not to have been successfully plugged by this neo-orthodox approach, and, indeed, they have let in so much water from the outside that the ship has veritably capsized. The first problem I have already noted, only to pass by it very quickly: this was the fact that no one could really carry through such an independent theological method. We have come to see that this fact has implications for the formulation of theological method itself. It was not a matter simply of being unable to realize an excellent ideal, as I suggested a moment ago; it was, rather, that, on reflection, the ideal itself made no sense.

For where is this "God's truth" which is to be the ultimate court of appeal for the theologian? Is it in the Bible? But the Bible is a collection of very human documents, shaped by the social and political history of Israel, of Babylon, of Egypt, and of other nations; far from being a pure distillate of God's revelation, it is an emergent from a particular cultural history in intensive and continuous interaction with neighboring cultures and peoples. As such it reflects the general sociocultural situation of the Hebrews and of the entire Near East. It is not, moreover, written in some peculiar heavenly tongue appropriate to the absoluteness of the truth supposedly contained in it but in the ordinary everyday language of a people, a language directly reflecting their own common life but also drawing on and ultimately derivative from the linguistic

resources of the pagan peoples around them. Or is the revelation located in Jesus Christ? But Jesus was a man shaped by
his culture and by the needs of his own time and can be
understood only in his own sociohistorical context; and
"Christ" or "Messiah" was a title developed in Hebrew history,
taking into itself certain political aspirations and hopes of the
Jewish people. Or perhaps the revelation is really located in
the faith of the church? But this again proves to be a sociohistorical phenomenon, varying and changing from time to
time and place to place, always much influenced by the concrete social conditions of the particular situation, hardly
specific and definite enough to serve as a norm or criterion for
precise intellectual work.

Thus, the notion of a culturally independent theological
norm—like the positivist criterion of meaningfulness—simply
proved unformulable and unworkable. Man's intellectual and
symbolical activities are so intermixed and interwoven in
human culture and in the human psyche that the kind of
independence and autonomy here envisaged could not be
clearly conceived or applied. A theological program based on
it was thus faulty, or, better, it was in fact not possible to base
actual theological work on such a method; the method did not
describe any possible theological program. It thus becomes
necessary to reformulate theological method in such a way as
to take explicit account of the fact that all theological activity
is participant in and dependent on, as well as (one hopes)
contributive to, the entire range of man's intellectual activities
and ultimately the whole of culture. The interdependence of
theology and other disciplines—as well as the independence of
theology—must be clearly formulated and utilized in any
workable theological method.

This discussion has already brought us to the other prominent leak in the theological ark of the last generation. By what
right, or on what ground, was any particular event, or doctrine,
or person to be regarded as ultimately authoritative for man,
even Christian man? In view of the interpenetration of all
aspects of culture, how is it to be decided that *this*, rather than
that, is properly to be regarded as God's revelation? Or, for

that matter, why should anything at all be regarded as God's revelation somehow in contrast with what is humanly discovered and humanly known? Are, after all, the words "God" and "revelation" anything more than cultural symbols that have become significant in a particular cultural history, just like any other words? Is there any good reason to give them all that authority and power, thus in turn giving a particular discipline especially concerned with them—Christian theology —special standing and special rights among men's intellectual exercises? The claims for a special theological method, as all nontheological outsiders saw from the beginning, rested on an entirely arbitrary and indefensible foundation which could stand unquestioned only as long as men took it for granted that God had in fact revealed himself in Jesus Christ. But when that assumption begins to be doubted—and who can any longer regard it as indubitable?—the whole enterprise falls to the ground. If theology wishes to use such terms as "revelation" and "God" it must show that they are appropriate and illuminating; it can no longer take it for granted that they are. The so-called God-is-dead movement in theology is the very obvious evidence of the complete breakdown of these supposedly rock-bottom assumptions on the basis of which the Christian theological enterprise had heretofore proceeded.

This means that theological method can no longer be formulated on the *basis* of God's revelation, as the entire neo-orthodox generation had supposed: it must now explore, criticize, and reconstruct or reconfirm that basis itself. This will require it to operate on a quite different basis, to set itself different problems, and to proceed in different ways. We may provisionally conclude, then, that whatever we may finally have to claim about the independence of theology, this may not be interpreted to exclude radical interdependence with and dependence on other intellectual activities, and it may not involve resort to arbitrary standards or courts of appeal; theology is one among men's intellectual activities, and it must be able to justify what it does and how it does it before the bar of ordinary human reason.

I I

Thus far we have noted—and rejected—two interpretations of theology: it is not, I have argued, to be regarded as the (or a) science of religion; and it may not be defined simply as interpretation or explication of Christian faith or the Christian revelation. How, then, is it to be understood? I return to my earlier suggestion that it is the interpretation of man, the world, and God from a Christian point of view. We are now in a somewhat better position to understand what this might mean.

In the first place, this definition suggests that theology is, and understands itself as, a *perspective* or point of view. It does not claim to be or to present the whole truth, or the only truth, or the ultimate truth, about man and his situation: it is, rather, one way of looking at the human condition, one way admittedly among many. It will, therefore, have to define its position and make its claims with particular care, both to distinguish itself from other points of view and to justify its own contentions. An acknowledgment that theology is a perspective can be made only from a position that also knows of, and to some degree participates in, other points of view that define things differently and perhaps even in contradictory ways. It can proceed only from a kind of self-understanding that has learned from the sociology of knowledge and of religion about the variety of points of view on ultimate questions that men take up in life, each having its own internal consistency and its significance and value to its adherent. Such a position will understand, moreover, that this variety springs not from men's sinful refusal to acknowledge God's truth, but rather from the concrete sociological and psychological conditioning of all men's efforts to grasp and interpret the truth, and is thus a function of the way we come to know anything at all, particularly anything of ultimate import. But such a sociologically and psychologically informed theology will also understand that its own form has been largely determined by the particular historical circumstances from which it has emerged. It will thus, in the first instance, see itself as one historical perspective among many, specifically, as that perspective which has emerged out of Hebraic history and received its defining norms in the early period of the Christian era, but which has continued to grow and develop down to the present. Thus, a kind of historical self-understanding will be fundamental to any theology that sees itself as a "perspective."

This has immediate implications for theological method. It means that Christian theology cannot proceed without taking historical stock of itself, without understanding, that is to say, from which of man's several historical traditions it has emerged and without grasping itself as in this way *historical* reality. Contemporary theological work begins in historical work, in the attempt to understand what Christian faith and Christian theology have been in the past, and why and how they have taken just this form, developed precisely this vocabulary and these methodologies, emphasized just these contentions and ignored those. Here objective historical and phenomenological work is of the utmost importance. It is not adequate to study biblical and church history simply as a more or less isolated stream of *Heilsgeschichte* which contains its meaning and significance in its own life. These historical streams must be seen in the context of the social and political developments that environed them and that influenced them in many respects, for the cultural and religious symbols and meanings that crystallized in these histories were created and developed through the same psychological and historical processes that create meaning for men everywhere. All of the tools of social, cultural, and intellectual history must be brought to bear, then, on the Hebraic-Christian history from which the Christian perspective emerged and in which it continued to be formed. For only in this way will the various features and dimensions of that perspective come fully into view, and only in this way will the relationship of that perspective to concrete human life—which is the real meaning of the perspective—become clear.

The purpose of such fundamental historical and phenomenological investigations, however, from the point of view of

Christian theology, does not lie simply in themselves, nor in modern man's interest in pursuing knowledge for its own sake. The purpose here is to lay a foundation for further theological work. As we have observed, Christian theology attempts to set out an understanding of man, the world, and God. The value of such historical studies to the theologian is that they help him to see more clearly and vividly just what the Christian understanding of God, man, and the world has been in the past, so that he is in a better position to grapple with its appropriate formulation for the present. If and as he masters the vocabulary and the conceptual distinctions that have proved helpful in delineating and interpreting this perspective in earlier phases of its development, he will be in a better position, and he will have better conceptual tools, for its contemporary reformulation. Indeed, without some such historical foundations, he would have no basis whatsoever from which to proceed, because, as we have noted, Christian faith and Christian theology are developing historical phenomena, and their very being, therefore, can only be grasped historically. But they are *developing* historical phenomena, living realities, and this means that their character and their appropriate formulation for the present and the future are not determined wholly by what they have been in the past. New problems arise, new social tensions appear, new cultural crises occur, and these all will have their effects on the Christian community and its theologians and must in turn be appropriated and interpreted theologically. The creative task set for the theologian is precisely to attempt to see and understand this emerging contemporary experience "from the Christian perspective," that is, in the light of the perspective of meaning derived from the Christian past.

In our time this has become a particularly delicate and difficult problem. What concretely does it mean to interpret the world and man from the Christian perspective? What actual difference does such a perspective make in the way things look? What distinctive stance in life does it require? What does it oblige us to believe, and how is such belief justified? If theology can no longer take it for granted that such questions can be answered by reference to the authority of divine revelation, how is it to proceed?

In order to deal with these questions, we must note again the peculiar self-knowledge of the contemporary theologian, that he is attempting to work within and set out "the perspective of Christian faith," one perspective among many. Now the concept of a perspective, as I am using it here, is not an originally theological notion. It is derived from psychological, sociological, and historical studies that uncovered the relativity of all human thought to the concrete conditions to which that thought is bound; and it attempts to grasp the variety of historically relative but philosophically coherent and intelligible positions that have emerged by use of a model derived from our visual experience, in which the same object appears quite different when seen from different angles or points of view. Each such "perspective" seems to have validity in its own terms and from its own vantage point, but it is not clear that any can claim final authority or truth. A perspectival approach, thus, taken without further qualification, seems to undercut completely the theological claims about God's revelation; indeed, some have drawn the conclusion that Christian faith is relevant and valid for, at most, Western man, other religious perspectives being appropriate for other cultures.

But to take such a position means that Christian faith in fact is *not* valid in its own terms, namely, in its claims to be a perspective uncovering man's true nature, his situation in the world, and the ultimate reality with which he has to do. It is, rather, a mythology within which some men find meaning for life, but which is neither more nor less objectively valid, that is, as an interpretation of how things really are, than are a number of other available mythologies. Its significance is exclusively subjective—what it provides for or gives to the subject in his quest for meaning in life—and so far as it makes objective or reality claims, it is to be rejected.

I would not deny that it is possible, even apparently quite appropriate, to move in this direction from a position that recognizes theology to be a perspective. But I would deny that

such a move is necessary, and I do deny that such a move is in
fact faithful to the Christian perspective, since that perspective
claims to be dealing precisely with matters of truth and
reality, not merely with questions of meaning in a highly
subjective sense. In the strong contemporary reaction against
the arbitrary authoritarianism of neo-orthodoxy it has too
often been assumed that one must move to the opposite
extreme of making no theological truth-claims at all. But that
is simply overreaction. A more appropriate response would
be to ask how questions of ultimate truth and reality in fact
get settled in a world in which men live within cultural and
religious perspectives, and not simply face-to-face with Reality
itself. And on the basis of an answer to that question, we might
explore the justification of the claims to truth of the Christian
perspective. + christologies + crucio lottries

III

Here once again the work of the phenomenologist of religion,
as well as of the psychologist and the sociologist of religion,
becomes important for the theologian. For their studies can
illuminate considerably the ways in which perspectives are
adopted by men and come to be regarded as true and valid, as
well as the reasons why such perspectives lose relevance and
authority and ultimately die out. That is, the sociological and
psychological processes, through which the diverse ways of
grasping the world and human existence become accepted as
meaningful and true, can now be described with some ac-
curacy; and the reasons for the breakdown and destruction of
such perspectives are also gradually becoming known, thanks
to the work of the sociologists and psychologists of religion. I
cannot rehearse such theories here, nor work out in detail their
applicability to the theological problem with which we are concerned, but let me make a general and oversimplified point.
We can say that religious perspectives develop in order to give
a coherent interpretation of life that will sustain the social
and personal order within which men in a given society are
living when they pass through crises such as death, suffering,

calamity, and the like;[2] in the religions such negative occurrences are related to positive experiences of meaning and value in such a way that the positive is seen to have greater significance for man than the negative.

Thus, in the biblical materials, God—the ultimate source of reality and the one who has made a covenant with Israel—is lord over the whole natural process; regular processes like rainfall and drought as well as terrifying events like earthquake or storm are under his control. Moreover, he is a God of justice who will ultimately right all historical wrongs and bring about happiness and peace for his people. Within such a scheme, the most powerful negative experience can be given a positive significance, thus reenforcing and deepening the scheme itself; the prophetic interpretation of the destruction of the twin Israelite kingdoms and the exile is a good example of this. Even such a basically pessimistic perspective as Buddhism achieves its power in this way, by interpreting the negativities of life in terms of what is known to be positive and good; here that ultimate good, however, is not a historical Agent, but the final overcoming of suffering that is Nirvana.

As long as a perspective is able to interpret persuasively the actual experiences of the men who know it and live within it, it will be taken by them as an appropriate interpretation of the realities of the human condition and the world in which man lives, that is, as true and valid. When, however, experiences do not fit well the categories provided by the perspective, or problems do not become intelligible when interpreted in its

[2] Note in this connection the definition of religion by Clifford Geertz: "a *religion* is (1) a system of symbols which acts to (2) establish powerful, pervasive and long-lasting moods and motivations in men by (3) formulating conceptions of a general order of existence and (4) clothing these conceptions with such an aura of factuality that (5) the moods and motivations seem uniquely realistic" ("Religion as a Cultural System," in W. A. Lessa and E. Z. Vogt, *Reader in Comparative Religion: An Anthropological Approach* [New York: Harper and Row, 1965], p. 206). Other particularly relevant recent books are Peter Berger, *The Sacred Canopy* (Garden City, N.Y.: Doubleday, 1967); Thomas Luckmann, *The Invisible Religion* (New York: Macmillan, 1967); Peter Berger and Thomas Luckmann, *The Social Construction of Reality* (Garden City, N.Y.: Doubleday, 1966).

terms, the perspective itself is threatened. At this point there may appear creative interpreters or prophets (theologians, if you like) who by stretching and reinterpreting the categories in new ways make them again serviceable, or else—if the crisis is serious enough—the perspective will die and another ultimately take its place.

The processes I have been describing here in vastly over-simple and general terms probably are known to all readers of this essay. What may not be so obvious is the significance these facts have for a contemporary understanding of the theological enterprise. If we agree that Christian theology also is the expression of a perspective, then we will have to admit that its social and cultural power derives in a similar way from its persuasiveness in dealing with human problems (and not simply from its being, in some undialectical sense, the expression of "God's truth"), and that it too will likely come to an end when it is no longer genuinely illuminating of man's condition. This perspective, then, like any other, is apprehended as "true" so far as it succeeds in actually illuminating men's situations in the world; it becomes questionable, and finally "false," when there are compelling experiences with which it cannot deal.

This insight now enables us to specify further the theological task, especially the task of ascertaining and demonstrating the truth of the Christian perspective in the face of other conflicting points of view also known by and available to us. It is the job of the Christian theologian to show that the Christian categories can in fact make sense of our contemporary experience, including our experience of a plurality of religious perspectives. Unless it can be shown that talk about God, for example, is required to do justice to certain features of our contemporary experience, that category cannot be sustained, and the Christian perspective will abandon it and become sharply different from what it has been in the past—the course advocated by the death-of-God theologians—or else that perspective itself will gradually die. Or again, unless it can be shown that the kind of meek, nonresistant love manifest in Jesus' suffering and dying on a cross is a significant key to the problems of disorder, suffering, hatred, and warfare in our world, this emphasis will continue to be displaced in the Christian perspective by ethical claims of a quite different sort, or the Christian perspective itself will not survive. Unless it can be shown that talk about man's fall and sin, about the creation of the world, about the sacraments, and so forth has some real bearing on contemporary human existence, they will each die away or they will contribute to the death of the Christian perspective itself.

Contrariwise, in those cases in which relevance and meaning for the understanding and effective control of contemporary life can be demonstrated, the categories and their perspective will appear to us confirmed in truth and significance. In particular, if it proves possible to grasp and interpret contemporary cultural pluralism in an especially significant way by reference to "God," the ultimate point of reference for Christian faith, and "Christ," the material criterion of meaning in terms of which "God" is understood, Christian faith will appear confirmed in its fundamental truth, and its categories will strike us as appropriate, meaningful, and valid. It is the task of the theologian to attempt precisely such reinterpretation in the face of contemporary problems and issues.

Reinterpretation of this sort will neither ignore the methods or conclusions of the scientific study of religion nor simply appropriate them. Rather, it will attempt to grasp the facts about human life as set out in these studies, together with the other social and human sciences, and give those facts a theological interpretation; that is, it will attempt to see them in terms of the fundamental categories of Christian faith. Thus, if it proves psychologically accurate to say that men's belief in God is grounded in part in their quest for security in a lonely world, it will become theologically necessary to attempt to grasp the human need for security as part of the anthropological basis of the knowledge of God. If it proves historically accurate to say that Israel's faith is to be understood as an appropriate and creative human response to the plight of a small nation crushed between the superpowers of the ancient Near East, theology will need to see such historical contingency as the actual vehicle through which God made himself known to man. If it proves sociologically correct to hold that Jewish and

Christian religion have functioned to give authority and meaning to certain modes of social organization in the West, just as other religious symbol systems and patterns of ritual have functioned elsewhere, then it will be theologically requisite to inquire whether God, and not merely a cultural system, is ultimately at work in such hallowing and sanctifying of certain specific sociocultural practices and institutions.

This does not mean that the theologian's task is merely to put a kind of pious frosting on whatever facts about man and the world the several sciences uncover. That would of course be trivialization and sentimentality in the highest degree. What is required of the theologian is that he show that the facts as known are susceptible to a theological interpretation that does not distort them, and that such theological interpretation goes beyond those facts to do justice to certain features of experience in a way that mere phenomenological description can never achieve.

Most notable of these additional features of experience is the fact that man is an active being, an agent, as well as a knower, a describer of what he sees. As an agent, who creates and continuously re-creates his culture and himself within that culture, he must constantly decide among alternatives confronting him. But such decisions require criteria, standards, norms, drawn not from the way things now are, but from the way they should be, the way man ought to move in order to remake them and to remake himself. There must be a vision of man that goes beyond the facts and a vision of the world that transcends anything the sciences can describe, and these visions and values provide bases for man's continuous active movement into the future. Whatever else the doctrine of God is about, it certainly is about that ultimate norm or standard in terms of which every given cultural situation or complex of fact, value, and meaning can be criticized, transcended, and transformed. Without such a point of reference, we become trapped within the scheme of value and meaning that constitutes precisely our perspective.

Men are condemned to fatally nihilistic relativisms by their perspectival condition, or to imperialisms that impudently judge all other perspectives in terms derived simply from their own, if there is no point of reference beyond all their perspectival meanings and values that relativizes them all. Such an ultimate point of reference, transcending every finite position and thus making it possible to judge and criticize them all, is what the word "God" denotes. If men were merely observing or spectating beings, it would not be necessary for them to have such a point of reference; everything about which they needed to speak could be dealt with in the descriptive terms made available by various scientific and phenomenological studies. But as active-choosing-creative beings, they must judge what confronts them and attempt to transform it in accordance with visions of what now is not. It is the task of theology to show how the conception of God (as grasped in the Christian tradition) provides for these needs of the self and the interpretation of experience in a way no descriptive science can, by grounding both value and being in one ultimate reality. I cannot here work this out in detail. I mention it only to suggest something of the way theology must go beyond mere interpretation of the facts provided by descriptive disciplines to provision of a basis for their assessment by man in his posture as actor and creator of culture.[3]

IV

I have been attempting to describe the task and methods of Christian theology as a human enterprise, to be judged by ordinary human canons of validity and significance and devoted to meeting specific human needs. Such theology is founded upon certain historical and phenomenological insights and studies in Hebrew-Christian history; it attempts to grapple with contemporary questions of orientation and meaning in the context of modern social and cultural problems and their scientific description and interpretation; and it speaks to the moral needs of the acting self and of modern complex society with the aid of psychological insight and sociological study. But it

[3] More detailed elaboration of this contention will be found especially in Chapters 5 and 10, below.

moves beyond all these scientific and phenomenological ingredients to a holistic interpretation of human existence and the world in which man finds himself through grasping that world as a dynamic, forward-moving historical process within which each man can find a meaningful life and to which he can significantly contribute. To the extent that theology is successful in dealing with all major dimensions of modern experience, it confirms the validity of its categories and thus resolves the central problem of the perspectival awareness underlying the contemporary theological self-consciousness, the problem of theological truth. It achieves this goal by, on the one hand, adopting scientific, phenomenological, and historical conclusions derived from a wide variety of sources, and, on the other, by going beyond all of these to provision for the self's needs to decide among alternatives and to create new futures. Contemporary man is highly dependent on scientific and other descriptive studies for his own self-understanding and his orientation in the world, and therefore a theology that is to meet his needs will necessarily incorporate what can be learned about the world and man from them. Theology must continue to work with its own independent method and problems, particularly with that central concept and problem, which is its unique task and responsibility, the idea of *God*. But for contemporary men these issues can never be pursued independently of the other cognitive enterprises in which we are engaged. In this respect modern theology is dependent upon scientific and historical studies.

It should now be clear, however, that theology will also have a particular usefulness or significance for the scientific study of religion. Though theology is far from being the science of religion—it is, as we have seen, an interpretation of man, the world, and God—it may provide indispensable material for scientific and phenomenological attempts to understand man. Christian faith, as noted earlier in this essay, is one religious perspective among others, and as such it is a proper object of investigation by the phenomenologist of religion; the work of the Christian theologian is important to the phenomenologist in determining the character, quality, and meaning of various terms and relations in the Christian symbol system, especially that most fundamental of those symbols, "God." If the Christian community belonged only to the past, were dead and gone, then it would not be necessary for the phenomenologist to attend to contemporary experiments in formulation and reformulation; his data would already all be in. But since the Christian community is living, and thus growing and changing both in its own internal life and in its relations to other communities and cultures, the scientific student of that community must come to terms with contemporary attempts at theological understanding, for they are the intellectual aspect of that community's movement into the future. The work of the theologian thus serves the phenomenologist of religion, and the philosopher of culture and of man, in supplying them with data for their work.

But there is a further general human significance to constructive theological work. The Christian perspective is, after all, meaningful to a great many human beings, or at least, so they say. It appears still to be an important way for men to find orientation in their world and meaning in life. As such it is well worth studying with care and attempting to reformulate with relevance. Were Christian faith completely dead, it might be studied only for its historical interest. Since, however, it is living and vital—however much it may appear threatened by contemporary intellectual and cultural developments—it is important to lay bare its quality and character, both that we may better understand those contemporaries who are Christians, and that we may see more clearly certain human possibilities open to us all that might otherwise be overlooked or neglected. That is to say, Christian faith and Christian theology should be of interest and importance not only to phenomenologists, attempting to sketch out various religious positions open to men; they have import for contemporary men generally, who are attempting to find orientation for themselves in a very confusing new world, for they claim to provide such orientation.

I conclude, then, by returning to the point with which I began. Christian theology is not the science of religion, and the scientific study of religion cannot become the basis for Christian theology. Nor can either of these disciplines be subsumed under the other. Rather, they are dialectically related. The scientific study of religion—and, indeed, of man and of the world generally—provides the theologian with much material that he must incorporate into his understanding of man and the world and enables him to come to deeper self-understanding of the perspectival character of his own activity. Constructive theological work in turn not only provides the phenomenologist with one more example of religious man at work, specifically, of contemporary Christian man attempting to orient himself in his complex scientifically described world; constructive theological work can also provide a framework of interpretation within which the phenomenologist or scientist can evaluate the meaning and significance of his own work and, perhaps, can himself find orientation in the world and meaning for life.

Romans 8:30
Matt 7:13?

Part II. God

3

Transcendence without Mythology[*]

Many have observed that modern man, more than the man of any other age, lives in a world from which God is absent, a genuinely secular world. Our forefathers had a sense of God's continuous providential guidance of history as a whole and of their individual destinies in particular; they found their lives meaningful because they were lived within the context of God's purposes, each man having his own unique place and task. But such meaning as most men of our time find is the this-worldly humanly created meaning emergent from ordinary social intercourse and cultural activity. For some this loss of a transcendent source and purpose has reduced human life to meaninglessness and absurdity, a pointless and empty burden simply to be endured (Beckett); others react with bitterness and revulsion (Sartre); still others seem to find sufficient satisfaction in their daily round of activities, punctuated occasionally by aesthetic experience or unusual excitement, not to miss or lament the dimensions of depth and transcendence and mystery in which previous generations found their lives ensconced. But in any case the radical "eclipse of God" (Buber) or even the final irretrievable "death of God" (Nietzsche) appears to be the most momentous theological fact of our age. Given this cultural context, it is little wonder that linguistic analysts find it dubious whether the word "God" has any

* This chapter was originally published in *Harvard Theological Review*, 59:105–132 (1966).

genuinely specifiable meaning,[1] and theological writers, in a desperate attempt to rescue the Christian faith from what appears to be its certain demise, seek wholly "secular" interpretations which go so far as to dispense with the word and idea of "God" entirely.[2]

I

A major problem with the concept of "God" arises out of the fundamental metaphysical-cosmological dualism found in the Bible (as well as in traditional metaphysics) and in virtually all Western religious thought.[3] This is the division of reality into "earth" and "heaven"—that which is accessible to us in and through our experience and in some measure under our control, and that beyond our experience and not directly open to our knowledge or manipulation. The latter "world" is, if anything, more real and more significant than the experienced world, since it is God's own abiding place (from whence he directs the affairs of the cosmos) and man's ultimate home. In the Bible this dualism is expressed in full-blown mythological terms. Heaven is a kind of "place" or "world" in certain respects like the places found in the world of experience; it is peopled by "heavenly beings" and even a "heavenly court" visualized in analogy with earthly persons and political structures; and God is the absolute monarch ruling the cosmos in a way analogous to an Oriental despot. Some writers, Rudolf Bultmann, for example, have supposed that if it were possible

[1] For a summary of the discussion, see F. Ferré, *Language, Logic and God* (New York: Harper and Brothers, 1961); and W. T. Blackstone, *The Problem of Religious Knowledge* (Englewood Cliffs, N.J.: Prentice-Hall, 1963). [The most thorough analysis now available of the logical issues here will be found in R. S. Heimbeck, *Theology and Meaning: A Critique of Metatheological Scepticism* (London: George Allen and Unwin, 1969).]

[2] See, e.g., Paul Van Buren, *The Secular Meaning of the Gospel* (New York: Macmillan, 1963).

[3] Karl Barth, who supposes himself not to be engaged in metaphysical or cosmological "speculations," nevertheless makes a considerable point of the essential duality of the world in the Christian view. Cf. *Church Dogmatics* (Edinburgh: T. and T. Clark, 1936–1962), III/1, 17–22; III/3, 369–531.

for Christian thinking to rid itself of this somewhat crude and unbelievable mythological machinery, faith in God would once more become a live option for contemporary man. But the difficulty is much deeper than that, for this elaborate and fantastic mythological imagery is simply a naïve and embellished expression of a more fundamental problem: the religious presupposition of a reality other than or "beyond" this world, the assumption that *the eminent reality with which we have to do —God—is somehow "out there"* (or "up there" or "down there" or "in there") *beyond the given realities of our experience.*

For the purposes of his "demythologizing" program Bultmann defines mythology as "the use of imagery to express the otherworldly in terms of this world and the divine in terms of human life, the other side in terms of this side."[4] But this leaves unquestioned the most problematic feature of mythological thinking: that there *is* an "otherworldly" or "other side" at all, which, in contrast with the "human," is to be viewed as "divine." Attempting to resolve the problem of myth by cutting away most of the minor mythological realities (demons, angels, and other supernatural and superpersonal powers), but continuing to speak of an "exalted Christ," of the "Word of God" as something that comes *to* man from some "beyond," and of "acts of God" that *transform* men and history, is to miss entirely the central problem posed by mythological language. For that problem does not arise from the mere picturing of another *world* ("heaven," "supernature") over against our world, in imagery drawn from within our world; the problem is whether there is *any significant reality at all* "above" or "beyond" or "below" the world we know in our experience, or whether life is to be understood simply in this-worldly, that is, secular, terms. Demythologizing that fails to come to terms with the ultimate metaphysical-cosmological dualism that is expressed in the mythology, and that is, in fact, at the root of all Western religious thinking, is not seriously facing up to the problem of the irrelevance of Christian faith and the Christian church in contemporary life.

[4] *Kerygma and Myth*, ed. H. W. Bartsch (London: S.P.C.K., 1953), p. 10, n. 2.

Men of other ages found it necessary to create and believe elaborate mythologies and metaphysics of the "beyond" in order to understand their world and themselves. Contemporary men in contrast—partially freed by scientific advance from the ignorance that mythological explanations attempted to fill, and through technological advance increasingly able to control forces that were to earlier generations simply mystery— find it more and more unnecessary and even ridiculous to make this dualistic assumption. They have learned in recent centuries that those claims to knowledge of reality that have warrant in this-worldly experience lead to prediction and control of their world, while speech about some "other world" or "supernatural reality" appears to be without warrant or significant effect, a merely traditional and probably superstitious usage. The authority of church and Bible no longer suffices to sustain the dualistic position; indeed, it is precisely the dubiousness to many moderns of the metaphysical dualism which these "authorities" so unquestioningly take for granted that can be credited in part for their obviously waning significance in modern life. We seem thus faced with two options. The dualism can be given up without remainder as an unjustifiable metaphysical vestige from previous stages of civilization[5]— and it is difficult to see how anything recognizably Christian would remain if one took this course without some qualifications. Or else we must find a way in the present situation to restate (in terms not simply presupposing the old dualistic mythology) the contention that the ultimate reality with which man has to do is somehow "beyond" that which is directly given in experience. That is, we must seek to show in terms meaningful for our own time how it is possible and why it is significant to speak not only of this world but of "God." It is to this latter alternative that the present paper is directed.[6]

[5] Auguste Comte more than a century ago, of course, already took this position, and he has proved to be the prophet of modern man in this respect.

[6] It should be observed that the present paper is concerned with the question of the *meaning* rather than the *truth* of statements containing the word "God." No attempt will be made here to prove either that God does or does not exist, that is, that the word "God"

II

We may begin our investigation by asking about the purpose or intention of "God-language." What function does the word "God" perform in religious and theological speech? That is,

does or does not actually refer to a reality. Questions of that sort can be faced only if we already know what we mean when we use the word "God"—the issue to which this paper is directed. (It should be evident that, certain neo-orthodox theologians to the contrary notwithstanding, prior discussion of the meaning of "God" is just as important for "Christian faith" as for "philosophy of religion," for it is meaningless to speak of "what God has done" or "what God has revealed" if it is doubtful whether the word "God" itself has any referential meaning.) It is my contention that the underlying assumption both of theists and a-theists is that "God-language" presupposes the validity of what I have above called the mythological-cosmological dualism between this world and another world, the holy and the secular, the eternal and the temporal, the absolute and the relative. Believers find themselves defending one or another of the several forms of this dualism; unbelievers (as well as many believers, if the truth be admitted) find the whole dualistic conception without sufficient warrant and possibly even a ludicrous vestige of earlier stages of culture. The question of the meaning and significance of speaking about God at all thus tends to get decided not in its own terms but on the basis of a prior attitude taken up toward the dualism of this world and the other. The purpose of the present paper is to show that the meaning of the word "God," even in its reference to the "transcendent," can be developed entirely in terms of this-worldly ("secular") experiences and conceptions—that is, in terms fully comprehensible and significant to the most "modern" of men—and that therefore the whole issue of a presupposed cosmological dualism, so problematic for modern man, can be bypassed. In English the word "God" is understood by some to designate a mere psychological projection of a father-image and by others to indicate the Father of Jesus Christ and the ultimate reality with which we have to do. Since we are here attempting to uncover the basis on which significant conversation between such diverse points of view may proceed, and are not trying to prejudice the case for one or the other of these alternatives, it is evident that our delineation of meaning will need to have great flexibility. Doubtless to believers the present analysis may seem to concede too much to psychological reductionism; to unbelievers, too much to outgrown superstition. My intention, however, is to favor neither view—that would be to argue the question of *truth* not *meaning*—but to provide a framework of meaning within which, therefore, genuinely significant conversation between them can once again proceed.

which experiences or problems *in this world* seem to require some people to talk about extramundane reality? And why do they think such an odd extrapolation or postulation is necessary? When one puts the question this way, the first thing to be observed is that the question about God-language has been transformed from a strictly logical to a quasi-historical form. The problem to which we shall initially address ourselves is not the abstract and general problem of proving to any rational mind the meaningfulness and even truth of the concept of "God"; it is, rather, the concrete problem of locating the context and situation in which the word "God" is used and found appropriate and meaningful. Clearly, only if this latter task is performed first can the former be undertaken with any hope of significant outcome. Indeed, it may turn out that this word or its context has a peculiar character that makes impossible such general logical justification.

In connection with what sorts of questions or problems, then, has speech about God or another world emerged and been used? The answer is not difficult to find. Such speech appears within the context of man's sense of limitation, finitude, guilt, and sin, on the one hand, and his question about the meaning or value or significance of himself, his life, and his world, on the other.[7]

On the one hand, man knows himself to be limited in many respects: God (or the gods, angels, demons, and so on) is seen as the reality that is the final limit to his being and power. This is the experiential dimension of the claim that God is creator, sovereign, lord of the world, and so forth: men experience themselves as "thrown" into a world (Heidegger) not of their own making and ultimately not under their control; they look forward to an end, death, which they may be able to defer slightly but which they can never avoid; they are hemmed in on all sides and determined by their peculiar aptitudes, tem-

[7] The emphases of biblical faith on salvation, deliverance, succor, abundant life, forgiveness, resurrection, atonement, eternal life, and so on all have this double reference, negatively to man's inadequacy and need, and positively to man's meaningful destiny and fulfillment.

peraments, and interests, by the position in society and history into which they have been born, by circumstances of all sorts completely out of their control. The details of the analysis and elaboration of this awareness of limitation and weakness will of course differ widely in different cultures and traditions, and the way in which the limiting factor(s)—God—is understood will vary accordingly, but the basic *fact* of man's finiteness is rooted in man's actual situation as a particular limited being in the world. When in the course of evolution man emerged to full consciousness and self-consciousness, it was inevitable that he would also become conscious of, and seek modes of interpretation of, this his finitude. The earliest forms of such interpretation were highly mythological and are no longer acceptable or meaningful to many moderns. But the problem that gave rise to those views remains, and talk about God in the contemporary context must be understood as a modern way of seeking to speak about these same issues. In this respect the idea of God functions as a *limiting concept,* that is, a concept that does not primarily have content in its own right drawn directly out of a specific experience, but refers to that which we do *not* know but which is the ultimate limit of all our experiences. While ancient man spoke with some confidence in his knowledge of this reality *beyond the limits* of his world—and it is just this which makes his thought "mythological" or "gnostic," and dubious to many today—most moderns are somewhat more fastidious and restrict themselves to positive affirmation about only what falls *this side* of the limits.[8] But it must be observed that we, like ancient men, are

---

[8] In this respect modern man appears to be more heir of the skeptical than the metaphysical tradition in philosophy. One remembers, for example, the speech of Hume's Philo at the end of Part 8 of the *Dialogues Concerning Natural Religion:* "All religious systems, it is confessed, are subject to great and insuperable difficulties. Each disputant triumphs in his turn, while he carries on an offensive war, and exposes the absurdities, barbarities, and pernicious tenets of his antagonist. But all of them, on the whole, prepare a complete triumph for the *sceptic,* who tells them that no system ought ever to be embraced with regard to such subjects: for this plain reason that no absurdity ought ever to be assented to with regard to any subject. A total suspense of judgment is here

also involved in a certain duality here, between what is in fact concretely experienced, and the limit(s) of all experience and knowledge.

On the other hand, as a being who lives in a world of symbolic meanings (that is, who is a linguistic being) and values (that is, who is a deciding and acting being, making choices between alternatives), man asks about the meaning and value of his own existence. His conscious experience and thought are made possible by his ability symbolically to compare and contrast the fragments and pieces of experience with each other through the creation of words and symbols and thus to build up a symbolical and ordered world of increasingly comprehensive wholes. His action in and measure of control over his world are made possible by his learning to create and define standards or criteria for evaluating alternatives before him, and his learning to discriminate with increasing precision between the realities of his experience in terms of these norms. It is only natural, then, that he should ask about the meaning of his own existence within this structured world in which he finds himself, and the value of himself and his activity in the midst of all these other valued realities. This question becomes especially urgent in the light of his ultimate limitation and powerlessness, which seem to suggest that no lasting meaning or value can be placed on his being; certainly he by himself could not be its adequate source or ground. Once more, then, an answer to this question could be found only *beyond the limits* of human possibilities and knowledge. Here again the mythologies of earlier generations were able to provide concrete answers. In the "other world," the world "beyond the grave," the inequities and injustices of this life are made right (doctrines of karma and the judgment of God, of heaven and of hell) and the value and meaning of human existence is assured. Though such affirmations could hardly be made sim-

---

our only reasonable resource. And if every attack, as is commonly observed, and no defence among theologians is successful, how complete must be *his* victory who remains always, with all mankind, on the offensive, and has himself no fixed station or abiding city which he is ever, on any occasion, obliged to defend?"

ply on the basis of this-worldly experience, the religious myths
provided a *gnosis* of the "beyond" (of God's nature and will,
or of the ultimate order of things) which gave adequate assurance. In contrast, contemporary man finds it exceedingly
difficult to speak with any confidence at all about that which
is *beyond* the limits of his world, although the duality (between
what is accessible to us and some ultimate limit) may be acknowledged.

It is in the context of these questions and problems about
man's finitude and the significance of his existence in the light
of this finitude that the meaning and use of the word "God"
should be understood. That is, our speech about this Other
arises because certain features of experience force us up
against the limit(s) of all possible knowledge and experience.
If there were no experiences within the world which brought
us in this way up against the Limit of our world—if there were
no point at which man sensed his finitude—then there would
be no justification whatsoever for the use of "God-language."[9]
This means that any persons (positivists?) who by temperament or training either do not often find themselves forced up
against these limits or do not choose to reflect on them when
they are will find speech about God seeming useless or empty.
Since it is in relation to this particular context of problems and
experience and language that "God" has meaning or justifiable
use, its significance or validity cannot be demonstrated to anyone who either refuses to acknowledge the legitimacy of the
context or denies any substantial interest in it. In this sense,
the problem of the meaning and importance of theological
speech depends upon matters of temperament and history.
But, though not everyone will acknowledge the significance of
questions about the Limit, to those who do, such questions will
appear to be of universal import; for every man (whether he
acknowledges it or not and whether he is interested in this or
not) stands under and within the limits here under consideration. It is not unimportant to raise the question, then, about
the degree to which one's understanding of the issues here in-

[9] The highly complex character of this "experience" of finitude
will be briefly analyzed in Section IV, below.

volved depends on the traditions that seem to him significant as well as the climactic historical occurrences in his own life.

III

We must now examine further the meaning of the term "God." Though the fact of ultimate limitations on our being and meaning provides the context within which religious language arises and has meaning, it is clear that more is intended by that word than simply the bare and abstract notion of Limit. It is not surprising that primitive man, in confronting this situation, created imagery (in analogy with certain concrete powers within his experience) by means of which the power of the ultimate Limit could be conceived; and so the mythological "other world" appeared as the home of the mysterious powers that invaded and controlled this world. Our modern problem with theological language arises out of the fact that we no longer find it justifiable or meaningful to speak of this other world and the powers that inhabit it. Even when, in more sophisticated interpretations, the plethora of mythological powers supposedly controlling human destiny is reduced to one—God (or, as in a contemporary highly bloodless form, "being-itself")—we are dubious of the claims to knowledge. And that for a rather obvious reason: if it is really the *limits* of our experience and knowledge with which we are here dealing, by what right can anyone speak of the nature or even the existence of reality beyond those limits? Here sheer agnosticism would seem to be not merely prudent but the only honest course as well.

Inasmuch as theological language often claims or pretends to speak of that *beyond* the limits of the humanly experienceable —even, upon occasion, claiming to know on the basis of "revelation" about the inner workings of the divine being(s)—it is not surprising that such talk seems highly dubious and even sheer nonsense to many. Limit means *limit*. And it is both deceitful and inconsistent on the one hand to justify talk about God on the ground of our limitedness, and then, on the other, to transcend those limits in order to spell out in some detail the structure of the reality that lies beyond them. Insofar as theological language is involved in this sort of self-contradiction and self-delusion, it very rightly has fallen into ill repute. If the experiential base that justifies the very use of theological terms is man's awareness of his own finitude, then the fact of that finitude must be consistently adhered to in that language, and the too easy transcending of finitude implicit in every form of mythology must be renounced. Because the awareness of the "boundary situation" (Jaspers) within which man lives was first expressed in mythological forms which themselves implicitly ignored that boundary,[10] it has been extremely difficult to discern clearly the experiential base that justifies theological language. Consequently it has been supposed, both within the theological community and without, that theology deals primarily in otherworldly realities. From this common assumption the religious have proudly drawn the conclusion that they have been granted a secret *gnosis* denied others, while the worldly supposed that theology dealt simply in old wives' tales and other superstitions about some "other world" which the imagination of man has fabricated out of whole cloth. Neither side was able to focus clearly on the actual base *in concrete experience* from which theological work proceeds, thus giving an interpretation of religious language that could justify its use to contemporary secular man. It is clear that if we have located correctly the experiential context of speech about God, the theological vocabulary will have to be rebuilt from the ground up with a much more sensitive ear

[10] It may be observed in passing that, despite all his strictures to the contrary, Jaspers also really allows his alleged "boundary situations" to be surpassable under certain circumstances in the experience of what he calls "transcendence" (see e.g., *Philosophie*, 2d ed. [Berlin: Springer Verlag, 1948], pp. 44 ff., 470, 675 ff.). In the respect and degree to which this is the case his conception and analysis of finitude represents one more attempt to deny its real meaning, and my more drastic interpretation of the "boundary situation" should not be confused with his. (For similar criticism of Jaspers, see also Barth's analysis in *Church Dogmatics*, III/2, pp. 109–121.)

to the epistemological consequences *for theology itself* of the fundamental religious situation of limitedness.[11]

It is not possible to undertake that project in any detail in this paper. The most that can be done is to analyze briefly the complex character of the awareness of our finitude and the special understanding of that awareness implicit in the use of the word "God." It must be clear, of course, just what I am attempting here. I am not seeking to develop a full-blown doctrine of God on the basis of a kind of natural theology of human finitude. Rather, I am trying to define with some precision the sort of "God-talk" which is justifiable and responsible from that base, as well as the limitations that must be imposed on theological speech when one seeks to avoid presupposing the traditional—and illegitimate in the modern view—mythology of two worlds. (If someone wishes to live and speak within that mythological framework, of course that is his business. I am here concerned with searching out the meaning that theological language can have for those of us who no longer find warrant for or meaning in that dualism.)

We begin then with a somewhat different duality than that of two-world thinking: the duality of experience and its Limit(s). Such meaning of the term "God" as derives from an alleged *gnosis* of some "other world," transmitted by mythological traditions, may not be admitted to consideration here, for our interest is in defining the meaning that the awareness of our finitude as such permits and requires.

IV

What kind of conception is this notion of ultimate Limit? Some existentialist literature seems to suggest that there is a particular immediate experience involved here, which is to be contrasted with other experiences of lesser limits. I do not think this is a very careful reading of the matter. All that we

[11] It goes without saying that my repeated use of such terms as "finite," "limit," and so on is meant simply to *characterize* man; the respects in which man's finitude might be either "good" or "evil" are not considered. The usage is intended as neutral description.

ever experience directly are particular events of suffering, death (of others), joy, peace, and so forth. It is only in *reflection upon these* and the attempt to *understand ourselves in the light of these happenings* that we become aware of our limitedness on all sides. Along with this awareness of our being hemmed in, powerful emotions of terror, despair, revulsion, anxiety, and the like, are often—perhaps always—generated, and this total intellectual-emotional complex may then be called the "experience of finitude" or awareness of the "boundary situation" or something of the sort. But it must be observed that this "experience" of radical contingency is not an *immediate* awareness of restriction, as when one butts one's head directly against a stone wall; it depends rather upon a generalization from such occasional immediate experiences of limitation to the total situation of the self. The self, in this way perceived as hemmed in on all sides, comes to a new and deeper awareness of its nature and powers: it is *finite*, master neither of itself nor of its world. Thus, the so-called experience of finitude or contingency, however powerful the emotions that accompany and deepen and reinforce it, has an intellectual root, and it is possible only because man is a reflective being. (Dogs also die, but this does not lead them to despair over canine life, because they, presumably, are unable to anticipate their own death imaginatively and reflect on its meaning.) As we shall see below, the peculiar character of this complex experience—being rooted in particular, simple experiences of restriction, but apprehended as referring to the contingency of the self (and of man generally) in every moment, man's boundedness on all sides—enables it to be the experiential ground both of theological conceptions and of nontheistic metaphysical schemas as well.

It is with the aid of concepts such as *limit* that the generalizing movement of consciousness from particular immediate experiences of restriction to the total situation of the self is made. This term, originally applying to physical boundary lines (for example, between fields or nations), here becomes used metaphorically to designate the self's awareness of being circumscribed or hemmed in. How is such restriction and limitation to be conceived? The imagery built into the notion of limit by its physical origins reminds us that every *actual* limit or boundary that marks off and restricts *real being* (in contrast to, for example, a mathematical limit or similar abstract "limiting idea") must itself be conceived *as a reality, as having some kind of substance and structure*.[12] Thus, a city wall is made of earth and stones, a fence of wire and posts. It is important to observe here, however, that only because we can examine the wall or fence from all sides, test it in various ways, and the like—that is, only because the limit is not an ultimate or absolute limit, but can be surpassed—is it possible for us to know the stuff of which it consists. If we could not in any way *get beyond* the limit we were examining, we would have no means of directly discovering its nature, but would have to construct the conception of it imaginatively out of elements more fully known in our experience.

Consider, for example, the situation of a man imprisoned in a cell outside of which he has never been and from which he cannot escape. If he seeks to conceive the restricting walls of his room—with their resistance to his efforts to push through them, their hardness and solidity and color—as (material) realities, he will be able to do so only in analogy with the experienceable (material) objects *within* the room. Thus, his conclusion that the walls are composed of some sort of *thickness* of material substance, however plausible, in fact presupposes an interpretation of that which is *beyond* what is directly experienceable by him, namely, the bare surface of the walls. The conception of the ultimate limit of his movements is con-

---

[12] I do not think the notion of a mathematical limit, which is always approached asymptotically but never actually reached, can serve as a root conception for the notion of *metaphysical limit* with which we are here working. For the awareness of finitude is not purely conceptual or hypothetical; it is an awareness of *my actual being* as here (in this time and place) rather than there, as restricted in this particular concrete way by aptitudes, interests, and training, as one who must and shall in fact die. It is the awareness of *my being limited* that we are here dealing with and thus in some sense an actual "encounter" with that which *limits me*. The notion of an asymptotic approach to a limit is simply not applicable, and we must revert to the physical experiences of limitation for our conceptual models.

structed imaginatively out of elements derived from objects within his experience that partially restrict and limit him; for the stuff or structure of the walls themselves—that "behind" their surfaces—cannot be directly known, though the restrictingness of the walls is, of course, directly experienced.

The same point about the way in which the notion of the ultimate Limit is conceived by analogy with certain relative limits known within experience may be made with reference to another illustration, the ancient image of the "end of the world"—a kind of final edge of a bottomless abyss beyond which it is impossible to go. In this case it is obvious that what is *beyond the Limit* is being imagined rather precisely in terms of the intramundane experience of dangerous cliffs and other places from which one might fall to his destruction. Even the abstract notion of limit itself, we may now recall, was drawn originally from the experience of (relative) physical boundaries; only by analogical extension of its meaning could it be applied to the self in such a way that the sense of being completely circumscribed and confined—the awareness underlying the concept of finitude—could develop.[13] It is hardly surprising, then, that when we seek to conceive this Limit concretely, as restricting and constricting our actual beings, images and notions drawn from concrete intramundane experiences of limitation provide the material making up the conception. Certain characteristics of known finite limits are abstracted from their context and are built by analogy into the notion of the ultimate Limit. Our problem, now, is to discern what experiences provide the images and what restrictions must be laid down governing their use in this way.

Let us recall what it is that is being limited here and see how

[13] In view of this complex structure of the concept of limit—it being derived from the experience of relative limits which can be surpassed, and then extended to the notion of ultimate Limit which cannot—we should really not be surprised that men of all ages have supposed they actually knew something of that beyond the Limit, and that they expressed this in what I have above designated as mythological thinking. The duality of conscious finite being and Limit very easily, and almost naturally, goes over into the dualism of this world and the other world. These facts also illuminate the roots and meaning of Kant's first antinomy.

its limits are in fact experienced. It is not property or a nation
or even the world with which we are here concerned, but the
self. The self's awareness of being restricted on all sides, rendering problematic the very meaning of its existence, gives rise
to the question: *What* is it that in this way hems us in? How is
this *ultimate* Limit, of which we are aware in the "experience
of finitude," to be conceived? There appear to be four fundamental types of limiting experience, and these supply models
with the aid of which the ultimate Limit can be conceived. The
first two are relatively simple: (a) selves experience external
physical limitation and restriction upon their activities through
the resistance of material objects over against them; (b) they
experience from within the *organic* limitation of their own
powers, especially in illness, weakness, failure, and exhaus-
tion. The other two are somewhat more complex: (c) they
experience the external *personal* limitation of other selves engaged in activities and programs running counter to their own
—the clash of wills, decisions, and purposes—but precisely
because matters of volition and intention are subjective, this
experience is neither simply internal nor external, but is interpersonal and social; (d) they experience the *normative*
constraints and restrictions upon them expressed in such distinctions as true-false, real-illusory, good-bad, right-wrong,
beautiful-ugly, which distinctions, though felt subjectively and
from within, appear to the self not to be its own spontaneous
creations but to impinge upon it with categorical demands
and claims.

The self is restricted in its actual willing and acting, in its
formulation of projects and its attempts to actualize them, in
each of these quite different ways. Each is the basis for a
peculiar experience of the nature of limitation, which cannot
be reduced to any of the others. Thus, for example, it is not
possible to understand the sense of being at cross purposes
with and thus restricted by another person, in terms simply of
the concept of *physical* resistance or limitation, any more than
the experience of utter weakness in connection with a severe
illness can be comprehended with categories derived from the
concept of logical necessity. Though these four modes of ex-

perienced limitation may sometimes be confused with each
other and often (or perhaps always) are experienced in complex interconnection with each other, they are obviously distinct and separate. In each case the *limiter* is conceived in
somewhat different terms so as to be appropriate to that of the
self which is actually restricted. Thus, material objects impose
physical restrictions, and physiological deficiencies limit our
organic capacities; other active wills are responsible for personal constraints, while values and ideals impinge with normative force. In a situation such as imprisonment I experience
physical restriction (the prison walls), but am also aware of the
personal constraint of other wills (those who built the prison
and put me in it), and perhaps of organic deterioration (increasing weakness owing to poor food and lack of exercise).
Each restriction is involved with the others and with the concrete situation of imprisonment, and some (such as physical
restrictions) may be the result of others (the conflict of wills)
and essential to the effective realization of those others, but
none of the limiters can be reduced to any of the others.
Escape from prison will not dissolve the conflict of wills, and
personal reconciliation will not correct malnutrition. In each
case the specific limiter restricting the self must be dealt with
appropriately to its own nature.

If we turn now from this identification of the variety of
finite limiters to the problem of understanding the ultimate
Limit, it will be clear that there are a number of possibilities.
The ultimate Limit could be understood analogously with any
one of the types of finite limiter, or through some combination
of several of them; but there is no way of grasping the nature
of the ultimate Limit simply and purely in its own terms. For,
in the first place, if this is really the *Limit* beyond which we
can never move, then by definition there could be no way for
us directly to apprehend its character; at best we could experience and know its "surface," that is, its mere impingement
as such, its limitingness, a quite abstract notion. But the
ultimate Limit—being that which is apprehended as the *real*
and *effective* restriction on our being and movement (no mere
"empty idea")—is grasped as concrete actuality impinging on

us, that is, not merely abstractly but as having some concrete character or nature. Moreover, in the second place, as the preceding analysis has shown, awareness of the ultimate Limit is no fifth entirely distinct type of direct and immediate experience of limitation; on the contrary, this awareness arises only mediately through complex acts that generalize the immediate and particular experiences of constraints upon the self into the "experience of finitude."[14] It is out of this complex experience that the question about an ultimate Limit over against the self first arises, and it is within this context that any apprehension or conception of the ultimate Limit will emerge.[15] Insofar as its

[14] It will be observed that, though in many respects my position resembles Schleiermacher's, at this point I am setting myself against his contention that we have a specific and unique sense of absolute dependence as such (cf. *The Christian Faith* [Edinburgh: T. and T. Clark, 1928], §§ 3–5).

[15] It might be helpful to summarize here the various phases of the complex process through which, according to this analysis, the conception of an ultimate Limit is formulated: (1) there must be particular concrete experiences of limitation (of the several types described); (2) the self must be sufficiently mature and reflective to be able to move from consciousness of these particular experiences to a more general concept of limitation or finitude; (3) the awareness of the significance that it is *I* who am in this inescapable way hemmed in must arise, together with the powerful emotions that contribute to the "experience of finitude"; (4) this awareness of my own radical contingency may then give rise to the question about *what* it is that so confines and limits me; (5) the ultimate Limit may then be conceived in terms of one (or possibly some combination) of the four types of finite limiter. It should not be thought that the complexity of this process in any way prejudices the legitimacy of the question (4) or the possible truth of the answer (5). For it is certainly conceivable that we are limited ultimately by some (one) reality, and, if so, that only through some such complex process could we—all our knowledge being rooted in experiences of the finite—come to know it. As we shall see below, if the ultimate Limit were personal (as the notion of "God" suggests), we would expect him to be known through complex mediatorial processes in any case (as is a finite person), and there would seem to be no reason why these processes could not include the sort here suggested (see note 26, below). On the other hand, it must also be admitted that there seems to be no compelling necessity to move from step (3) in the above process through (4) and (5). One could claim (positivistically), if one chose to do so, that the only *what* that limits me are the four types of finite limiter as experienced in (1), and that there is no

character or nature is explicitly conceived at all, it will evidently be understood then, with the aid of one or more of the actually experienced finite limiters (the experiences of which are the only concrete sorts of limitation we know), and will be interpreted in terms of implications derived from that (or those) image(s). Moreover, since there is no possible way to prove the special appropriateness of any one or combination of the finite limiters to perform this function (again, that would presuppose a direct knowledge of the nature of the absolute Limit, which, as we have seen, is not available), it is evident that any particular concrete conception of the ultimate Limit may be quite arbitrary.[16] Despite this difficulty we cannot avoid conceiving the Limit as concrete, for if it is apprehended at all, it must be apprehended as that which in fact constricts and constrains the actual concrete self.

Any of the types of finite limiter could serve as the model in terms of which a conception of the ultimate Limit might be developed, but difficulties arise when any one of them is used exclusively. Thus, when physical limitation is taken as the fundamental analogy, a materialistic world-view results and man's being is understood as simply a function of the physical universe. This is a common enough view and has much to commend it, notably the obvious dependence of all man's functions

---

reason to suppose there is some one reality beyond and behind these which is the *ultimate Limiter*. The fact that the present analysis of the consciousness of finitude lends itself to such varied sorts of interpretation is no shortcoming: it means, rather, that significantly different perspectives—from positivism to a variety of types of metaphysics and Christian theology—can enter into common discourse with the aid of this framework, and this is precisely what we are seeking to make possible with this analysis (see note 6, above).

[16] It is, of course, better that we be aware of these peculiar difficulties in the conception with which we are dealing here than, in ignorance, simply refuse to face the question at all. In this respect Kant, who saw that we could never resolve the antinomies and problems of metaphysics but who also saw that we could never cease struggling with these issues (see, e.g., *The Critique of Pure Reason*, A849/B877–A851/B879), was much wiser than many of his latter-day (positivistic, existentialistic, and fideistic) followers.

on his physical being. However, it is very difficult to see how the other types of limiter are to be understood simply in physical terms. This problem is often dealt with in modern times through some conception of emergent evolution, but the problems here are immense and probably insoluble from a purely materialistic point of view. Hence one may be led, as with A. N. Whitehead or Henri Bergson, to seek a resolution of the difficulties with some sort of organicism or vitalism. Yet it is difficult to see how the notion of organic limitation is really helpful in developing a conception of the world that does justice to the other limiters. Similar problems arise with the various forms of idealism, which take normative limitation to be the most fundamental.

However, our objective here is not to resolve these difficult problems of metaphysics but rather to examine the grounds for speech about God when the traditional mythological dualism is given up. The ultimate experiential ground for such speech should now be evident. Talk about God appears when the ultimate Limit is understood on analogy with the experience of *personal limiting* as known in the interaction of personal wills. In this respect religious faith opts for one particular metaphysical alternative from among the several available. This metaphysical decision is not of mere speculative interest, however, for the option involved is active will, that over against which a self can live in interaction and intercourse and communion. The other options understand the ultimate Limit in terms of an image of dead being or passive structure (as a quasi-physical limiter or like certain aspects of a normative limiter), or else as a vital but unconscious and certainly purposeless force (like an organic limiter or certain other features of a normative limiter). Though each of these interprets certain dimensions of our experience significantly, none comes directly to grips with our distinctive experience as persons in communities, as conscious, active, deciding, purposing beings living in a symbolical world that provides the context and the possibility for continuous communication and intercourse with others. The interpretation of the ultimate Limit in terms of

this social level and dimension of our experience—which, however dependent it may be on the others in many respects, is the
presupposition of our having any experience (properly so
called)—is the metaphysical prerogative of theistic religion
and defines its peculiar character. The religious attractiveness
of this metaphysics—in that the ultimate context of human
existence is here seen as personal and purposive volitional activity and not dead matter or unfeeling logical structure or
unconscious vital power—makes theism relevant to the existential problems of the person in a way unmatched by any of
the other metaphysical alternatives.[17] Hence, it appears naturally as the essential ideological dimension of most religious
faith. But precisely this same attractiveness makes theistic
belief seem dubious to many, in that the powerful desire of
man to find genuine purpose and meaning in his life here
seems too easily and happily fulfilled. The intrinsic anthropomorphism of this perspective thus makes it at once suspect
and seductive. (This, of course, really does not bear directly
on the question of its actual truth, since *all* the metaphysical
alternatives conceive the ultimate Limit with the aid of a more
or less arbitrarily chosen finite model.)

V

When a personal limiter is the analogical basis for understanding the ultimate Limit, a doctrine of God results. The
ultimate Limit is then conceived in quasi-personal terms to be
understood most decisively with notions drawn originally from
the language used to deal with interpersonal experience. It is
clear that this conception is the one operative in the biblical
tradition where God is spoken of as lord, father, judge, king,

[17] If in this paper I were seeking to give an argument for the
truth of theism, instead of limiting myself to an analysis of the
experiential bases for—and thus the root meaning of—the word
"God," it would be necessary and appropriate to expand and develop some of the implications of these sentences. (See also note
19, below.) [An expansion of some of these ideas will be found
in Chapters 5 and 10, below.]

and he is said to love and hate, to make covenants with his
people, to perform "mighty acts," to be characterized by mercy,
forgiveness, faithfulness, patience, wisdom, and the like—all
terms drawn from the linguistic region of interpersonal discourse. Moreover, the biblical God is understood not to be accessible to man's every whim; he is not some structure or
reality immanent in human experience and thus directly
available to man. On the contrary, he resides in lofty transcendence, whence he acts in complete freedom to change the
course of history or to reveal himself to his people through his
prophets. Now it is clear that this image of inaccessible transcendence and freedom made known and effective through
explicit acts of communication and power—through words
and deeds—is built up analogically from the model of the hiddenness and transcendence and freedom of the finite self, who
also can (in some significant measure) hide himself from his
fellows and remain inaccessible, except as he chooses to manifest himself through acts and words.[18] Though other terminology and images are also found in the biblical materials, there
can be no doubt that personalistic language and conceptions
most decisively shape the biblical view of the ultimate Limit.

I contended earlier in this paper, however, that the biblical
and Christian traditions appear determined in large part by a
metaphysical-cosmological dualism characteristic of mythology and no longer meaningful to many moderns. Moreover, it
has often been held that precisely the anthropomorphic image
of God as personal is an especially crude example of the
mythological thinking of primitive man and therefore to be
regarded as only symbolic or picture language, of significance
in worship or prayer, but not adequate for precise theological
or philosophical work. We must now ask, therefore, how far

[18] For a full discussion of this claim that genuine transcendence
is intrinsically a personalistic notion and can be consistently developed only in connection with a personalistic conception of God,
see my paper on "Two Models of Transcendence," published in *The
Heritage of Christian Thought: Essays in Honor of Robert L. Calhoun*, ed. R. E. Cushman and E. Grislis (New York: Harper and
Row, 1965). [The relevant parts have been reprinted as Chapter 4
in this volume.]

a personalistic conception of God is essentially bound up with an inadequate mythology, how far it may be an independent and justifiable interpretation of the ultimate Limit.

It should be evident that to conceive the ultimate Limit personalistically is formally neither more nor less mythological than to conceive it on analogy with any of the other types of finite limiter. Each has its own peculiar appropriateness to certain dimensions of the self's experience of limitation, and each has difficulty in interpreting the other dimensions. With respect to the experience of limitation itself, then, no reason for preferring any of the four to the others can be given.[19] Moreover, inasmuch as it is necessary to grasp the ultimate Limit in terms of *some* model if it is to be adequately conceived at all, the attempt to grasp it personalistically should not be rejected as mythological (in the dubious sense of claiming unwarranted knowledge of that *beyond* the Limit) in any way not also applicable to every other attempt to apprehend and understand our finitude.

In a manner not characteristic of the other finite limiters, however, the personalistic image lends itself to a reopening of the question not only of the Limit, but of what is beyond it. For (as noted above) it interprets man's relationship to that which ultimately limits him as being like his relationship to the finite selves with which he interacts. Such selves always transcend in their subjectivity and freedom what is directly accessible to one in his experience (that is, their bodies) even though they "come to him" and communicate with him in and through this physical dimension of their being that is open to his view. What one directly experiences of the other are, strictly speaking, the external physical sights and sounds he makes, not the deciding, acting, purposing center of the self— though we have no doubt these externalities are not *merely*

[19] It might be noted here, however, that inasmuch as the personalistic model involves the notion of a self whose active center is *beyond* that which is directly experienced, the latter being conceived as the vehicle or medium of the self's action or revelation (see below), there is a certain flexibility and breadth in theism enabling it to deal with the diverse types of finite limiter somewhat more easily, perhaps, than can other kinds of metaphysics.

physical phenomena, but are the outward and visible expression of inner thought, purpose, intention. Thus we do not speak merely of "sights and sounds" in this case but of the "sights and sounds which *he* makes" in *his* attempt to act or to communicate. In our interaction with other persons we presuppose a reality (the active center of the self) *beyond* that which we immediately perceive, a reality encountered by us and known to us not simply in physiologically based perception (though that is of course also involved) but in and through the language that we jointly speak.[20] It is in the act of communication that we discover that the other is more than merely physical being, is a conscious self; it is in the experience of speaking and hearing that we come to know the *personal* hidden behind and in the merely physical.[21] This is the most powerful experience we have of *transcendence of the given* on the finite level, the awareness of genuine activity and reality *beyond* and *behind* what is directly open to our view.

When this type of complex interrelationship is used to interpret the ultimate Limit, it is clear that an active reality (or "self") beyond the Limit—beyond what is directly experienceable as such—will be implied. A self in its active center is never directly open to view,[22] but is known only as he reveals himself in communication and communion. Likewise, on this model God cannot be identified with what is accessible to or within our experience, not even with the ultimate Limit of our experience; rather this Limit must be grasped as the *medium* through which God encounters us (as noises and gestures are

[20] To avoid confusion in this already complex analysis, I shall use the term "encounter" to designate the linguistic-experiential ground of our knowledge of other selves, reserving the more general term "experience" for the sensory-perceptual foundations of our knowledge of physical objects (including the bodies of persons qua their purely physical character).

[21] For a more linguistically oriented treatment of these problems, which comes to fundamentally similar conclusions on the basis of careful anlysis of personalistic modes of speech, see Stuart Hampshire, *Thought and Action* (New York: Viking Press, 1960).

[22] [For some qualifications on this way of putting the matter, see the Preface.]

media for finite selves), God himself being conceived as the dynamic acting reality beyond the Limit.[23] In this way a certain reference to reality beyond the Limit of our experience is intrinsic to the personalistic image, and therefore such reference need not depend upon nor involve a reversion to mythology. It must be emphasized, however, that reference of this sort to transcendent reality is justifiable only when the ultimate Limit is understood in terms of a personal limiter, for only in the interaction with other selves do we encounter an active reality that comes to us from beyond what is accessible in experience. Organic, physical, and normative limiters can all be interpreted exhaustively in terms of what is given in and to experience (though it is not essential to do so), and it is mythology, therefore, if one speaks of a transcendent extraexperiential reality on the basis of one of those models; a personal

[23] In an early paper Paul Tillich seemed to be taking a position close to the analysis of this essay. "The non-symbolic element in all religious knowledge is the experience of the unconditioned as the boundary, ground, and abyss of everything conditioned. This experience is the boundary-experience of human reason and therefore expressible in negative-rational terms. But the unconditioned is not God. God is the affirmative concept pointing beyond the boundary of the negative-rational terms and therefore itself a positive-symbolic term" ("Symbol and Knowledge," *Journal of Liberal Religion*, II [1940], 203). Tillich, however, failed to refine his analysis and develop his insight. Thus, the peculiar character of "boundary experiences" remains unanalyzed here, and the "boundary" can even be interpreted in terms of such positive images as the (almost hypostatized) "unconditioned" or "ground"; this blurs its radical character as the ultimate unsurpassable Limit. Again (similarly to my analysis), "God" is distinguished from "the unconditioned" as "a positive-symbolic term" pointing beyond the ultimate boundary, but Tillich fails to see (either here or anywhere else in his writings) that this is because of the peculiar character of the transcendence known only in interpersonal relations and is thus intrinsically connected with the personalistic overtones of the term "God." In his later writings, where Tillich apparently gives up the view that the "non-symbolic element in all religious knowledge" is a special experience and holds instead (sometimes) that we can make at least one non-symbolic *statement* about God (see, e.g., *Systematic Theology* [3 vols., Chicago: University of Chicago Press, 1951–1963], I, 238–241), there remains little resemblance to the view I am trying to develop in the present essay.

limiter alone necessarily and intrinsically involves genuine transcendence.[24]

Correlative with this reference to a locus of reality beyond the Limit there must be a conception of revelation. We know the transcendent reality of other selves only as they act toward and communicate with us, as they reveal to us their reality and character and purposes in word and deed. So also, only if we are prepared to acknowledge some genuine encounter with God through his own actions directed toward us is it appropriate to speak of the ultimate Limit in personalistic terms, that is, with "God"-language. By definition we could know nothing of any personal being beyond the Limit of our experience if that being did not in some way manifest himself to us through our experience or its Limit.[25] Once again, the organic, physical and normative analogies for understanding the ultimate Limit require no doctrine of revelation, nor is any appropriate to them. This is the mode of knowledge characteristic of interpersonal communion, and it is when such encounters are taken as the model for understanding the Limit of all experience that the category of revelation is required.[26] Thus, to

[24] For further discussion, see my paper, "Two Models of Transcendence." [Chapter 4, below; see also Chapters 5 and 7.]

[25] Since, according to the present analysis, every *positive* doctrine of God must rest on revelation, it should be clear both why no real doctrine of God appears in this paper (no concrete revelation being expounded here), and that the present analysis of "limit" is not to be confused with the "negative way" *to* God.

[26] It will be observed that, according to the analysis presented in this paper, the "encounter" with God actually rests on a double mediation, whereas our encounters with finite selves involve only the single mediation (of noises, visible gestures, and the like) discussed in the text: (a) the ultimate Limit is not immediately experienced, but is known only through the mediation provided by reflection on and generalization of particular experiences of limitation (see note 15, above); (b) the "selfhood" or "nature" of God is not immediately experienced or directly encountered, but is known through the mediation of the ultimate Limit. This does not mean, however, that an "encounter" with God is really the product of a rather long chain of somewhat dubious inferences and no encounter with a reality at all. Rather, as the encounter with other selves makes clear, such communication through media is the mode in which realities transcending the reach of our immediate experience are known to us. In such an encounter, of course, I do not attend

speak of God acting or God revealing himself is not necessarily to make a mythological statement presupposing an unjustified and unjustifiable metaphysical-cosmological dualism; such forms of conceptualization and speech are necessary if and whenever a personal limiter is taken as the model for grasping the ultimate Limit.

VI

Most attempts to locate the experiential referent or basis for the term "God" heretofore have accepted the framework of what I here called metaphysical or mythological dualism and then tried to justify it in terms of some sort of direct "experience of God," or "apprehension of the infinite," or something similar. For those who had such experiences or intuitions,

---

directly to the mediating processes (the noises the other is making); rather, I am conscious of *him,* of the speaker. Insofar as I must attend to his *words,* consciously, in bewilderment about their meaning, making deliberate inferences, the process of communication is halting and ineffective. Only if I can and do "leap beyond" the media to the self who is mediated through these words is there significant encounter with the other. In most of our intercourse with others this leap is made in the most natural fashion; this is why we say we *know* the other *person,* and not merely the noises he makes. In a similar way, God is never directly "experienced," but is "encountered" (as is appropriate to his transcendence) only in and through media. (The *double* mediation involved in this case, in contrast with finite selves, is appropriate to the fact that this is *God,* and not merely some intramundane reality, of which we are here speaking.) If the media are the focus of attention here, of course the encounter with God will seem problematic and unreal; as with a finite self, only as and when a "leap beyond" the media (although through the media) occurs will the encounter with God be felt as genuine; only then could one properly speak of *God* being encountered. Theologically such moments are referred to as "revelation," that is, God's self-manifestation. It is only because men have believed these to have occurred to themselves, or others, that talk about "encounters" with God—and thus talk about "God"—has appeared and continues to be sustained in human discourse. *Faith,* we can now see, is that stance in which the "experience" of the ultimate Limit is apprehended as the medium of the encounter with God (see Section VI, below); *unfaith* is that attitude which, unable to "leap beyond" the ultimate Limit, finds itself always attending instead to the mere Limit as such.

these analyses doubtless had meaning and significance; but for others of a more secular or this-worldly temperament or turn of mind, this seemed to be nothing more than paying rather extravagant "metaphysical compliments" to certain dimensions of experience. The present analysis does not rest on the assumed validity of some esoteric experience of the otherworld or the supernatural or even the "numinous" (Otto). On the contrary, I have claimed that the experiential root of the notion of God is simply the awareness of Limit or finitude (known in some form by every man). In and of itself this awareness does not presuppose or imply some "infinite" or "unconditional" being. Indeed, only when it is grasped and interpreted in concrete personalistic terms does the Limit become understood as the expression of a being transcending our world, that is, of an active God.[27] Thus, the constitutive *experience* underlying the word "God" is that of limitation; the constitutive *image* which gives the term its peculiar transcendent reference is personalistic. These fused into one in the concretely religious apprehension of our finitude provide us with the root referent for the word.

This double rootage accounts for the fact that, on the one hand, the presence or action of God is sometimes said to be immediately "experienced" or "known," and, accordingly, doctrines of religious experience are developed. On the other hand, it is often maintained that the knowledge of God rests on "faith" or "belief," and that he cannot be experienced directly at all. If, as I am arguing, the most we could be said to experience directly here is our bare finitude as such—and even this is a complex sort of "experience" that is never apprehended concretely apart from the image of one or another of the finite limiters used analogically—then the truth in both claims can be understood: the encounter with God will involve

[27] It might be argued that it is no accident that such impersonal philosophical notions as "infinite" or "unconditional" reality, "being itself," and the bare notion of "transcendence," appear always as demythologized or depersonalized versions of the more anthropomorphic god(s) of a religious tradition, and that in their impersonal (sometimes called "superpersonal") form they are in fact denying the vital root on which their very life and meaning depend.

both the "experience" of our finitude and the faith-interpretation through which this limitedness is apprehended as owing
to an active will over against us. Since in the actual encounter
with God these two elements so interpenetrate each other as
not to be separately distinguishable,[28] there is little wonder
that conflicting views about the relative importance of "experience" and "faith" appear. The faith-interpretation, of
course, is shaped by the concrete historical tradition within
which one stands. If one stands within the Christian tradition,
which knows of a loving and powerful Creator, it is hardly
surprising that he will tend to see the course and destiny of his
own being—its limits on all sides—as determined by the activity of God: God's mercy and benevolence toward him will be
felt in that which seems good in life; his judgment and wrath,
in the painful and constrictive.[29]

I conclude, therefore, that God-language is not necessarily
hopelessly mythological and old-fashioned, but that, if carefully defined and restricted, it has a genuine basis in our awareness and knowledge of the Limit. This of course does not mean
that the door is opened wide again for the well-structured
"other world" of much traditional Christian thought. We have
found it possible and legitimate to speak only of the reality
that ultimately limits us on all sides—that is, God—in this way.
Of the existence beyond the Limit of finite beings alongside
God—angels, demons, supernatural powers of all sorts, or the
departed spirits of the dead—we know nothing and can know

[28] See note 26, above.

[29] If we have correctly identified the experiential elements underlying the term "God," the doctrine of God must always deal in some
fashion with the notion of transcendent reality (even if only to
refer it to some "depth" in everything that is) and with the way in
which this transcendence is known to us (that is, with "revelation"). However, such highly problematical negative notions as
"infinite" and "unconditional"—probably rooted ultimately in "mys-
tical" experience of the "supernatural"—would perhaps not need
to be given the constitutive role in a doctrine of God that they have
so often played in the past (though they might well have a certain
secondary and interpretative role to play); and the meaning of the
doctrine would not in that way be placed so completely out of reach
of those whose direct experience seems to them limited to the
finite and contingent.

nothing. There is no warrant in the present analysis, then, for reintroducing the "mythological world-view" in any form at all.[30] Since historically Christian theology grew out of and accepted rather uncritically the cosmological dualism underlying and expressed in that world-view, and in many details seems still to presuppose it, it is necessary to think through the whole of the Christian perspective afresh, sifting out all mythological elements to arrive at what of Christian faith modern, this-worldly man can affirm. Only when this winnowing has been performed will we be in a position to see whether the essentials of Christian belief in fact depend on the acceptance of a mythology meaningless and even ridiculous to moderns, or whether Christian faith can be a live issue in our secular culture.

I have tried in this paper to show that there is some justification for continuing to speak of a personal God even though the mythological framework characteristic of earlier speech of this sort be completely abandoned. This of course in no way can or should be construed as a kind of proof of the existence of such a God. As we have seen, there are other ways of conceiving the ultimate Limit which may in some respects seem more credible. All that I have attempted here is to show that "God-language" has its roots in concrete (secular) experience

[30] It should perhaps be observed that my contention that such a doctrine of God would not be mythological rests on a distinction between "mythological" and "analogical." A *mythological* doctrine of God *begins in* and *presupposes* what I have called the cosmological dualism of "this world" and "another world," "this side" and "the other side." For such a presupposition there seems little warrant. An *analogical* doctrine of God makes no such presupposition, but results when (the experience of) finitude is understood in personalistic terms. Thus, an analogical doctrine, being experientially rooted, can be carefully disciplined and controlled methodologically; with mythology the rootage is so vague and legendary that strict methodological control is almost impossible. For the position I am taking here, only if the Christian *doctrine of God* itself— worked out in strict accord with the foundations of theological knowledge as sketched in this paper—were to require the reintroduction of certain features of the otherwise discarded mythical world-view, would it be justifiable to reinstate them. But this is as it should be: Christian faith is first of all faith in *God*—and all else that must be said theologically should follow from this premise.

and that its cognitive meaningfulness can be defended, even granting the premises of "secular man"; whether it is *true* or not is another question. Our analysis has brought us into a position from which we can see what would be required if the truth of this claim were to be affirmed, however. Only on the ground that God had in fact revealed himself could it be claimed he exists; only if there were and is some sort of movement from beyond the Limit to us, making known to us through the medium of the Limit the reality of that which lies beyond, could we be in a position to speak of such reality at all; only if God actually "spoke" to man could we know there is a God. It is of course the Christian claim that God has acted to reveal himself and continues to do so. Whether that claim is true or not—and the grounds on which one might decide its truth—cannot be discussed here; a full systematic theology would be required to deal with it. This paper should have made clear, however, that genuine knowledge of God could not be affirmed on any other basis than such revelation, and that the Christian claim is, therefore, directly relevant to the general philosophical question of God's existence.

4

Two Models of Transcendence[*]

When we assert God's "transcendence" we are indicating something specific about God's relation to the world of our experience. In order to make clear just what is intended here, it is useful to consider the principal models of transcendence which are exhibited in ordinary (finite) experience and on the basis of which conceptions of divine transcendence can be (are) developed. In this essay I shall try to show that such models are to be found particularly in the language dealing with the striving of the self for goals not presently accessible, and in that pertaining to the experience and knowledge of other persons.[1] Let us turn first to the peculiar character of our experience of other persons.

---

[*] Though written some years earlier, this essay was first published in *The Heritage of Christian Thought: Essays in Honor of Robert L. Calhoun*, ed. R. E. Cushman and E. Grislis (New York: Harper and Row, 1965). The opening pages of the essay as originally published, which purported to discuss the contemporary analysis of "the problem of theological meaning," have been eliminated here because it is clear to me now that they reflected too uncritically an almost positivist criterion of cognitive meaning, even as they were attempting to propose an alternative approach. What remains has also been revised. Although this essay suggests a more subjectivistic understanding of the self than I now hold, its basic contentions about two conceptions of transcendence are, I believe, largely correct.

[1] To these two might be added the awareness that the "I" always transcends every given experience as its subject. However, precisly the elusiveness and unobservability of this "I" render all conceptions here highly problematical and therefore hardly suitable for the purpose of exemplifying and clarifying the already too obscure notion of transcendence.

I

It is often supposed that our knowledge of persons, like our knowledge of "things," is ordinarily or typically interpretation of and inference from sense data. But in fact, as a moment's reflection will show, though certain aspects of our knowledge of others are so rooted, the most important knowledge that we have of our friends (as well as our enemies)—that is, of persons as persons—is derived from *their acts of revealing or unveiling themselves to us when they communicate with us.* In this respect knowledge of persons is radically different from knowledge of objects. The latter knowledge depends exclusively on what we do to obtain the knowledge—perceive, infer, develop experimental testing procedures—and not at all on an act performed by the object known. But knowledge of persons depends quite as much on what *they* do—speak honestly and openly with us, or deliberately conceal from us how they feel—as on what we do.[2] Such knowledge arises out of the process of communication in which both knower and known actively participate, mutually revealing themselves to each other. Here another understanding subject provides us with, not mere sense data to interpret, but meaningful words and other gestures to understand, and it is through our understanding of his deliberate communication that we come to know him. This knowledge, then, arises out of a complicated interpersonal process involving the communicating, under-

----

[2] "All knowledge of persons is by revelation. My knowledge of you depends not merely on what I do, but upon what you do; and if you refuse to reveal yourself to me, I cannot know you, however much I may wish to do so. If in your relations with me, you consistently 'put on an act' or 'play a role', you hide yourself from me. I can never know you as you really are. In that case, generalization from the observed facts will be positively misleading. This puts the scientific form of knowledge out of court in this field. For scientific method is based on the assumption that things are what they appear to be; that their behaviour necessarily expresses their nature. But a being who can pretend to be what he is not, to think what he does not think, and to feel what he does not feel, cannot be known by generalization from his observed behaviour, but only as he genuinely reveals himself" (John Macmurray, *Persons in Relation* [London: Faber, 1961], p. 169).

standing, and interpreting of meaningful symbols; its deepest root is not a (solipsistic) interpretation of, or making inferences from, mere sense data.

I cannot within the limits of this essay provide detailed analysis of this process of interpersonal knowledge. We are concerned here with observing only one point: that insofar as our knowledge of another self emerges within the process of communication, we are here encountering a reality which is, strictly speaking, beyond the reach and observation of our senses, which, therefore, must be understood in contrast to objects of ordinary sensory perception. For interpersonal knowledge depends on the *other's act* and not simply our observation, that is, on something intrinsically inaccessible to us, something that we cannot at will make accessible. If we consider briefly what occurs in ordinary conversation, this will be clear. In speaking to someone, we "throw" meanings, as it were (we do not simply make noises) out beyond the circle of our own world, to a personal center transcending our direct experience and not open to our view, but which we believe capable of apprehending our meaning. Only the other's body is visible to us, and thus within our world in the sense of being directly accessible to our senses, not the dynamic self with whom we are seeking to communicate, though we usually think of that self as somehow "in" the body confronting us.[3] However, we put a question to the other precisely because the world accessible and open to us—and specifically, our direct perception of the other person—does *not* present us with the answer, and we must depend on the other self freely and honestly to respond to our query.

Our encounter with another self in the process of communication is thus an encounter with a reality that is in a certain sense beyond our direct reach and observation. We could not know this reality did he not choose to reveal himself to us from this beyond. For this reason the other self is always mystery in some significant sense, always unknown (however well known), always transcendent of our world. The other self

[3] [For qualifications on this way of putting the matter, see the Preface.]

can, if he chooses, refuse to reveal himself to us, remaining almost completely out of our reach even though his body is directly at hand. Despite this inaccessibility, to speak of the other self as real and as encountered by us, in the moments he reveals himself, is certainly reasonable and proper. In this experience-of-inaccessibility-except-in-moments-of-revelation we are provided with a model for the peculiar meaning of our word "transcendence."

There is another dimension of the experience of selfhood to which the concept of transcendence can also be meaningfully referred. A self has the power to act. That is, a self is able to formulate objectives, to set them as goals to be realized, and then to organize his life in such a way as to move toward and often to realize them. A large part of our lives consists in just such teleological activity, directed and guided no doubt by a wide variety of values, goals, interests, and loyalties. In each case, however, the end sought clearly transcends the immediate present experience of the self as the goal or ideal toward which he is striving, but its significance for the self is not less on that account. Indeed, it is precisely because the goal is not present, but is thus transcendent, that the self works toward it. This type of transcendence we can conveniently designate as "teleological" to distinguish it from the "interpersonal" transcendence which we have just considered.

Teleological transcendence is to be contrasted with interpersonal in a number of respects. Transcendence of the latter sort, for example, is more nearly unqualified than the former. The other self in certain respects forever escapes my grasp; even in moments in which he reveals himself to me, I am aware of a deep, impenetrable mystery beyond the revelation. In goal-seeking activity, however, the transcendence is often only temporary. If I set myself the task of making a table, my objective transcends the present realities of my experience, but with the completion of the project the transcendence is overcome.

Of course, teleological transcendence can be much more enduring than this, as in the self's experience of striving toward the realization of ideal values like truth, justice, or beauty.

Inasmuch as these objectives are never perfectly realized, they are experienced as always transcending the concrete world of our experience and thus eluding our grasp. This does not mean, however, that in its teleological activity the self sometimes experiences transcendence to be as "objective" as in interpersonal relations, although idealism has supposed this to be the case. The goal of the self's striving, whether material or ideal, is always in some sense posited by the self as *his* goal. However much one might wish to maintain with the idealists that values "lure" us, the actual imagining or conceiving of the values, as well as the work involved in moving toward them, is entirely the activity of the self. In this sense the self's striving is always toward a reality contained within its world, at least its world of ideals.

In contrast, however, another self is over against me, not as a goal I project, but as a reality impinging on me. The other can and does speak and act toward me in ways completely out of my control and in no way dependent on my teleological activity. He reveals himself to me, or refuses, as he chooses. Doubtless my activity with reference to this other is often teleological—as when I deliberately seek to make another my friend—and thus teleological transcendence is involved too, but the more fundamental transcendence here does not in this way depend on my activity; it depends rather on the fact that the center of the other self is forever outside my grasp, a reality with a life and activity of his own that becomes open to me only at his will. Precisely because the other is himself an active power, he is objective to me in a way that my values and ideals—however significant they are—can never be.

We have, then, two quite distinct models on which concepts of transcendence can be built, each rooted in living concrete experience, open and accessible to every man.

II

It has not often been noted that these two models of transcendence lead to quite diverse theological conceptions. If one makes teleological transcendence the model, one is led toward a theology of *being*. The ultimate reality will be understood as that good "which moves [all other things but is] itself unmoved."[4] All finite reality will be viewed as necessarily grounded in this ultimate reality, and as, in turn, striving toward it. This final *telos* should not be viewed anthropomorphically any more than the objects of the self's striving are normally conceived as other selves: it can be viewed ethically as the ultimate good, aesthetically as perfect beauty, or intellectually as being-itself or the ground of being or the absolute idea. Only when notions rooted in interpersonal transcendence are surreptitiously introduced is this ultimate reality conceived as personal, acting or loving, in short as "God," in anything like the Jewish or Christian sense. "It is not that the Supreme reaches out to us seeking our communion: we reach towards the Supreme; it is we that become present."[5] Personalistic notions of ultimate reality are, moreover, usually viewed by theologians of this perspective as somewhat embarrassing anthropomorphisms, to be tolerated primarily because of man's "religious" needs (that is, for subjective reasons) rather than because the understanding of reality requires it.[6]

[4] Aristotle, *Metaphysics*, Bk. XII, 7.

[5] Plotinus, *The Enneads*, trans. by Stephen MacKenna, rev. ed. (London: Faber, 1956), VI, 9, par. 8.

[6] It will be observed that Paul Tillich's whole theological program rests on the model of teleological transcendence. Thus, the "method of correlation" with its view that human existence has a certain instability and thus inevitably poses questions driving us beyond the finite to its transcendent ground (*Systematic Theology* [3 vols., Chicago: University of Chicago Press, 1951–1963], I, 61–66) is simply a reformulation of this model rooted in the self's striving. It should occasion no surprise, then, to find Tillich maintaining that the only literal statement one can make about God is that he is "being-itself," all other statements, including specifically religious statements, being symbolic (*ibid.*, pp. 238–241); nor is it surprising to discover that revelation for him is not so much the act of a personal being who transcends us, as an act in which the self transcends itself in "ecstasy" (*ibid.* pp. 111 ff.). Similarly, in the "traditional theism" of Eric L. Mascall, teleological transcendence is the determining model before which theological notions rooted in interpersonal transcendence must give way: "Certainly we must admit that, from the point of view of Christian devotion, the fact that God is Love is all-important. . . . But the attribute that is primary from the point of view of devotion may

On the other hand, if the theological model for the conception of the divine transcendence is drawn from interpersonal relations, a considerably different picture results. God's independence from our world and all our striving can be emphasized much more decisively, because here God is viewed as an autonomous agent capable of genuinely free *acts* (not merely "activity"). Correspondingly, of course, the divine reality is viewed more anthropomorphically on this model, since in our finite experience only persons enjoy this kind of fully objective transcendence. Here, then, God (in analogy with persons) is believed able to love and forgive, as well as punish and destroy, and knowledge of God results from his special act or acts of revealing himself; indeed, without such self-disclosing action no knowledge of him would be possible. Inasmuch as the term "God" ordinarily carries precisely these personalistic connotations—rooted in religious experience and devotion—and is even used as a proper name, it seems to me it should be reserved for theological conceptions developed on the basis of this model of interpersonal transcendence. "Being" is the much more appropriate term for theologies grounded on the model of teleological transcendence.

The philosophical significance of the conflict between the positive-historical theologies of revelation and every form of "natural theology" can now be clarified. Since with the analogy of interpersonal transcendence the referent for the word "God" becomes known primarily through divine acts of revelation, there is no real place here for a natural theology in the usual sense. Everything that is known about God—even the bare, formal meaning of the word "God"—develops in a concrete history of revelation, just as our knowledge of other persons—indeed, even our knowledge that there are such realities as persons—develops only in and through their revela-

---

not necessarily be primary from the point of view of theology or of philosophy. For God has other attributes, such as power, wisdom and justice, and it does not seem possible to derive these from the fact of his love. Is there not something even more fundamental, from which love and all these other attributes can be deduced? . . . [This] formal constituent of deity is Being" (*He Who Is* [London: Longmans, Green, 1943], p. 11).

tion of themselves to us. Moreover, just as in the history of our relations with others we come to know them as they and we mutually reveal ourselves—and that history then provides the context in which new encounters occur and are understood—so our knowledge of God also develops historically, and this historical deposit provides the context for each new stage of religious awareness and theological understanding. Thus, Moses is the indispensable historical presupposition for Isaiah, and Isaiah for Jesus, just as Jesus is for Paul, Paul for Augustine, and Augustine for Luther and for us. For a philosophy or theology rooted in the model of interpersonal transcendence, the actual positive course of history is of philosophical importance since it is within this interpersonal history—and here alone—that the divine is apprehended.

There would seem to be no *prima facie* reason why a full-blown philosophy or theology might not be developed on the basis of this model. It would, however, be a kind of radical historicism quite unlike much traditional thinking about God (which has been rooted in the teleological model or in an uncritical mixture of the two models),[7] and it would be necessary to face much more seriously than anyone has yet done certain difficulties arising out of the basic anthropomorphism of the view. Our experience of the transcendent reality of other selves is always mediated through their bodies—through the words they speak or write or the gestures and other motions they make. How, then, is God's reality mediated to us—through his "body," perhaps the world? If so, what otherwise appear simply as ordinary physical events would have to be interpreted as linguistic symbols, and there seems little ground for that. Or is it possible, in developing the analogical meaning of interpersonal transcendence, to disregard the physical dimensions of interpersonal intercourse—dimensions that appear indispensable on the finite level? If this way is taken, then it must be shown both legitimate and possible to abstract the

[7] The teleological model has been so much used in Christian theology that Heidegger, for example, takes it for granted that this is fully definitive of transcendence and that precisely this definition is peculiarly Christian (see *Sein und Zeit,* 7th ed. [Tübingen: Niemeyer, 1953], p. 49).

actual encounter with another in his transcendence from the sensory seeing, hearing, and touching through which such encounters appear always to be mediated in our finite experience. But this may prove exceedingly difficult, if not impossible.[8]

When the teleological model is followed, on the other hand, it is assumed there is an appropriateness or fitness of the Infinite Source and Goal to finite striving and needs, much as food proves to be an appropriate satisfaction for hunger. "Our hearts are restless till they find their rest in thee."[9] This structure becomes, then, the pattern in terms of which God's relation to the world is everywhere understood. History itself must transpire within the framework of this "cosmological idea."[10] Thus, it is in terms of this finite-Infinite relationship that the word "God" is given its root meaning, not in and through events of revelation. It is little wonder that for philosophers to whom this pattern appears virtually self-evident, rather considerable claims can be made about the extent of our knowledge of God quite apart from his revelation, as in traditional "natural theology."

It is somewhat curious that the more anthropomorphic of the two models (and thus the one that seems to imply that God is most like us and presumably most easily knowable by us) is at the same time the model with which a more unqualified kind of divine transcendence can be affirmed. For here God is the impenetrable mystery, known only in and through his revelation in concrete historical events. In contrast the model of transcendence that eschews anthropomorphisms of all sorts and regards God simply as *Being* turns out to be the one in which God is less hidden and less mysterious. For with teleological transcendence the fittingness or correspondence of the transcendent goal to the striving of the finite self is always

[8] These difficulties and others, involved in utilizing the experience of interpersonal encounter as a basis for speaking of God, have been made especially clear by Ronald W. Hepburn, *Christianity and Paradox* (London: Watts, 1958), Chaps. 3, 4.

[9] Augustine, *Confessions*, Bk. I.

[10] The term is Austin Farrer's, in *Finite and Infinite* (Westminster: Dacre, 1943), Pt. I.

implied, and with it a certain proportionality between the experienced finite order and the Infinite.

Of course, more recent thinkers operating with this model of transcendence (for example, Paul Tillich) have been much more aware that if transcendence is, after all, real *transcendence* of our experience and knowledge, the pattern cannot be so clearly perceivable as earlier theologians had supposed. But this insight into the difficulties of "natural theology" has been purchased at a high price. For, taken together with the fact that teleological transcendence is not easily reconcilable with a strong doctrine of revelation (which is, as we have seen, rooted in the other model), it means there is no real basis for our alleged knowledge of God. It should not be surprising, then, that many moderns have become increasingly dubious about the meaningfulness of all theological and religious language. When it became clear that teleological transcendence— far from making it possible to talk about God on the basis of our finite experience and knowledge—could be fully understood in terms of the imaginative and projective activities of the self (Feuerbach, Freud), it simply seemed no longer reasonable to try to speak of a radically transcendent reality— God—at all.

It is, I suspect, partly the failure of theologians themselves to realize the significantly differing implications of the two models of transcendence that has led to the present serious questioning whether notions like "God" have any specifiable meaning. If the theologians had from the beginning taken the position that the model of transcendence appropriate for their work was interpersonal, it would have been clearer that the question of the reality of God—and, likewise, of the meaning of the word "God"—could not be answered by reference to an inspection of the finite experience directly open to everyone, but could be explored only within the context of a "history of revelation."

But can we in fact give any meaning to the claim that God has revealed and does reveal himself in history? That question is very difficult to answer. We shall attempt to explore some aspects of it in Chapter 7.

5

God as Symbol

God is symbol for God.
Paul Tillich[1]

God, we have seen,[2] is to be taken as in himself transcendent of the entirety of man's world. He is not to be identified with any particular object in the world or any dimension of experience: to do so would be to demote him from the Creator of all that is to a part of the world (that is, of creation). This means that the referent of the word "God" cannot be indicated ostensively in any ordinary way. We are never able to point to this or that object or quality of experience and say, "That is what the name 'God' denotes." Any such direct identification of God with a particular in the world would be idolatrous.

I

To what, then, does this name refer? Proper names ordinarily designate beings locatable in space and time and precisely specifiable. "John is the third person from the left over there." "London is the capital of England and lies at 51°30′ latitude and 0° longitude." "George Washington was the first President of the United States, born 1732, died 1799, lived at Mt. Vernon." "Pegasus was a winged horse in a Greek myth related by Hesiod."

In some cases, as with "John," it is possible to point directly

[1] *Dynamics of Faith* (New York: Harper and Brothers, 1957), p. 46.
[2] See Chapters 3, 4, above.

to a particular physical object or person to which the name corresponds. If one then wishes to give a full description of that which the name designates, he can observe John carefully, measure him in various ways, interrogate him, and the like. John is directly available for examination.

With fictional beings it is similarly possible to indicate rather simply the body of literature within which the character is found; the name "Pegasus," for example, designates not a physical object but an imaginative construct created by poet or mythmaker. Information about the referent of the name will then be gained by study of the appropriate literary documents (or monumental remains), and nothing can be known beyond what they provide. For in this case the name indicates only a character found in those documents.

In the case of historical figures (no longer extant) the matter is somewhat more complex. George Washington cannot be directly pointed out nor information about him gained by direct inspection, but neither is he simply to be regarded as the creation of poet or storyteller, fully available in a particular novel or myth. We are dependent on records, reports, letters, and other documentary remains for our information about Washington, but we are certain that he is not exhaustively described in these materials: Washington was much more than, and doubtless in some significant respects quite different from, the person we are able to reconstruct imaginatively on the basis of the historical evidence available to us. No doubt John, present in the same room with us, also transcends our knowledge in many crucial respects, but when new and paradoxical data about him come to light, he is available for further questioning and observation as we seek more adequate understanding. Though we know him only through the complex composite image we gradually build up through our interaction with him,[3] we never take that image as final and complete but always leave it open to the modifications that new encounters might necessitate.[4] With George Washington, however, this

[3] See R. D. Laing, H. Phillipson, and A. R. Lee, *Interpersonal Perception* (London: Tavistock Publications, 1966).

[4] This is obviously a rough generalization: some persons are

potential input of new data through further encounters does not exist. Our understanding of him will have to be constructed entirely on the basis of extant historical evidences (assuming no further new documents are to be discovered), carefully sifted and evaluated by the best historical reasoning we can bring to the task, and any reasonable inferences that this evidence warrants. Though the name "George Washington" denotes a particular person who lived in a particular time and place, everything we know and can say about this referent will be based on our own historical reconstruction of that personage. In this sense (as with a fictional character) the name could be said actually to refer for all practical purposes to our imaginative construct rather than to the "real" Washington no longer accessible to us. All of our operations, attitudes, and ideas with respect to this name will be oriented by this construct of the historical imagination, not by the man himself. I wish to distinguish, therefore, between the *real* referent of the name of a historical figure (or the "real Washington") and the *available* referent (the "available Washington"). Only the latter can in any way affect our attitudes, action, or thinking: thus only the latter can be of real significance or importance to us.

If we return now to the name "God," we will see that the matter is even more complicated and difficult. Although (like John) God is taken to exist (in some sense) and be present, he is not available for our direct inspection or querying. "God" thus functions more like a historical or fictional name: what it denotes is grasped not directly in experience (as a present object or person) but largely verbally or intralinguistically,[5] with the help of various partial descriptions or characterizations.

---

quite "open" with respect to the emergence of the new in others, while others operate much more with stereotypes and relatively fixed images. There are also important moral considerations here: to treat another as a (creative and free) person, and not a mere dead object to be manipulated, *requires* one to take up a stance of openness toward the other. For our purposes at the present juncture, however, such matters need not be pursued.

[5] Cf. Paul Ziff, "About God," in *Religious Experience and Truth*, ed. Sidney Hook (London: Oliver and Boyd, 1961), pp. 195–202.

As with a historical name, it is useful here to distinguish between the available referent (our imaginative construct of God) and the real referent. The real referent for "God" is never accessible to us or in any way open to our observation or experience. It must remain always an unknown X, a mere limiting idea with no content. It stands for the fact that God transcends our knowledge in modes and ways of which we can never be aware and of which we have no inkling. The objects of our experience, particularly persons, also transcend in often surprising ways our knowledge (as noted above), but with God this transcendence and hiddenness is far more unqualified. For other persons are, after all, in many crucial respects accessible to us for observation, encounter, dialogue; and reports of historical figures are similarly based on such direct experience. God is never directly available in this sense and has never been. No supposed voice of God that we hear (or others in the past may have claimed to hear) can definitely be established to be such. Any supposed knowledge of God always remains unverifiable and controversial and may be completely mistaken. It is part of the profound mystery and meaning to which the word "God" points that man can never claim here adequacy of understanding and certainly no mastery or control. ". . . how unsearchable are his judgments, and his ways past finding out" (Rom. 11:33 KJ). The religious significance of the unspecifiability of the real referent for "God" is precisely this sense of an unfathomable depth of mystery and meaning, and this is an important dimension of the meaning of the word. But, conversely, this implies that the real referent can never be more than a limiting concept for us, a strong reminder that our ideas and experience are far from adequate: for all practical purposes it is the *available referent*—a particular imaginative construct—that bears significantly on human life and thought.[6] It is the "available God" whom we have in mind when

[6] It should not be forgotten that all I have said here about God's mystery transcending all our experience and knowledge—that the real referent for "God" is not accessible to us—is itself part of the available referent for the word in Western traditions, and a very important part indeed. This complex double-layeredness of the

we worship or pray; it is the available referent that gives content and specificity to any sense of moral obligation or duty to obey God's "will"; it is the available God in terms of which we speak and think whenever we use the word "God." In this sense "God" denotes for all practical purposes what is essentially a mental or imaginative construct. This does not mean, of course, that believers directly pray to or seek to serve some mere idea or image in their minds—that would be the crassest sort of idolatry; it is rather that what their images and ideas are *of* is the *available God,* not some utterly unknowable X.

This fact, that the God actually available to people is an imaginative construct, does not necessarily mean that God is "unreal" or "merely imaginary" or something of that sort. That question remains open for further investigation. As we noted, the available George Washington is also an imaginative construct, and that in no way prejudices the issue of whether there really existed at one time a man referred to by that name. But our knowledge of that real Washington will never exceed our knowledge of the available referent, and this imaginative construct is in fact the vehicle of whatever knowledge we come to have of the real man. Similarly with God. Whatever knowledge we may claim to have of him, it will be mediated through, and never go beyond, the imaginative construct that is our available God. The "real God" must always remain a transcendent unknown, a mere point of reference. This emptiness and formality does not, however, make the notion of the real God useless: it plays the indispensable role of relativizing and restricting all our claims to theological knowledge.

II

Once we understand that and why the available God is a construction of the human imagination, a number of issues become somewhat clarified. It is not difficult to understand, for example, why talk about God is perennially unconvincing to

---

available referent will have to be analyzed in more detail as we proceed.

many. Recognizing that the real referent intended by the word is never accessible, skeptics can always claim that God is nothing but a figment of the human imagination, and there is no possible way effectively to dislodge them from this position. In the nature of the case—in order for God to be *God*—he cannot be available to man's every beck and call: for he is the Transcendent One. In principle, therefore, there can be no coercive disproof of theological skepticism. But, for precisely the same reason, the skeptic's demand for some sort of ostensive indication of the object of faith will never appear to the believer as particularly apposite or profound. For faith understands that whatever else the word "God" might suggest, it emphatically does not denote a reality in this (or any other) way under human control. The skeptic's demand for proof or evidence in any ordinary sense thus begs the fundamental question. The *real* referent for "God" must never be confused with any experiential objects or mental constructs that we can directly and easily indicate. The debate between believers and unbelievers, therefore, is often not clearly joined: the skeptic attacks every available God as merely a product of man's imaginative activity, while the believer claims the real God— that which he intends—far from being a human creation, is in fact the single self-subsistent ultimate Reality on which all else depends for its being, "the Creator of all things visible and invisible." *sane + insane, psychically ordered or chaotic,*

In Flesh op angel realm?

This complex double-layeredness of the referent for "God" also illumines an important difference between theology and philosophy. While the philosopher can remain content with the task of analyzing and describing what is given directly (and indirectly) in human experience, the theologian has as the principal object of his inquiry this imaginative construct, God. His task is to examine the available (traditional) formulations of the concept, develop criteria for criticizing them, and propose more adequate reconceptions. But what criteria are there for assessing the validity or appropriateness of this creation of the human imagination? On what grounds does one conclude that this or that formulation (available referent) is more adequate or truer to the real God, when precisely that real referent is never directly accessible but must always be grasped only and entirely through the very conceptions and notions under scrutiny? And what justification can one offer for proposals for reconception or reformulation when any and every such proposal will inevitably be simply one more creation of man's imagination and can never be laid alongside the real referent for assessment and criticism? I do not say there are no criteria or grounds for the critical and constructive work of the theologian,[7] but it is obvious they will necessarily be much more tenuous and problematical and controversial than those to which the philosopher appeals (however complex and lacking in agreement the latter may be). There will always be a variety of imaginative constructs available for consideration, each with its adherents and advocates but none able fully to justify itself against its critics. And there will always be alternative methods of theological criticism and construction to be examined, none able fully to argue its claims or demolish its opponents. Since theology deals with what are wholly imaginative constructs, and itself consists in considerable imaginative constructive and reconstructive activity (and not simply in phenomenological description of what is given to man in experience, or even analysis and reconception of that given), its rational side must ever remain elusive and inconclusive in a way simply not true of philosophy. Despite the problematic character of theology, however, the theologian cannot simply resign from his task, for the imaginative constructs with which he is concerned are believed to be a (or perhaps even the most) significant clue that man has to the Real.

III

When I say the notion of God is a creation of the human imagination, it should not be supposed that I mean a theologian is free to let his fancy flow, creating whatever images or notions please him. The theologian is not a poet or artist in this sense at all, producing works of beauty or meaning out of

---

[7] I have made some specific proposals for such criteria in my *Systematic Theology* (New York: Scribner's, 1968), Chap. 4.

his own resources of creativity. The conception of God is obviously the product of a long and tortuous history and has been shaped by the experience and reflection of many peoples.[8] What has been handed down to us is the work of the collective imagination of generations of men who have been deeply involved with their whole being: it is not the creation of a few men of genius, a kind of *objet d'art* the multitudes can admire or ignore as they please. The concept of God defines and orients a whole way of life and understanding of the world.

It is a commonplace that man is fundamentally a symbolic or linguistic being.[9] The entire cultural world within which he is immersed from birth consists of symbols and signs, artifacts, institutions, and other structures of meaning in which and by means of which he orients himself in life. Unlike lower animals, the patterns of whose lives are determined largely biologically and instinctually, man's existence is given shape and form by the society and culture within which he lives and which he must acquire after birth by complicated processes of learning. These vast and complex orders of language and symbolization, of social roles and institutions, have of course themselves been created by men and developed over many generations. No mature man observes and experiences a naked and unadorned world; each sees and lives in a world ordered by the categories that have become basic in his culture and interpreted by the traditions and myths inherited from his past. Our intuitions and understanding of complex and difficult notions like reality, truth, and goodness, as well as our experience and appreciation of what is supposedly primary and obvious—parents, food, the awareness of the color green—are all shaped and ordered by the language we have learned and the patterns of social interaction we have acquired. And these in turn vary widely in the world and through history.

It would not be appropriate here to attempt to analyze the fabric or structure of meaning that constitutes culture and

[8] See Chapter 7.

[9] I cannot develop this in detail here. For fuller discussions, see my *Systematic Theology*, esp. Chap. 23 (also Chap. 2), and *Relativism, Knowledge and Faith* (Chicago: University of Chicago Press, 1960), esp. Pt. 2.

society and enables man to be man.[10] It is important to observe, however, that there is no egalitarianism of meaningfulness or significance within any given culture, so that all words are equally useful and important, and all symbols, myths, and values equally significant. The web of meaning is structured hierarchically, lower-level conceptions and values depending upon and being legitimated by weightier and more comprehensive symbols, myths and views of life and the world.[11] The religion of any given culture usually provides the most far-reaching of these latter, thus profoundly influencing the fundamental attitudes toward life of the members of the society, informing the very quality of existence and affecting behavior at all levels.

In Western culture the symbol with the deepest significance and greatest power to legitimate and sustain others is God. This was precisely expressed centuries ago in Anselm's classical definition: God is "that than which nothing greater can be conceived."[12] But putting the matter in such abstract and general terms really fails to reveal the full significance of the notion for the whole structure of meaning, and it is not surprising, therefore, that Anselm's crystallization of the concept did not appear until the end of a long religious development in which God was conceived much more concretely by means of a group of characterizations or partial descriptions.

Thus, for example, God had long been regarded in the West as "the Creator of the heavens and the earth." Whatever exists depends upon him for its being, not only in the sense that it "rests" upon him as a house upon a foundation, or that he has been the instrumentality through which it came to be as the (immediate) cause of an effect. Rather, he has "acted inten-

[10] See, e.g., Alfred Shutz's "phenomenology of everyday life" in *Collected Papers* (3 vols., The Hague: Nijhoff, 1967–   ); Claude Levi-Strauss, *Structural Anthropology* (New York: Basic Books, 1963); Erving Goffman, *Interaction Ritual* (Garden City, N.Y.: Anchor Books, 1967); Peter Berger and Thomas Luckmann, *The Social Construction of Reality* (Garden City, N.Y.: Doubleday, 1966).

[11] See Peter Berger, *The Sacred Canopy* (Garden City, N.Y.: Doubleday, 1967).

[12] *Proslogium*, Chap. 2.

tionally" to bring the world into being, as an artist works to bring forth his masterpiece; without this deliberate and purposive activity it would not exist at all.[13] Whatever exists in experience or the world depends absolutely on the divine volitional activity.

Again, God is often addressed or referred to (in the Bible this is the most common appellation) as "the Lord." Here the conception of his absolute mastership is what is intended, his sovereignty over the world, his guidance of historical and natural process, his ability to work out his will in creation, finally, "in the end," achieving his purposes. But this still puts the matter too abstractly. God is also man's Lord, the One before whom each must bow down, the One whom he must serve obediently and with gratitude, the One for whom man—every individual man—exists. All of life, therefore, is to be ordered to the divine will, and all of man's activities are to be put into God's service. *But we still rushed to choose things?*

multi will

The meaning suggested by the word "God" in the West—the available referent for the term—is of course not exhausted by such metaphors emphasizing "absolute dependence" (Schleiermacher). God is also said to be a Father who loves his children (especially in Christian writings) and a Husband whose heart is broken by his unfaithful spouse, mankind (see Hosea). He is faithful to man, trustworthy, loving, forgiving, merciful, and kind: one bound to men with bonds of affection and tenderness, one whom man can love with his whole heart. But he is also absolutely just and righteous, the Holy One who governs his universe with unblemished moral rectitude and demands "perfection" of men (Matt. 5:48): before him one feels deeply his own lowliness, guilt, and sinfulness. *+ He can wipe out of baby in 7 days...*

We could continue at length, exploring the meaning and implications of these characterizations and introducing many others prominent in the tradition, but that is not our purpose here. Perhaps enough has been said of the complexity and full-

---

[13] For a full discussion of the theological concept of creation, see my *Systematic Theology*, Chaps. 9, 20. Other characterizations of God, some of which are touched on here, are discussed in some detail in that volume, esp. in Pt. 1.

ness of the notion of "that than which nothing greater can be conceived" to suggest that that reality is grasped (by believers) as intimately related to every aspect and feature of the world and every dimension and quality of experience. Anyone who takes the notion of God seriously will apprehend the whole structure of meaning within which he lives as oriented toward and grounded upon this most profound resource of meaning and being, and the available God will thus be grasped, phenomenologically speaking, as himself "objective" and "real." Indeed, God will be the most objective or real element of the believer's phenomenological world, for, as the source and ground of all else, he provides the order or structure of all that has meaning and can be experienced, and he gives direction and purpose to the historical process. Thus, although *formally* (like any other cultural element) the available God is a human construct, created by men in the process of dealing with the exigencies of life, *materially* he is grasped as the most Real of all the realities of experience and the world. (It should not be forgotten here that men never "encounter" or "know" or "experience" any absolutely extracultural realities: all are apprehended through and interpreted in the cultural process. Thus, to have the highest degree of objectivity and reality within a cultural system is to have the highest degree apprehensible or knowable by the men living within that system.) From within such a perspective, therefore, God is the most real being, Creator and Lord of the world, an autonomous and self-sufficient Agent on which all else depends. Even for the unbeliever or skeptic the meaning and connotations of the name "God"[14] are still sufficiently powerful in contemporary Western culture that it is not difficult imaginatively to sense his claim to absolute uniqueness as the foundation on which the whole structure of meaning rests, and empathetically to feel how life might be experienced from such a perspective.

[14] If anyone feels uneasy regarding my interpretation of the proper name "God" as having "meaning" and "connotations," I refer him to the very helpful discussion of proper names in Paul Ziff, *Semantic Analysis* (New York: Cornell University Press, 1960), pp. 93–108.

semi subjective

Since God is a fundamentally personal reality (one who can properly be characterized with such anthropomorphic terms as "father," "lord," "loving," "righteous," "forgiving"), the world created by him and lived in by men is itself experienced and conceived in personalized terms: it is infused with meaning and purpose because its very being and the direction of its development have been "meant" or purposed by God. In this perspective man is no lonely spirit somehow caught up in an alien nature, whether this be conceived in modern terms with man the more or less accidental product of an impersonal evolutionary process, eventually certain to be destroyed by some cosmic catastrophe, or in the ancient Platonic and gnostic terms with man thought to be a heavenly soul somehow become imprisoned in an alien body. Rather, man can here feel and live as one at home in the world, for the nature that is his environment is itself the expression of the personal purposive activity of God, a context created to facilitate the emergence of finite personal beings.

Such a sense of fundamental at-homeness in the world is scarcely possible to men apart from (at least implicitly) theistic assumptions, for nature as we observe and construct it in physics and biology is not pervaded by personal and purposive order but rather by impersonal determinisms (or, alternatively, mere chance) which appear destructive of personal meaning. These processes can be apprehended as fundamentally supportive of strictly personal existence and meaning only if, at some deeper level than meets the empirical and scientific eye, they are grasped as themselves expressive of the same underlying personal activity that has called finite persons into being. In this respect one could say that to live in the world not in rebellion or cynicism or resignation but accepting it as the appropriate and meaningful context for moral and personal existence is in effect to take God as more than merely cultural artifact: it is to believe in God (in a practical sense).[15] For

[15] See below. Many persons who deny that they "believe in God" in fact manifest such belief in this sense of accepting the world as the appropriate home for man in his personal and purposive existence, and accordingly taking up a responsible and creative

such a stance God is the most adequate and vivid symbol or image for ordering and orienting life.

---

moral stance in life. That persons should fail to recognize, or that they should even explicitly deny, beliefs that they hold and that significantly order their lives should really not be surprising. We have too long supposed that our most basic beliefs lie directly accessible to consciousness. But the whole contemporary philosophical analysis of belief as fundamaentally a disposition of the self rather than a conscious "mental act" or occurrence goes against such traditional views. "If '*A* believes that *p*' is a dispositional statement about *A*, how is it possible to know or find out that *A* does believe that *p*? On the traditional occurrence analysis, there is always one person, namely *A* himself, who can find this out directly, by introspection. All he has to do is to consider the proposition *p* and notice what is going on in his mind. Does he or does he not have the experience of assenting to the proposition? . . . But if '*A* believes that *p*' is a dispositional statement about him, the situation is entirely different. *A* himself is no longer in a privileged position. Any knowledge he can have about his own dispositions is as indirect as the knowledge which other people can have about them. A disposition, whether it belongs to an inanimate object or to a person, whether it is one's own or someone else's, is not something which can be known 'just by inspection' either of the introspective or the perceptual kind . . . . such dispositional statements . . . are inductive . . . . I learn by an inductive process that I am timid or resentful and very liable to put the blame on others when things go wrong . . . . what is a person disposed *to*, when he believes a proposition *p*? . . . One answer is that they are actions: to believe a proposition is to be disposed to act as if the proposition were true" (H. H. Price, *Belief* [London: George Allen and Unwin, 1969], pp. 248–251. To be fair to Professor Price I should note here that he carefully qualifies this notion in his discussion; the above quotation oversimplifies his full position, but I think it represents it well enough for my purposes here.) Price shows that the understanding of belief as dispositional is able to take account of the full phenomena of belief much more adequately than the older conception of it as principally conscious occurrence or process; for example, it can deal with the problems of "unconscious beliefs," "half-beliefs," and the like (see *ibid.*, pp. 299–314). But on this view explicit assent to a proposition must be regarded as only one criterion among several of belief. Other criteria are provided by feelings, hopes, fears, and the like, and perhaps the most important is a person's actual actions ("Actions speak louder than words"). It is really quite in order, therefore, and in accord with our customary usage of the word "belief," to take into account a man's feelings about life, his fundamental moral stance or posture, and his decisions and actions—as well as what he explicitly affirms—when judging whether he "believes in God" or not.

IV

I have been trying in the preceding paragraphs to sketch briefly something of the meaning and implications of the word "God," to describe the available referent for the term and the way this impinges on the quality of experience and understanding of the world. It is important that we recall now that we have been describing the *available* referent of the name (not the real referent). The available referent is that structure of meaning which has developed over many centuries in the West, growing out of certain Hebrew (and also Greek) roots. It is carried in the culture as the meaning of "God" and is elaborated and developed in many ways in literary documents and works of philosophical and theological reflection, as well as in religious liturgies and institutions, moral practice and reflection, and the ordinary work and speech of everyday life. It is thus empirically accessible to us in the way that other structures of meaning in a culture are accessible: first, through our becoming native speakers of a Western language and participants in Western culture; and, second, through sensitive and careful historical and phenomenological studies which uncover and verify delicate shades of meaning and broad implications and ramifications that might otherwise be overlooked. It should be possible for believers and unbelievers alike to reach considerable agreement in descriptions of the available God, and methods of historical and phenomenological investigation are at hand to help arbitrate differences of opinion.

As we have seen, however, the available referent is not exhausted by its material content or meaning. In addition it makes the peculiar formal claim to be inadequate to the real referent in a way entirely unique among the words in Western languages: God is ultimately profound Mystery and utterly escapes our every effort to grasp or comprehend him. Our concepts are at best metaphors and symbols of his being, not literally applicable. In theologically sophisticated writers this peculiar feature of the notion of God is often worked out in elaborate doctrines of symbol or analogy; in the ordinary believer it is felt as a profound strain of humility at the very heart of piety. What are we to make of this? Does it simply wipe out all that has been said about God as finally to be canceled in the glorious final Negation that is the Absolute? Or is this a kind of inner contradiction in the meaning of the word that renders talk of God ultimately nonsensical?

Neither of these alternatives need be chosen, for neither properly indicates the actual situation. We have already observed that what is meant by "God" is so bound up with every dimension of experience that it decisively affects and forms the very apprehension and understanding of the world and the objects within it. The word "God" not only designates a transcendent reality never accessible to our observation or even our speculation; it also implies an ordering of the world in personalized and purposive terms. Though God himself may escape our every attempt to search him out, the world that we can and do experience can be apprehended as his.[16] That is, we can perceive it and live in it as created by God and ordered to his purposes, though we may not be able to prove either that this is in fact true of the world or that God does himself exist.[17]

The matter may be compared to the convergence of a number of main highways toward a city lying some distance off the map. There is an order in the converging lines which can be clearly perceived, but the ground and center of that order (the point of intersection) is not open to view. We can, if we choose, orient ourselves and our travels by reference to the sup-

[16] See Ludwig Wittgenstein on "seeing as" (*Philosophical Investigations* [Oxford: Blackwell, 1958], II, xi). See also John Hick, "Religious Faith as Experiencing-As," in *Talk of God*, Royal Institute of Philosophy Lectures, Vol. 2 (New York: St. Martin's Press, 1969).

[17] See in this connection John Wisdom's parable of the gardener in "Gods," in Antony Flew, *Logic and Language*, First Series (Oxford: Blackwell, 1960). Also see Raeburne Heimbeck's critical discussion of that parable and its use in recent analytic philosophy (*Theology and Meaning* [London: George Allen and Unwin, 1969], pp. 78 ff.). It might be well to point out here that "seeing-as" (seeing x as y) does not necessarily imply a distortion of, or even an interpretation "read into" but not fully justified by, "the facts." J. L. Austin has observed, for example, that "We sometimes say that we see a *person* 'as he really is'—'in his true colours' . . . " (*Sense and Sensibilia* [London: Oxford University Press, 1962], p. 101n.).

posed city off the edge of the map, even though we have no further chart that actually shows that the city is there or just what are its contours and character. In such a case what we *believe* about the city will have definite practical effects in life: it will determine the direction we choose to travel; it will shape our expectations and hopes and goals; it will lead us to discipline and prepare ourselves in certain ways and to cultivate certain appropriate stances or attitudes. All this can and will be effected by the "available city"—our beliefs about it— even though the real city never comes into view. When one considers that faith in God is interconnected not only with belief-systems developed through centuries of tradition, but also with elaborate and important social institutions and communities, effective and meaningful ritualistic practices, elevating and demanding moral and ethical claims, and whole systems of subtle and sophisticated philosophical and theological reasoning and reflection, all interlaced and mutually supporting and reinforcing each other, it is clear that evidences of (the available) God are everywhere to be found in human life and culture.

Whether the city of God exists somewhere off the map or not, and regardless of its actual contours and character, there is a pattern of roads leading in its (supposed) direction and ordered by its (supposed) demands. The available God functions as an ordering principle for life in this world, whatever may be the case about the extraworldly reality of the real God. Moreover, all of this can be empirically studied and known by appropriate sociological, psychological, and historical methods. There are many data immanent in the world for understanding what faith in God consists in and for grasping what and who God himself is supposed to be.

But what light does all this throw on the real God, on whether there actually is a transcendent referent appropriately symbolized by the available God? None whatsoever in any objective or verifiable sense. In principle, as we have seen, the real referent is beyond our direct observation or encounter. Then does not faith in him finally come to nothing? Have we not reduced it to a merely subjective phenomenon, deluded so far as it believes itself actually to make objective transcendental reference? I think not: that way of putting the matter oversimplifies. The analysis thus far leads to two conclusions: First, there is an empirical, worldly, describable side to faith in God, namely the attitudes, values, institutions, and beliefs which are engendered by and with such faith, and the available God himself. Life is perceived, ordered, and lived in certain specifiably characteristic ways when God is taken to be real and significant, and there is nothing ultimately mysterious or ineffable about this at all. Second, the final or ultimate or metaphysical meaning of such an ordering of human existence and experience remains unknown and unknowable (in principle). That is, despite everything, man remains finite and limited in perspective and understanding, never attaining to final knowledge of the meaning of his life or the world. Theologically speaking, man remains always a creature, never reaching the ultimate insight or understanding proper only to God. A man's resolve, therefore, to order his life according to the demands of theistic faith (or according to any other pattern, for that matter) always remains a leap of faith, a willingness to commit himself to a pattern of life as right and good even though he is unable metaphysically or logically to ground such a commitment. "There is only one proof that the Eternal exists: faith in it."[18]

We have not escaped from the subjectivist trap—there is no escape from it—but we now can understand it better. It is precisely man's finite closed-in-ness that is discerned and appreciated in the ancient religious insight that "we walk by faith, not by sight" (2 Cor. 5:7). That is, the question of a man's fundamental orientation in life—his deepest commitments and ultimate values—is not decided by rational assessment of

[18] Soren Kierkegaard, *Purity of Heart Is to Will One Thing* (New York: Harper, 1938), p. 84. Such genuine commitment may, of course, come to have the character of self-fulfilling prophecy: as experience and activity are increasingly ordered according to the requirements of faith, life's meaning becomes increasingly grasped in reference to God; and God himself is apprehended as the foundation of it all, as the Ultimate Reality on which all else depends.

the (metaphysical) structure of the world and a judgment about the form of life appropriate to that structure. It is determined on other grounds. This does not mean that we are condemned to live in a nihilistic darkness with no compass or lodestar. As we have seen, though "God" cannot be *proved* to have the real referent that the name claims to denote, faith certainly can and does treat God as providing the focus for orientation in life. This suggests that it is a mistake to deal with the meaning of this term chiefly speculatively and theoretically, asking whether our available referent in fact "corresponds" to what "really exists" somewhere "out there"; the meaning of this term is to be found primarily in its practical import for life, its way of ordering society and the world and the demands it lays on selves and on communities.[19] + *misfires*

There is no way to establish the "truth" of the notion of God by ordinary rational or philosophical argument: that is in principle impossible. The only relevant question of truth that can be directly considered here concerns that ordering of life and the world which faith imposes: is such an ordering appropriate to the world as we experience it and to the nature of our human existence, or does it involve misapprehensions of our situation and result in a stunting of human life and its ultimate breakdown? Is some other fundamental paradigm or "root metaphor"[20] more apposite or adequate for grasping the world so as to enhance and deepen human life, or does the theistic imagery and pattern most effectively perform this function? If the latter, then a theistic world-view—whatever be the truth about the transcendental reference of its talk of God—would

[19] This, I take it, is the truth lying behind Richard Braithwaite's claim that the meaning of religious statements is to be found in their moral import (see *An Empiricist's View of the Nature of Religious Belief* [Cambridge: Cambridge University Press, 1955]). However, Braithwaite's analysis of the question of religious truth-claims is too cavalier and unsubtle. An attempt at a more careful analysis, which recognizes that there are certain senses in which religious propositions claim to be true (to life or the world) and can be confirmed or disconfirmed in (moral) experience, is provided below.

[20] See Stephen Pepper, *World Hypotheses* (Berkeley: University of California Press, 1942).

be at least most "true to life," the most adequate and appropriate way to grasp self and world. And if this truth about life and the world seems indissolubly connected with talk of God, then such talk has a certain fittingness and justifiability, even though the implied transcendent referent can never be verified. If our map, with the highways converging toward some supposed city beyond its borders, proves a good guide to life in this world, accurately indicating available watering places and sources of food and warning of dangerous cliffs and mosquito-infested swamps, it is a valuable and true map and well worth using—even though we have no way of discovering just what beyond its borders gives the map's roads and contours a form and pattern most readily interpretable by us as approaching a hidden city.

V

God is the anchor-symbol for a whole way of life and world-view. But how does one assess the appropriateness of a "way of life" or a "stance in the world"? It is important that we note that this is a fundamentally *practical* (not speculative) question. It has to do with how I do, can, and should order my self and my activity. It has often been (mistakenly) supposed that to deal with such problems one can and must first take up the stance of a neutral and impartial observer or spectator and investigate the "nature" of the world and of man, so that it becomes possible to judge whether particular proposals for posture and life are usable and fitting. This has led into metaphysical issues so paradoxical and difficult as to cause many philosophers to despair of their solution and to conclude that man's very concern with them was based on mistakes and is ultimately pointless. But man is most fundamentally a practical or active being, and his spectation occurs as but one moment within, and mode of, his all-comprehensive activity. In this respect moral questions (What ought I to do? How ought I to comport myself?) are *prior* to questions of truth and being (What is the world really like? What is man?) and cannot be suspended until the latter are answered. (Indeed, the very at-

tempt to formulate all such questions and to answer them
itself consists of *actions*, deliberately ordered in ways deemed
appropriate or "right."[21]) Man created the world of symbols,
within which he continues to live, first and most importantly as
a structure within which to orient his action: because he has
language, man is able to attend to and reflect upon what is not
immediately present in experience, anticipating imaginatively
a variety of possibilities, deciding among them, and ordering
his activity accordingly. Only secondarily and reflexively can
that symbolical world itself be made an object of investigation
with a view to seeing whether our symbols and concepts appropriately "correspond" to "reality."[22] We shall attempt here

[21] "The most characteristic fact about actions is that they
can—in various specific ways—go wrong, that they can be performed incorrectly. This . . . is as true of describing as it is of
calculating or of promising or plotting or warning or asserting
or defining . . . . These are actions which we perform, and our
successful performance of them depends upon our adopting and
following the ways in which the action in question is done, upon
what is normative for it. Descriptive statements, then, are not
opposed to ones which are normative but in fact presuppose
them: we could not do the thing we call describing if language
did not provide (we had not been taught) ways normative for describing" (Stanley Cavell, *Must We Mean What We Say?* [New
York: Scribner's, 1969], p. 22). Kant first clearly made this
point about the priority of practical activity over speculative.
(See esp. his discussion of the "primacy of the pure practical
reason" in the *Critique of Practical Reason*, Pt. I, Bk. II, Chap. 2,
Sec. 3.) This entire section of the present essay is heavily
indebted to Kant's analysis.

[22] A spectating approach is, of course, appropriate for formulating most questions of truth about particulars *in* the world, such
as tables or electrons. Here I can compare one particular in my
set of symbols with one particular in what I (symbolically)
designate as "the world." But this stance breaks down—or
rather, we deceive ourselves—if we suppose we can examine
the validity of our symbolical system itself in such a spectating
way. (See in this connection Thomas Kuhn's study of the
immense problems that arise when the whole framework of
scientific investigation begins to break down and a "revolution" to quite new ways of formulating problems, setting experiments, and grasping data is required [*The Structure of
Scientific Revolutions* (Chicago: University of Chicago Press,
1962)].) I cannot jump out of the symbolical structure within
which I live, and in terms of which I have my most fundamental
and primitive awareness of self and world, in order to see

to get clear the practical or actional function of the mythological and metaphysical maps and models with which man has pictured the world and himself.[23]

It must be emphasized first that such maps or models are necessary if man is to act at all. Animals simply behave in accordance with impulse or conditioned response, but men have the ability to choose among alternatives and in some degree to determine their own courses of action. They cannot avoid repeatedly asking themselves: Why do this rather than that? Why discipline or train myself in this way rather than that way, or not at all? What styles of life are open to me, and which should I adopt, and why? These questions admit of no answers apart from some conceptions of the sort of being man is and the possibilities open to him, as well as notions about the character of the world within which we live and the possibility of altering that world in accord with our ideas and purposes. It

---

whether it "corresponds" to some "objective reality" over against it. ("Corresponds" and "objective reality" are themselves highly abstract concepts in my symbolic-linguistic world, presupposed in this very attempt to formulate the relation of the symbolical or linguistic order to the nonsymbolic.) Human existence always falls within such a symbolical order, and it is this structure of symbols—including grammar, syntax, logic, meaning—which defines and articulates the world of our experience. Because the symbolic order is a web of complex interrelations and interconnections, no simple one-to-one theory of reference or meaning does justice to the linguistic facts even in the case of particulars (see Ziff, *Semantic Analysis*); with a complex foundational symbol like God, expecting to discover some ostensive corresponding referent is to make a fundamental category-mistake.

[23] Every culture has its mythologies and world-views which interpret what man essentially is and how he can best comport himself in order to realize or fulfill his nature. When these, or their refinement into complex and subtle metaphysical and theological conceptions, were treated as simply descriptive of how the world "really is," insoluble problems and paradoxes arose, leading often to cynicism and despair about metaphysics and theology. These difficulties appeared because the primarily practical function of such conceptions—to orient human action—had been forgotten, and it was supposed that their chief purpose was to provide an impartial spectator's knowledge of an objective world. We shall, in what follows, attempt to hold to a practical or actional stance, seeking thus to bypass the difficulties rooted in a spectating approach.

is true, of course, that the inevitability of our making assumptions about these matters does not certify them "valid" (in some "objective" or "verifiable" sense). But it is equally true that the problematical status of such claims (in a rigorously scientific or philosophical sense) in no way prevents, or can prevent, our presupposing their appropriateness whenever we take up our stance as agents and proceed to act. What we necessarily presuppose about ourselves and our world when we act has considerable independence from, and is certainly not a simple derivative of, our "demonstrable" scientific and philosophical "knowledge" gained through spectation.

Were we simply spectators of life and the world, observers of the passing scene, there would be no need to reach conclusions about what the world and we ourselves are like until all the evidence was in. We could observe what goes on around us, and within us, for all eternity, and we could construct innumerable theories explaining and interpreting our observations and experience, but we would never have to commit ourselves to any particular view as adequate or true. We are, however, whether we like it or no, actors in the world, not merely spectators of a passing panorama. We have no way to withdraw from the necessity to choose among various alternatives confronting us, thus committing ourselves, our efforts, and what is dear to us to this course of action or that, and working toward the achievement of this particular goal and the defeat of that other proposal. Even the attempt to withdraw from certain sectors of active life, such as the political as with some of our contemporary youth, involves a decision and certain kinds of action; "dropping out" of life entirely, suicide, is itself a choice and a deed. As actors willy-nilly, we are not permitted the luxury of waiting until we are certain about the metaphysical nature of human existence and its context before committing ourselves to one view or another. We must act, and we must choose—and in doing so we will have committed ourselves to the view that man is just one more animal, or to the claim that he is really an immortal soul of immeasurable value, or that he is a finite person with capacities for freedom and creativity and love as well as evil and destructiveness, or to some other view; and we will have construed the world within which we live as a fundamentally material order ultimately impermeable to human and humane values and meanings, or as an order of beauty, goodness, and truth, or as a moral universe within which responsible, just, and loving action makes ultimate metaphysical sense, or in some other way. Our action, so far as it is conscious and deliberate, will be attuned to and expressive of these metaphysical commitments and construals, for they will provide the cognitive context in terms of which we understand and interpret what it is we are doing and how we are going about doing it. Even though we have not been able to satisfy ourselves as spectators of the world and of man that the interpretation we accept is the final and lasting metaphysical Truth—and I am enough of a skeptic and positivist to believe that finite man will never reach that goal—we have to stake ourselves, our lives, and all that is dear to us on one or another view and act and work from one day to the next in the terms it lays down for us.

I cannot here spell out the details of the conceptions of man and the world presupposed by action itself; nor can I argue their philosophical propriety.[24] I do wish, however, to indicate some-

[24] I hope to be able to do this in the future. Suffice it to point out that the very posture of an agent poised to act presupposes that he conceives the (metaphysical character of the) world in certain definite ways. For example, if the world were taken to be a completely determined unalterable structure on which no decision or action of men could have any effect, an actor's posture would be nonsensical: there would be no point to men's making plans or exerting efforts intended to transform the world. In such a situation men could at most conceive themselves as spectators of the passing scene, never as actors in or on it. If the human experiences associated with acting—speaking and listening, observing, planning, studying, imagining, deciding, intending, working—are to be rendered intelligible, it is necessary to conceive man himself as an active agent, in some measure free, creative, and self-determining, and the world in which he lives as plastic and open (to some extent) to human intentions and purposes. The whole vast literature in the "philosophy of action," rooted in the work of the later Wittgenstein and J. L. Austin, has surely made that point clear. It can be argued, I think, that every deterministic world-view is rooted in a spectating stance and the correlative assumption that the spectated world is the real world. There is no place in such a world for human

thing of the significance of the notion of God for man as actor. We have seen that speech about God is not confined in its meaning to reference to a transworldly being: it also implies a definite conception of the world within which man lives and of man himself. The world and man exist in a larger context— the personal purposive activity of God—and they must be understood as ordered and shaped by this activity and oriented toward its goals. In a theistic view human life falls ultimately within a context of personal and purposive order (not some subpersonal species of order, whether that be conceived materialistically, vitalistically, or logically). And this personal purposive order itself underlies and undergirds and expresses itself through all other forms of order in the world.

Talk about God, thus, involves a claim that every level of man's being, including the highest or most comprehensive—his full being as person or agent—is grounded metaphysically, in ultimate reality. It is not only man's physical being or organic vitalities that are thus grounded, the higher reaches of the human spirit being merely epiphenomenal or at most a more or less accidental emergent from a cosmic or life process indifferent to them and with no interest in sustaining them: the whole of man's being, including his valuing, purposing, meaning-creating, and meaning-craving self, has an ultimate metaphysical foundation.[25] A doctrine of God (or of the gods, in a polytheistic system) means that meaningful or purposive forms of order are not confined to human history and society,

---

action. But if action is logically prior to spectation—spectation itself being a form of action and inconceivable otherwise—then this whole approach and all that it entails is misconceived. It is necessary to understand man and the world first from the point of view of the possibility and reality of action; only then are we in a position to see the significance and proper use of conclusions rooted primarily in spectation.

[25] In contrast, to take up a materialistic stance (for example) is to see everything, including the obviously personal, as ultimately grounded in meaningless matter-in-motion or energy; this leaves both the organic and the personal without metaphysical support for their specific characters. To take a positivistic stance is to attempt to ignore the question about the character of the world and thus simply to live and act in a kind of daze with reference to it.

but pervade the cosmos to its deepest roots. In this way the conception of God (as ultimate cosmic Agency) provides a view of the world as a universe of action, a universe within which man as agent can quite appropriately feel "at home." Human agency is no mere excrescence in an otherwise nonpersonal, nonagential world.

Further, it is not mere neutral, amoral action that is sustained metaphysically by the Western conception of God. God is conceived as the absolutely *moral* being, invested with perfect righteousness and love, and demanding the same of his devotees. This has been understood materially in a variety of ways in the course of Hebrew-Christian history—sometimes not reinforcing what we today might regard as particularly profound moral insight—but it has meant that morality, and not merely action, has the deepest possible metaphysical grounding, in the Creator of the world. This conviction was so strong in Hebrew culture and its descendants that the growing moral insight of the great prophets and others led to development not only in Israel's moral awareness and practices; it resulted in continuous revision of the understanding of the very character and will of God himself. God increasingly appeared as one who was educating his people to ever deeper moral awareness and who demanded of them increasingly profound righteousness, and men felt obliged to respond to God accordingly. Faith in God as a moral being in this way contributed substantially to the transformation of man into a fully moral—and in the modern sense, personal and human—being.

Believing in God thus means practically to order all of life and experience in personalistic, purposive, moral terms, and to construe the world and man accordingly; the meaning and significance of human action and ethics are thus enhanced by being grounded on an adequate metaphysical foundation.

VI

But why construe the world in this way—as a moral universe —especially in view of the well-known theoretical difficulties about the existence of God? At this point we can easily be tempted into making a mistaken move. We may either attempt to argue the existence of God on theoretical grounds (in order to justify such a construal of the world) or else we may move in a purely fideistic direction and simply proclaim our belief that God exists despite all difficulties inherent in the notion. Both of these moves make the same mistake: they take the central problem to be the existence of a being with such and such properties called "God." But this is to focus attention primarily on the theoretical question of the real referent for "God," a question that is in principle unanswerable, as we have seen. Theistic (and atheistic) philosophies usually approach this question speculatively; fideism resolves it simply by fiat. But none of these approaches prove convincing; moreover, practical faith in God seldom (if ever) rests on their claims and demonstrations. The available God functions as anchor-symbol for a stance that takes the world to be pervaded by personal and purposive meaning, whatever be his reliability as clue to the existence and nature of a transcendent being. God serves as the supreme symbol for a life-policy of humanizing and personalizing the world.

From a practical point of view, one does not ask first whether it is true that God exists (a speculative question), but rather whether this is an appropriate life-policy for men to adopt. Here we are concerned with the kind of symbolical scheme that will make possible a meaningful, fruitful, and supremely human life. Should our frame of orientation be one that leads us always to invest every item of experience with personal or quasi-personal meaning, or one that leads us to depersonalize? We are not so much concerned here with "how things are" as with the kinds of policies we should adopt. The primary question, therefore, is not what is true, but what is right.[26]

[26] It is worth noting that "believing-in" something (as contrasted with "believing-that" something is the case) often expresses adherence to some sort of policy. Thus, as Price has pointed out, to say, "I believe in classical education," or "I believe in taking a cold bath every morning," is to express a maxim or methodological rule, not a proposition directly claiming truth. ". . . believing in a policy or procedure is very different from believing

An analogy may be helpful. If we ask whether it is *true* that there are such things as quasars or negative matter or even electrons, we might scarcely know how to answer. These are all imaginative constructs that seem to help deal with certain features of experience, but we do not know if or how they correspond to what is the case. If we ask, however, if it is right to explore the world in terms of the conceptions of quasars and electrons, an affirmative answer seems easy and obvious. It is appropriate to act in terms of any constructions that enable us to deal productively and creatively with our world. Thus, certain ideas may be important to and valuable for action even though their precise truth-value is unknown or even unknowable. And if so, it is *right* to determine action in accordance with them. In this sense "right" ideas do not necessarily coincide with "true" ideas; certainly they are not limited to the latter. In a similar way, it may well be right to act in accordance with the conception of God and what that implies about our world and ourselves even though we are unclear whether or in what respects that notion is true.[27] If the idea of God helps

---

that something is the case" (*Belief*, p. 124; see also pp. 426–454). It is quite appropriate, of course, to ask for one's reasons for advocating or adopting a given policy, but this is not the same as asking what evidence there is for it, as if it could be true or false. To say, "I believe in God," I am suggesting, is more an expression of a life-policy one has adopted, an expression of how one does, or ought to, comport oneself, than it is an expression of what one believes factually to be the case.

[27] Of course the questions of right and truth are not entirely independent of each other: it would not be *right* to believe in God if we knew it were *true* he did not exist. Indeed such a position would involve the self in the contradiction of knowing the world to be one thing but construing it as something quite different. What sort of consistent or meaningful action could follow from such a stance? We would be drawn in contrary directions. If we could know (scientifically, speculatively) that the world is fundamentally and to its very roots a material order, then we would not be able, and it would not be right, to construe it as an essentially moral order (that is, as personal and purposive). Metaphysically construing the world in a certain way is legitimate and necessary only because, first, the fundamental order of things remains ambiguous to us despite our every attempt to reach clear and convincing conclusions about

to sustain our action and ourselves as agents, helps to further humanize and develop man, enhancing his moral sensitivity and stiffening his will to live responsibly, then it is right to allow that belief to shape one's policies of action. That is, it is right to act in accordance with that belief, to believe in God (in a practical sense).[28]

VII

God is a symbol—an imaginative construct—that enables men to view the world and themselves in such a way as to make action and morality ultimately (metaphysically) meaningful. The justification for speaking of and believing in God is thus primarily a practical one: a world under God is a moral universe, a universe in which action and morality make metaphysical sense, and in which, therefore, our own feeble impulses toward the moral life are supported and reinforced. Commitment to God, faith in God, belief in God are practical postures of a self striving to represent to itself with the only kind of imagery or symbolism available a world in which moral action and seriousness about life make ultimate sense.[29] Doc-

---

it (note Wittgenstein's observation that "seeing as" is possible and required not in situations of perspicuity but of fundamental ambiguity, for example, the "duck-rabbit," in *Philosophical Investigations*, II, xi), and, second, there is no possible way for us to avoid deciding and acting in the world, to avoid construing it in one way or another so as to get on with our lives. If human life, character, and growth are sustained by metaphysically construing the world theistically, that is, having personal and purposive meaning, rather than some other way, then it is justifiable or right to do so, even though we do not, and in principle cannot, know whether God exists.

[28] Even though the notion of God has in this way important practical validity or significance, this does not mean that it can be taken as true in some theoretical sense (cf. Kant). The partial independence of *right* and *true* means that it is no more justifiable to assume that an idea deemed "right" (as a basis for action) is "true," than to hold an idea must be metaphysically or scientifically true in order for it to be a right or proper presupposition of action.

[29] When we once understand that the idea of God has in this way a fundamentally practical, rather than speculative, use and mean-

trines of God as "Creator" and "Lord" of the world attempt to elaborate and explicate this vision of life and reality,[30] and thus they too have a practical significance and warrant. But when any of this language is taken as literally referring to and

---

ing, it becomes more evident why belief in him is always precarious and dubitable and always involves a definite act of will. Faith in God is not merely the acceptance of the truth of an idea or a set of ideas; it involves committing one's whole self to a definite style of life and particular way of construing the world. The world can well be construed in other ways, and there are many prepared to argue it ought to be construed otherwise, and other forms of life may certainly be attractive. But despite all such uncertainties and counterpressures on the self, faith in God is the resolve to commit oneself to this highly personal and responsible form of life and to regard the world as a fundamentally moral universe in which such a life is both intelligible and reasonable. This should not be understood to imply, of course, that believers may not also be rogues, sinners, or hypocrites of the worst sort. Indeed, precisely because the believer's world is fundamentally *moral* in structure, it may lend itself to more frightful (moral) distortions and corruptions than any other; the evidence of Christian history is not particularly reasurring in this respect. But the point is that within this world-view, in contrast with some others, all such hypocrisy and evil will be interpreted as not being restricted in significance to the human historical order, but of cosmic meaning and import. Doctrines of God's righteous wrath and long-suffering love, as well as of heaven and hell, make precisely this point, thus raising to a qualitatively new level the meaning and significance of human moral (and immoral) activity.

[30] Any ambiguous situation or reality that is "seen-as" or interpreted-as something definite or specific requires some elaboration in order to make clear just how it is being understood. As Peter Slater has pointed out, "In the simple case of the duck-rabbit, we have to be able to show how we would continue the drawing to specify the posited identity; and this is easily done by adding lines to the drawing to render it an unambiguous representation of a duck or a rabbit. In the case of seeing something as symbolic of the nature of the whole [of reality], what corresponds to adding lines to the drawing is the process of further specifying the symbolism to show its application in our lives. To see the world as God's creation, for instance, and really to see it in this way, we need to specify what it might mean to live as God's creatures in this time and place" ("Parables, Analogues and Symbols," *Religious Studies*, 4:30 [1968]).

describing some transcendent being outside of or beyond the world, we have moved out of our depth.

Does this mean, then, that the conclusion is, after all, that God really does not exist, that he is only a figment of our imaginations? If those words are intended to put the speculative question about the ultimate nature of things, then, as we have seen, there is no possible way to give an answer. If they are intended, however, to suggest that commitment to God is an inappropriate (moral) stance in life, indeed is delusory, they are mistaken. For our ultimate commitments must be assessed in terms of their potential fruitfulness as life-policies, giving order and meaning to life and drawing us into ever more human and humane levels of existence. God, particularly God conceived as absolutely loving and self-giving, has that sort of power.[31] He is a worthy symbol therefore—it is doubtful

---

[31] It must be acknowledged, of course, that not every conception of God is morally supportive and productive. Indeed, it is possible—and this has happened all too often in Western history— that the conception of God may weaken man's moral sense and cut the nerve of his striving for moral responsibility. When the notion of God as Agent and as the locus of all true goodness and righteousness is accentuated to the point of implying that men have no real or effective agency at all, and that they are completely unclean and sinful with neither moral insight nor the possibility of any moral achievement, the role of man's moral consciousness in defining the character and activity of God may atrophy completely and God be viewed as simply an arbitrary and imperial Tyrant who rules the world. Moreover, whatever this Tyrant does, no matter how much it contradicts or offends our moral sensibilities, will be regarded as "right" and "good," and even "loving" and "kind," because by definition God is held to be the very epitome of righteousness and goodness. Thus, for example, what Paul apparently regards as the completely arbitrary hardening of Pharaoh's heart by God is nonetheless accepted by him as legitimate and morally appropriate behavior because it has been performed by the one who cannot possibly be reproached or held morally blameworthy (see Rom. 9:14 ff.). What would in human beings be taken as clear examples of injustice, evil, narrow-mindedness, even malevolence, is called, when God does it, goodness, love, mercy, and the like. In this way a powerful theological contradiction to man's own moral insight and sensitivity is built up, and this can corrupt and seriously weaken human moral awareness. Augustine, for example, can believe there is great rejoicing in heaven—the heaven of the God of

there can be any more adequate—for that to which one com-
mits himself without qualification and in terms of which he

---

mercy and love—over the torture and torment of sinners in
hell, and it is possible for men like John Calvin and Jonathan
Edwards to contemplate the damnation of the vast majority of the
human race without a shred of sympathy because it is a direct
expression of God's "righteousness" and "love." The confusion and
damage this works in man's moral consciousness and understanding can be seen clearly in Hugh of St. Victor who did not
hesitate to say that God "wills evil to be, and in this He wills
nothing except good, because it is good that there be evil" (quoted
in John Hick, *Evil and the God of Love* [London: Macmillan,
1966], p. 97). With God himself, believed to be the very source
of all morality and goodness, behaving in such ways, is it any
wonder that Christians have been capable of the worst sorts of
fanaticism, persecution, and inhumanity in his name? As J. S.
Mill queried: "Is there any moral enormity which might not be
justified by imitation of such a Deity? And is it possible to adore
such a one without a frightful distortion of the standard of right
and wrong?" ("Utility of Religion," in *Three Essays on Religion*
[New York: Henry Holt, 1874], p. 114). This moral ambiguity
in the conception of God has of course been present from the
beginning, when YHWH appears as a mighty warrior who
arbitrarily favors the Hebrew people over others and destroys
their enemies without mercy, commanding them to do the same.
And it reappears in accentuated form in some Christian views
of atonement where salvation depends entirely on what Christ
has done (often to appease a vengeful Father) and not at all on
what man is obligated to do, thus making both man's agency and
his morality completely irrelevant to the ultimate state of his
soul. It is clear that not every conception of God—not even
every "Christian" conception—helps to support, sustain, and
develop man's moral sensitivity and activity by providing the
indispensable metaphysical foundation for a vision of the world
as a moral universe, an order within which personal existence
finds ultimate metaphysical sustenance, and humane and humanizing action is not only right but ultimately reasonable. For this
reason (as well as others) a contemporary Christian doctrine of
God dare not be constructed on the basis of an uncritical use of
either traditional or biblical imgery: all such must be thoroughly
criticized and reformulated in the light of criteria based on the
image of that helpless, nonresistant suffering figure dying on
a cross. Only such a radically loving, forgiving, suffering God
can metaphysically sustain and further enhance our moral
sensitivity in face of the terrifying evils in today's world. (For
an example of an attempt at such reconstruction of the Christian
doctrine of God, see my *Systematic Theology*, Pt. I; see also
Chapter 8, below, on "God and Evil.")

orients all his activity. In any other sense than as the appropriate object of ultimate loyalty and commitment, unqualified devotion and love, God need not exist.[32]

It might be supposed that all this talk of God as an imaginative construct, a symbol for a way of ordering life and the world, is a far cry from the "living God" of Abraham, Isaac, and Jacob, known by his "mighty acts." Besides such imagery the God spoken of in this essay may seem bloodless and dead, a creation of man with no powers of his own. But that would be a mistaken interpretation. *All* conceptions of God (as we noted early in this essay), including that of scripture and faith, must be understood as creations of the human imagination: the "real God" is never available to us or directly knowable by us. (Even the distinction between the real and the available God is necessarily a characteristic of the available God.) It is the content of the notion of God, not the manner in which that notion is created and shaped in human consciousness, that determines whether God is a proper object of worship and devotion. To interpret God, as I have done in this paper, not as merely the idea of an absolute being, but as implying a conception of the universe as through and through moral, a world within which personal and purposive action is continuously effective and determinative, is to conceive God as living and active at every point in reality. Men can pray with conviction to such a God; they can cry to him in their hour of need; they can throw themselves on his mercy in their despair; they can give themselves to him with full devotion. The so-called re-

---

[32] For C. S. Peirce it is precisely in such commitment and devotion that belief in God consists. ". . . any normal man who . . . [pursues] the hypothesis of God's Reality . . . in scientific singleness of heart, will come to be stirred to the depths of his nature by the beauty of the idea and by its august practicality, even to the point of earnestly loving and adoring his strictly hypothetical God, and to that of desiring above all things to shape the whole conduct of life and all the springs of action into conformity with that hypothesis. Now to be deliberately and thoroughly prepared to shape one's conduct into conformity with a proposition is neither more nor less than the state of mind called Believing that proposition, however long the conscious classification of it under that head be postponed" ("A Neglected Argument for the Reality of God," *Hibbert Journal*, 7:98–99 [1908]).

ligious needs of man to which talk about God is supposedly primarily directed can in fact be met only by a God conceived as the sustainer and guarantor of a thoroughly *moral* universe.[33]

To speak of the anthropological bases of man's awareness of and thought about God as located in imagination and cultural tradition, as I have done in this essay, prejudices the ultimate ontological status of God no more than to speak of seeing as located in the eye and nervous system argues that the trees and flowers are all illusory. There are, of course, special problems connected with the "objectivity" of the "real God" that do not obtain for the flowers and trees, as we have seen, but these are just as much rooted in the theological claims about God's greatness, mystery, and transcendence as in any epistemological or logical difficulties. To regard God as *merely* imaginary is to collapse the double-layeredness of the notion of God entirely into the available God. That is certainly possible—every atheism goes that way—but it is just as much a falsification of what is meant by "God" as the naïveté which identifies the available God too easily and directly with the real referent of the name.

The biblical God does not differ from the one described here by virtue of his impressive ontological independence and self-subsistence: it is simply that he was imagined, believed in, and responded to as existent and real by the men of the Bible. And one might expect that for any modern to commit himself and his life to God in decisive fashion, he would similarly have to imagine him as independent and real, no mere human creation.[34] But it might be hoped that a modern believer would be

[33] As Kant suggested, "though *fear* first produces *gods* (demons), it is *reason* by means of its moral principles that can first produce the concept of *God*" (*Critique of Judgment*, Bernard trans. [New York: Hafner, 1951], p. 297); "for the concept of the Deity really arises solely from consciousness of these [moral] laws and from the need of reason to postulate a might which can procure for these laws, as their final end, all the results conformable to them and possible in a world" (*Religion within the Limits of Reason Alone,* Greene and Hudson trans. [Chicago: Open Court Publishing Co., 1934], p. 95).

[34] How such a notion works itself out in conceptions of God as genuinely "acting" in the world and "revealing himself" to man may be seen in Chapters 6 and 7, below.

sophisticated enough to recognize the highly problematical and constructive character of his theological notions, and thus would not—as perhaps earlier generations all too often and too easily did—allow his faith to be bound up with literalistic mythology. A good grasp of the significance of the distinction between the real referent and the available referent for "God" would help, I think, to make that possible.

Part III. God and the World

6

On the Meaning of "Act of God"*

What we desperately need is a theological ontology that will put intelligible and credible meanings into our analogical categories of divine deeds and of divine self-manifestation through events . . . Only an ontology of events specifying what God's relation to ordinary events is like, and thus what his relation to special events might be, could fill the now empty analogy of mighty acts, void since the denial of the miraculous.

Langdon Gilkey[1]

The concept "act of God" is central to the biblical understanding of God and his relation to the world. Repeatedly we are told of the great works performed by God in behalf of his people and in execution of his own purposes in history. From the "song of Moses," which celebrates the "glorious deeds" (Exod. 15:11) through which Yahweh secured the release of the Israelites from bondage in Egypt, to the letters of Paul, which proclaim God's great act delivering us "from the dominion of darkness" (Col. 1:13) and reconciling us with himself, we are confronted with a "God who acts."[2] The "mighty acts" (Ps. 145:4), the "wondrous deeds" (Ps. 40:5), the "wonderful works" (Ps. 107:21) of God are the fundamental subject matter of biblical his-

* This paper was originally published in *Harvard Theological Review*, 61:175–201 (1968).

[1] "Cosmology, Ontology, and the Travail of Biblical Language," *Journal of Religion*, 41:203, 200 (1961).

[2] See the well-known book of that title by G. Ernest Wright (London: SCM Press, 1952).

tory, and the object of biblical faith is clearly the One who has acted repeatedly and with power in the past and may be expected to do so in the future.

I

However hallowed by Bible and by traditional faith, this notion of a God who continuously performs deliberate acts in and upon his world, and in and through man's history, has become very problematical for most moderns. We have learned to conceive nature as an impersonal order or structure. The rising of the sun, the falling of the rain, the development of the solar system and the evolution of life, catastrophes like earthquakes or hurricanes as well as the wondrous adaptations and adjustments through which the myriad species of life sustain and support each other, terrifying plagues and diseases as well as powers of healing and restoration—all are grasped by us as natural events and processes. All are understood to proceed from natural causes and to lead to natural effects; in no case is it necessary to invoke the special action of God to account for such occurrences. Indeed, we have learned, especially in the last three or four hundred years, that it is precisely by *excluding* reference to such a transcendent agent that we gain genuine knowledge of the order that obtains in nature, are enabled to predict in certain respects the natural course of events, and thus gain a measure of control over it. The deliberate exclusion of reference to the action of God in the understanding of nature does not, of course, involve a claim that nature has become transparent to man, that there is no longer mystery in this world before which we must stand in awe. But it does mean that a particular kind of mystery is excluded: it is not to an inscrutable but personal will, apt in any moment to act in new and unpredictable ways, that such features of our world are to be referred, but simply to the mystery and obscurity of the cosmic process itself, whose infinite scope and impenetrable depths our limited minds cannot fathom.

It is precisely this question about the kind of mystery which

nature manifests that is at issue in the modern theological discussion of miracle. The proponents of a doctrine of miracle as
interruption of natural order claim that any view holding that
such deliberate acts of God do not (or cannot) occur reduces
or obscures the genuine mystery in our lives, hidden ultimately
in God's inscrutable will; for it involves the claim that the basic
(and inviolable) order or structure of nature is in some real
sense discernible by us. But those who deny the appropriateness of this view can claim that it is precisely the doctrine of
miracle that refuses to face the mystery of existence, for it
disposes too easily of the unusual or uncomprehended by referring them to that which is supposedly known and can be
trusted, the will of a God who loves and redeems his creatures;
thus, the proponents of a doctrine of miracle erode the genuine
mystery of our existence, seeking to overcome their anxieties
as personal beings in an impersonal world by the postulation
of a purposive and personal God as its Creator and Lord. In
this argument it is clearly the opponents of miracle who have
won the day. Few any longer are disposed to explain the occurrence of particular events by referring them directly to God's
intervention in the natural order. Although many theologians
still wish to say such occurrences are possible "in principle"
(for "with God all things are possible," Matt. 19:26), it is clear
that both their practical decisions and actions and their theological theories are controlled by the assumption of the fundamental autonomy of natural order. In view of the fact that this
is completely inconsistent with the supposedly authoritative
biblical conception of God as one who continuously *acts* in and
upon nature as its Lord, it is little wonder that contemporary
talk about God sounds hollow and abstract, and for many of
us has become uncomfortable and difficult.

A frequently proposed way out of this dilemma is to concede
that nature, as we experience it and have learned to describe it
in science, is indeed autonomous and self-contained, but that
God acts in man's history, revealing himself, covenanting with
man, rescuing men from the various forms of bondage into
which they have fallen. Though nature may be ruled by impersonal iron necessity, history is the realm of freedom and pur-

pose in which values are cherished and ends are pursued; though teleological conceptions may well obstruct and even make impossible the work of the natural scientist, without such categories as *purpose* and *act* the historian could not even begin his work. Hence, if God is to be conceived as one who acts, it is in terms of our experience of history that we must understand him: he is one who acts through the events of history as history's Lord. Although in our understanding of nature we are instructed by modern secular science, in our interpretation of history we can be believers.

The shallowness of this proposal—though it has often been enunciated in the desperation of contemporary theology—should be immediately apparent. In the first place, no one conceives of or experiences "history" in this kind of sharp isolation from "nature." All historical events take place within the context of natural process and order and involve the movements and reordering of physical bodies and material objects of many sorts. Moreover, many natural events—one needs think only of rainfall and drought, earthquake and disease, birth and death—have significant historical consequences. It is impossible to speak of history as though it were a realm of freedom and decision entirely separate from nature. Certainly the biblical perspective is not characterized by such nonsense. It is a measure of the desperation of contemporary theology and faith, in the face of the power of the modern scientific world view—a desperation already manifest in Kant's metaphysical agnosticism[3] to which such theological views are heavily indebted—that this way out was attempted at all. It will not do to speak of God as the agent who made it possible for the Israelites to escape from the Egyptians, if one regards it as simply a fortunate coincidence that a strong east wind was blowing at just the right time to dry up the sea of reeds. The biblical writer's view is coherent and compelling precisely because he is able to say that *"the Lord* drove the sea back by a

[3] It should be recalled here that according to his own testimony in the first *Critique* Kant had "found it necessary to deny *knowledge,* in order to make room for *faith*" (B xxx [Kemp Smith trans.] (New York: Macmillan, 1929); cf. B xxivff.).

strong east wind" (Exod. 14:21); that is, it was because, and only because, God was Lord over nature, one who could bend natural events to his will, that he was able to be effective Lord over history. *so was Eve arguably*

In the second place—even if the sharp bifurcation of nature and history could be made intelligible—referring acts of God to historical events really helps little to resolve the fundamental problem. For the modern experience of and interpretation of history, just as surely as the modern view of nature, is entirely in terms of intramundane powers and events. We may well agree that history is a realm in which decision and action, pursuit of ends and appreciation of value and meaning, have genuine reality and effectiveness; we may be prepared to argue that some measure of genuine freedom and creativity must be presupposed to account for the creation and cumulation of culture, teleologically modifying nature in such diverse ways. But this certainly does not incline many of us to speak of *God's* free and creative activity in and through the historical process. Indeed, the orientation of the modern historian explicitly precludes such extraworldly reference: his task is to explain and interpret the movement of man's history entirely by reference to the interaction of human wills, the development of human institutions and traditions, and the effects of natural events and processes, that is, exclusively in intramundane terms. Doubtless he may refer to historic decisions and to creative ideas and imaginative visions, but these are always the work of human political or military leader, artist or philosopher or dreamer. Never does he invoke a transcendent agent to explain what has occurred, and never does he suppose it necessary, or even intelligible, to refer to some injection into the human historical process from beyond in order to understand even the most radical historical reversals or the most creative beginnings: all are to be understood by reference to human powers and actions in the context of the natural world.

It is not out of some unbelieving perversity that the modern historian thus thinks and writes; rather, since this is the way we in fact experience history, this is the only way in which it is intelligible to us. Nor is this an attempt to ignore or reduce the mystery of the historical movement in which we are immersed by disregarding its depths and obscurities; few would claim to understand "where history is going" or "the pattern of history." The mystery remains. But it is the mystery and obscurity of human creativity and willfulness, the mystery and incomprehensibility of cosmic process, not the mystery and inscrutability of the purposes and will of a personal and loving God who is moving the world toward a consummation known only to him.

Inasmuch as our modern experience and understanding of history is quite as secular as our experience and understanding of nature, the concept "act of God" can no more readily be interpreted by reference to historical events than to natural. But since the root metaphor that informs the Western notion of God and gives it its special character is that of a supreme Actor or Agent, it is little wonder that the notion of God has become empty for us, that "God is dead."[4] An agent is experienced and known in and through his acts; since we no longer grasp events as genuinely acts of the transcendent God, the Agent himself has faded away for us into little more than a word inherited from our past. In this situation three alternatives confront us. The first, and probably most common, is to grant that "God is dead," that is, that life is to be understood in humanistic and naturalistic terms; if the word "God" is used at all, it will only be in perfunctory and conventional ways, not out of the awareness and conviction of a genuine trans-human agent. The second, followed, for example, by Paul Tillich, is decisively to reinterpret the notion of God in such a manner that the conception of agent is no longer implied; then the reality of God will be sought in other dimensions of experience than "acts." The third, which I shall attempt here, is to subject our ordinary notion of "act" to a reexamination to see whether it is possible to reinterpret the conception of "God's act(s)" in a sense to some extent continuous with ordinary

[4] There are, of course, many other contributing factors to contemporary unbelief, such as the experience of massive evil in our time. But the problems with which we are concerned in this paper have a certain logical, if not existential, priority over such difficulties.

usage but nevertheless theologically significant and philosophically intelligible.

If the conception of God's "act" can be developed as the fundamental metaphysical category for interpreting his relation to finite beings, the theological task is much facilitated. God himself can be viewed as *Agent,* one who has intentions and purposes that he realizes in and through creation; thus his creative, providential, and redemptive activity can be rendered intelligible in fairly straightforward terms, reasonably continuous with biblical language. Such a defining image of God is not only advantageous when interpreting the heavily anthropomorphic terminology about God's love, mercy, justice, and wisdom; it also provides a way to interpret his transcendence,[5] thus preserving his radical independence and aseity even while making possible an understanding of his relation to the world. Furthermore, if it is possible to understand God as an active being in this quasi-personal sense, it is much easier to work out the complex metaphysical problems having to do with his relation to other agents, men.[6] Conversely, if "act"-language is abandoned in theology, or is subordinated to the language of being or cause or process, it becomes difficult to regard much of the traditional terminology as anything more than poetic metaphor or outright equivocation. *as in much dogma?*

II

An act (as we ordinarily think of it) is something done or performed, a deed; it is a particular and generally a specific

[5] See my two papers, "Two Models of Transcendence," in *The Heritage of Christian Thought*, ed. R. E. Cushman and E. Grislis (New York: Harper and Row, 1965), and "Transcendence without Mythology," *Harvard Theological Review* 59:105–132 (1966). [Reprinted as Chapters 4 and 3, respectively, in this volume.]

[6] When "act"-language is used in this way to interpret ultimate reality, freedom and creativity are given significant place on the metaphysical ground floor, in contrast with cosmologies that make either causal or teleological order (or some form of chance or indeterminism) fundamental. Thus, such a position can provide a metaphysical grounding for human freedom and creativity which is simply unavailable to other cosmological or theological positions.

event brought about by an agent. Acts may be of shorter or longer duration, and although an act always has a certain unity governed by the end or objective that is being pursued, it need not be completed in a single unbroken stretch of time, but may be interrupted and then resumed (as with the act of building a house or writing a book). But in all cases a particular act has a certain unity and specificity; it is some particular thing achieved, a definite deed done. It is not mere activity, but activity bound together and given a distinct order and structure by the intention of an agent to realize a goal.[7]

The goal seeking characteristic of an act must be distinguished from the immanent teleology that Aristotle ascribed to living organisms. The latter simply follow patterns built into their very structure and handed on from generation to generation: thus the acorn becomes an oak which again produces more acorns. In the case of an act, this ruling pattern does not exist; instead, the agent deliberately posits the end he intends to realize—and it may be something quite new, which had not existed before or which he had not done before. Thus, an act involves an element of creativity not characteristic of lower forms of life than man. The cumulation of such (creative) acts produces the *historical* order, culture, a new order of being superimposed on the process of life and not to be simply identified with it. To understand the teleological movements of living organisms, which involve the repetition of unfolding patterns long since established—the acorn simply becoming another oak—it is necessary only to postulate that the same pattern somehow be transferred from generation to generation. The purposive movement of an act, however, inasmuch as it is no mere repetition of previous pattern but involves creative production of the new, cannot be understood in this way. In this case there must be an *agent* who performs the act,

---

[7] [The notion of an *act* is really much more complex than can here be described. (See A. R. White, "Introduction," in *The Philosophy of Action* [London: Oxford University Press, 1968], for an outline of this complexity. Other essays in this volume, as well as those cited in Chapter 8, note 8, should also be consulted.) I have attempted here only to point to dimensions that may help to clarify the notion of "act of God."]

a reality in which is lodged the teleological intention to be realized through it. Such an agent must be capable both of formulating the intention to be realized in the future (he must have powers of imagining the presently nonexistent) and of working through time in such ordered fashion as to realize his goal. The successive moments of time here are bound together not by a preestablished pattern implanted in the organism but by the purposive activity of the agent. Thus, *act* and *purpose* should not be reduced to Aristotle's notion of the teleology at work in all organisms; our proper model here is human purposive behavior.

Acts may be broken down into constituent acts (or subacts), each of which makes its necessary contribution to the larger act. Thus, my act of constructing a bench will include within it many subacts, hammering, sawing, measuring, and so forth. Each of these, involving as it does its own unification of activity toward a particular goal, can be considered an act in its own right. Fastening one board to another is a particular act, but so is driving in each of the nails used to secure that board; we may, if we choose, regard each blow on the head of a nail as itself a distinct act. But there is a limit below which acts may not be further analyzed into constituent acts. We would not, for example, regard the movement of the hammer through each separate inch of the path toward the head of the nail as a distinct act; such fractions of activity in which no end, not even a subordinate one, is attained, though essential constituents of the act of hitting the nail, are not themselves acts. To be regarded as an act, the movement must realize some posited objective, however slight or unimpressive, such as striking the nail. The same sort of rule governs the upper limit of the size and inclusiveness of an act as the lower: so long as the subacts are bound together into a single overall teleological unity, we may speak of them as one act. Thus, building a house is a particular act, but it may be viewed as part of the larger act (if done with this larger end in view) of establishing a village or even founding a nation. Moreover, several individuals, or even groups, can participate in the same act, if their activity is ordered toward a common end (cf. an "act of Congress"). We would be hesitant, however, about describing the complicated and long historical process of, for example, the rise of science as *an act*. This is not because of its complexity per se, but because the many constituent events of this development can hardly be conceived as ordered toward and controlled by some definite end posited by some particular individual or group: it is difficult to see this process as *an act* performed by *an agent* (even a collective agent). Although many acts doubtless contributed to this development, the peculiar kind of unity to which the term "act" points does not characterize the process as a whole.

An "act of God," now, in the literal meaning of the phrase, would be a deed performed by God, an event that did not simply "happen," but that was what it was because God did it.[8] Certainly this is the picture of the "mighty acts of God" found in scripture. Here God does things just as do men: he enters into battle, he makes covenants with his people, he builds and destroys cities and nations, he cares for the poor and helpless and brings to judgment the wicked, he comforts the afflicted, he causes the sun to shine and the rain to fall, he brings plagues and destruction but also healing and well-being, he has created this very world in which we find ourselves, and he will yet create new heavens and a new earth. Each of these is a particular act done by God either simply on his own initiative to further his ends or in response to something done by men.

It may be supposed that the difficulty we moderns feel with such talk of God's acts arises simply and entirely from our unwillingness or inability to think in terms of supernatural causes of historical events. And thus, on the one hand, traditionalists may declaim in the name of faith against what they regard as modern unbelief, while, on the other, secularists will

---

[8] We can still sense something of this meaning even in the conventional or legal usage of the phrase to designate a terrible catastrophe—such as being struck by lightning or destroyed by storm—although such events are now understood to be due entirely to impersonal natural causes; their unexpectedness, man's powerlessness before them, their terrifying impact on human affairs may still evoke some sense of a powerful and inscrutable will working its way through the events of nature.

laugh at the naïveté of those who suppose God really does something. These contrary positions both arise from the common assumption that an act of God is to be thought of as a particular miraculous event that God directly causes,[9] and as long as this conception is left undisturbed, the impasse cannot be resolved. In order to do so, it will be necessary both to analyze with more subtlety certain roots of the modern difficulties with the notion of God's acts and also to elaborate more fully some of the implications of the previous analysis of an act for the notion of God's act.

III

The modern difficulties here do not arise exclusively, as is often supposed, from our unwillingness to believe in some transcendent *cause* of events; they arise quite as much from our inability to conceive *these events themselves,* in view of the way in which we (necessarily?) conceive nature and history. In this paper I shall confine myself largely to the second problem, leaving questions about the mode of God's causal impingement on the world for treatment elsewhere.[10]

According to the modern view, events are not conceived as

[9] It may be observed here that though Aquinas worked out an elaborate doctrine of "second causes" which he held were the usual media of God's work, he maintained that God could and sometimes did work directly and immediately, and this possibility was regarded by him as theologically indispensable (*Summa Theologica,* I, Q 105), as indeed it is if one works with a theory of second causes like that of Thomas. But it is precisely this way of conceiving God's direct and immediate action in particular events that is no longer plausible or intelligible.

[10] Though I would not be inclined simply to adopt A. N. Whitehead's or Charles Hartshorne's organismic models for rendering intelligible God's impingement on the world, certainly much is to be learned from their careful and detailed treatments of this matter. The principal difficulty with them, it seems to me, is that God's effective initiative and autonomous agency are rendered highly problematical, and I am concerned to keep these at the very center. [As suggested on pp. 158–159 below, I am now quite doubtful that it is logically consistent with the meaning of "God" to speculate on the means or modes of his direct impingement on the world.]

individual atoms that are more or less independent of the natural and historical context or web within which they fall. All events are so interrelated and interconnected in many complex ways that to think or to describe any particular event always involves us in reference to those events which preceded it as necessary conditions for its occurring, to those events which surround it and thus specify it by both defining its boundaries or limits and providing the context within which it falls and the background against which it is perceived and known, and to those ever widening circles of events which it will condition and shape in a variety of ways. One of the greatest of Kant's achievements in the first *Critique* was his demonstration that we not only think in terms of such an interconnected and unified web of events, but that such a unified whole is a necessary condition for having experience at all; that is, it would not even be possible to experience totally isolated and unconnected particulars. The success of modern natural science in describing, predicting, and in some measure controlling events in the natural order is due precisely to the discovery of ways to discern and formulate fundamental structural regularities obtaining between events (laws of nature), but this growing success makes it increasingly difficult even to conceive what an event occurring somehow independently of this web might be.[11] A

[11] For example, is it even possible, any more, to think clearly what is meant by the "virgin birth"? It might be supposed that this idea is clear enough: it involves conception without the activity of a male partner. But how are we to think of such conception? Are we to suppose that at some point a male sperm appeared within Mary's womb, there fertilizing an egg? If so, how are we to think of this? Were the requisite number of atoms and molecules created instantaneously and out of nothing within Mary's body and somehow infused with life? How is it possible to conceive this in view of the assumptions (indispensable to science) about the conservation of mass-energy, and of the slow evolution of life? If we do not suppose a male sperm was somehow created in Mary's womb, do we think of this conception as without benefit of fertilization at all? Or did the egg fertilize itself? I am far from contending that any or all of these questions can be or need be answered; my point is that the way we have come to think of conception and birth under the tutelage of modern biology makes it inevitable that such questions will arise. For we cannot clearly think (though we can, perhaps, *imagine*)

similar development has occurred in historical work. The great achievement of modern history is its success in developing methods of analysis, criticism, and evaluation of the "sources" with which the historian works, methods that enable the historian to give a wholly satisfactory and convincing interpretation of the order and character of the events with which he is dealing without reference to anything beyond the historical process and its natural context. The presupposition of modern historical understanding (as of scientific knowledge) is that each new event emerges out of, and can and must be understood in relationship to, the historical context in which it appears. Though the event may qualify and transform the future course of that history in significant ways, it never appears within the historical process as an inexplicable bolt from the

---

what an event without prior finite causes and conditions would be (and in many cases, as in conception, we know much about what these essential conditions are), and so, no matter at what point in the process of conception and birth we begin, we inevitably and necessarily inquire about the antecedent conditions. *The very definition or concept of event implies for us such connection with indispensable antecedent (finite) conditions*, and it is no longer possible for us to think an "event" as simply supernaturally caused. That is, for us all chains of events, such as the growth of the boy Jesus, presuppose preceding chains of events, such as the development of Mary's pregnancy, and these in turn presuppose other chains; and this continuous recursive movement may not be halted simply arbitrarily. The question, then, is whether it is even possible to conceive clearly the idea of a supernaturally caused event, or (what is the same thing) the occurrence of a finite event without adequate finite causes, or whether such a notion is not quite as self-contradictory as the notion of a square-circle. Cf. Schleiermacher: "every absolute miracle would destroy the whole system of nature. . . . Since . . . that which would have happened by reason of the totality of finite causes in accordance with the natural order does not happen, an effect has been hindered from happening, and certainly not through the influence of other normally counteracting finite causes given in the natural order, but in spite of the fact that all active causes are combining to produce that very effect. Everything, therefore, which had ever contributed to this will, to a certain degree, be annihilated, and instead of introducing a single supernatural power into the system of nature as we intended, we must completely abrogate the conception of nature" (*The Christian Faith* [Edinburgh: T. and T. Clark, 1928], §47, 2).

blue. When a historian has to deal with remains so fragmentary that he is unable to propose a hypothesis about their proper place in the continuing movement of history, he never assumes this was because of some supernatural origin; to do so would imply a conception of breaks in the historical process that would vitiate even the possibility of knowledge of the past. His conclusion (rightly) is that we simply do not have sufficient evidence to say what happened here. But there is no question in his mind (or ours) that if we did have the requisite evidence, we would be able to understand in intrahistorical terms the events in question. Not only is secular history written in terms of such assumptions; the whole enterprise of modern biblical criticism and interpretation proceeds (quite properly) on the same basis.[12] Without such assumptions about the continuity of the historical process, the analogy of preceding events and periods with our own (secular) experience, and the necessity of criticism of documents, it would not even be possible to think what a historical event is, as Ernst Troeltsch long ago clearly perceived.[13]

It should not be supposed that this modern conception of nature and history as a web of interrelated events that must be understood as a self-contained whole is a somewhat arbitrary move, that we could just as well, if we pleased, go back to earlier notions of a much looser weave in the nature of things such that occasionally events without finite cause might appear. The development toward the modern conception was a necessary and natural one fostered by an increasing awareness of the conditions of knowledge and experience, and the tremendous growth of modern scientific and historical knowledge is both its consequence and confirmation. Nor should it be supposed that the discovery of certain indeterminacies on

[12] A good recent analysis that shows clearly why this must be the case, as well as how theologians and biblical historians have often sought to evade the full implications of this matter, will be found in Van A. Harvey, *The Historian and the Believer* (New York: Macmillan, 1966).

[13] See the essay, "Über historische und dogmatische Methode in der Theologie," *Gesammelte Schriften* (4 vols., Tübingen: Mohr, 1912–1925), II, 729–753.

the microatomic level opens the door once again to the older conception. I have not been arguing for a (quasi-mechanical) *determinism* of all events by their antecedents, but rather that the modern pursuit of knowledge presupposes the interrelation and interconnection of all events in an unbroken web. That there may be some measure of "play" or indeterminacy on the atomic level, and that there is genuine creativity and self-determination on the human level, I am quite prepared not only to admit but to argue. But this indeterminacy and this freedom occur within and are continuous with contexts such that statistical descriptions can always be made and are usually quite precise, and (in the case of human actions) understanding in strictly human terms is demanded. My point is that it is precisely the gradually developing awareness of the interconnected web of events which has made possible the high-level description and understanding characteristic of modern science and history. Therefore, it is no longer possible for us to think (when we think clearly and consistently) of individual or particular events somehow by themselves: every event is defined as a focal point in a web that reaches in all directions beyond it indefinitely;[14] it is never grasped (in our modern experience) as an independent substance that can exist and be thought by itself alone.

This being the case, we can see why we have great difficulty with the traditional notion of "act of God." This phrase seems to refer to events that have their source or cause directly or immediately in the divine will and action rather than in the context of preceding and coincident finite events: indeed, the finite nexus apparently need not be thought as conditioning the newly injected event in any significant way, though a chain

[14] It is, of course, A. N. Whitehead who has worked out most fully both the necessity of conceiving events in this way and also the full cosmological implications of such a conception. (See, e.g., *Science and the Modern World* [New York: Macmillan, 1925], esp. Chap. 7; and the doctrine of "actual occasions" in *Process and Reality* [New York: Macmillan, 1929].) One may learn much from Whitehead's ontological and cosmological analysis and construction even though one does not wish to commit oneself to his theology.

of consequences within the finite order presumably ensues from it. Acts of God in this sense, seen from man's side, are absolute beginning points for chains of events that occur—not at the "beginning" of the world and history—but *within* ongoing natural and historical processes. It might be supposed this could be made intelligible by viewing the movement through time of nature and history under the metaphor, for example, of a flowing river, with new streams (acts of God) from time to time emptying into the onward flow, thus becoming part of the cumulating rush of waters; but here also, we must remember, such streams can always be traced by a recursive movement to their (finite) sources somewhere back in the hills, precisely what this notion of God's acts renders impossible. I want to emphasize that the problem we are considering does not arise in the first instance out of difficulties connected with conceiving a transcendent agent; it is rather the difficulty—even impossibility—of conceiving the *finite event itself* which is here supposed to be God's act. That is, the problem is not that such acts invoke a no longer believable mythology of some being beyond this world (however serious that problem may itself be); it is rather that what is said to happen *in this world,* in our experience, is not intelligible. An "event" without finite antecedents is no event at all and cannot be clearly conceived; "experience" with tears and breaks destroying its continuity and unity could not even be experienced. It is incorrect to suppose, then, that all that is required here is a reformulation of our categories so as to make room for an occasional act of God; the problem is that certain logical preconditions of connection, continuity and unity must obtain if there is to be any experience at all (Kant), and precisely these conditions are contradicted by the notion of particular "acts of God" being performed from time to time in history and nature. Or, to put the matter in a somewhat different way: it is impossible to conceive such an act either as a natural event or as a historical event, as occurring either within nature or history; in short, it is impossible to conceive it as any kind of event (in the finite order) at all. Our experience is of a unified and orderly world; in such a world acts of

God (in the traditional sense) are not merely improbable or difficult to believe: they are literally inconceivable. It is not a question of whether talk about such acts is true or false; it is, in the literal sense, meaningless; one cannot make the concept hang together consistently.

IV

Having noted certain difficulties for the modern consciousness with the notion that God performs particular more or less individual acts in history, let us return to the earlier analysis of *act* to see whether there are possibilities of reformulation. I will be able to present here only in brief outline a way to conceive God's act in analogy with human acts and yet consistently with the requirements of modern scientific and historical work; many important details, relating both to the (analogical) concept of God as Agent and his mode of affecting finite processes, remain to be worked out.[15] However, if the proposed reconstruction is successful, the (analogical) concept of God's act can be utilized as the fundamental metaphysical category for interpreting his relation to finite reality, that is, as the form of all his diverse relations to the world, the schema that gives them intelligible unity. If we are going to understand the fullness and diversity of creation in its manifold relations to the one God, we must have a concept that is at once general enough to cover the infinite complexity and many-sidedness of those relations and still gives them a sufficiently unified form to be intelligible. I suggest that the notion of *act*, having the specificity of referring immediately to an agent and

[15] For some suggestion of my way of treating some, though by no means all of the problems connected with conceiving God as Agent, see my two papers on personalistic conception of divine transcendence ("Two Models of Transcendence," and "Transcendence without Mythology") [and also Chapters 7 and 8 of the present volume]. Much remains to be done, however, especially on the problem of conceiving God as *effecting* his purposes within and for history. Resolution of this issue will depend in part on the success with which one is able to conceive how a human agent effects purposes, and then drawing out the analogy to interpret the divine activity. [See addition to note 10, above.]

yet the generality of comprehending all the relations into which an agent can enter, can provide the basis for developing an analogical concept appropriate to perform this function.

Two points particularly must be recalled from the earlier discussion. First, comprehensive or complex acts may be analyzed or broken down into constituent elements and sub-elements, some of which are themselves simpler acts, some biological or physical processes or motions; or, stated conversely, simple or particular acts are often phases of overarching complex acts—we will call these "master acts"—which unify and order various sorts of behavior and otherwise disconnected stretches of time. Second, that which makes an act an *act* is the deliberate ordering of behavior toward the realization of a previously posited end. I want to argue now that the customary interpretation of certain relatively restricted events —the crossing of the Red Sea, the dispersing of the hosts of Sennacherib, the virgin birth or resurrection of Jesus—as particular acts of God is too simple. For it overlooks the significance of the relation of "simple acts" to "master acts."

It is the master act, rather than each simple act taken by itself, that renders any given piece of activity intelligible. Simple acts, being constituent phases of a complex act, are always secondary and derivative, for they are not performed simply for the sake of their own end but rather as a step toward the master end: the nail is not hammered simply to get it into the board (that is a subordinate objective) but in order to build the house. Doubtless certain subordinate acts must be performed in order to complete the complex act, but they have their purpose and gain their character from the latter, and we can be said to "understand" them only when we see them in the light of the master end. Thus, we do not find it particularly illuminating to say simply, "The carpenter is driving nails," for that in itself is hardly meaningful activity; rather, it is when we see that the carpenter is nailing together boards in order to construct a house that we understand what he is doing.

If we are to understand properly the phrase "act of God," then, we should use it first of all to designate the *master act* in which God is engaged, not the particular and relatively limited events that might first attract our attention. The latter must be regarded as secondary and derivative, to be grasped and interpreted in the light of God's master end, not in their own terms. This means for a monotheistic theology that it is *the whole course of history,* from its initiation in God's creative activity to its consummation when God ultimately achieves his purposes, that should be conceived as God's act in the primary sense. In the biblical documents God is not portrayed as one who performs relatively disconnected and unrelated acts that lead in no particular direction or toward no definite goal; he is one who planned "the end from the beginning" (Isa. 46:10), and his activity throughout history is ordered toward his ultimate goal, the final establishment of that "kingdom which has been destined for [his creatures] from the creation of the world" (Matt. 25:34 Goodspeed). Even the appearance of Jesus Christ far down the course of history "was destined before the foundation of the world" (1 Pet. 1:20), and what he brought into history is to be understood as but a foretaste of the final glorious consummation. The movement of history as portrayed in the Bible is no mere succession of events— not even a succession of "acts of God"—leading to no clear goal or end: from its beginning and throughout, it is given shape and direction by the ultimate objective that God is bringing to pass. Since, as we observed previously, activity proceeding from a single agent and ordered toward a single end, no matter how complex, is properly to be regarded as *one act,* this whole complicated and intricate teleological movement of all nature and history should be regarded as a single all-encompassing act of God, providing the context and meaning of all that occurs. It is, of course, an act that has not yet run its course, an act that will not be finished until the eschaton.

This conception of God's master act does not encounter the same difficulties with the modern presuppositions about the unity and structure of nature and history as did the notion of various relatively independent act-events. For here God's act is not a new event that suddenly and without adequate prior conditions rips inexplicably into the fabric of experience, a notion consistent neither with itself nor with the regularity and order that experience must have if it is to be cognizable. Rather, here God's act is viewed as the source of precisely that overarching order itself: it is God's master act that gives the world the structure it has and gives natural and historical processes their direction. Speaking of God's act in this sense in no way threatens the unity and order of the world as a whole.[16]

It is meaningful to regard the fundamental structures of nature and history as grounded in an *act* (of God), however, only if we are able to think of them as developing in time. An act is intrinsically temporal: it is the ordering of a succession of events toward an end. If we could not think of the universe as somehow developing in unidirectional fashion in and through temporal processes, it would be mere poetry to speak of God's act. For this reason, prior to the late nineteenth and early twentieth centuries, while a static-structural view of nature prevailed, it was very difficult to think of nature as ordered by God's act in any further sense than being created (and sustained) by him. But a scientific revolution occurred in the nineteenth and twentieth centuries: geologists began to see the earth not as a more or less static given, but as having a history through which it developed during many ages to its present form; biologists came to see life not merely as a structure of species, but as a unitary evolutionary process in continuous development from lower forms to highly complex ones; and astronomers even discovered that the supposedly eternally stable heavens actually manifested a continuously expanding movement through billions of years, seeming to go back to some primeval originating "explosion." In short, scientists

[16] John Macmurray even argues that the "only way" in which we can conceive the world as a unified whole is by thinking it as "one action" (*The Self as Agent* [London: Faber and Faber, 1957], p. 204). For if the overarching unity of the world were conceived simply in terms, for example, of the category *process*, it would be "a world in which nothing is ever done; in which everything simply happens; a world, then, in which everything is matter of fact and nothing is ever intended. We should have to assert, in that case, that there are no actions; that what seem such are really events" (p. 219). That is, the concept of process cannot comprise the unity of the entire world because it cannot contain our own actions as part of that overall unity.

came to think of nature, in all her levels and forms, as in historical process, as moving and developing and evolving in time. Thus, to conceive the whole cosmic movement as comprehended within a single "act" through which God is achieving some ultimate purpose is consistent with the modern understanding of nature as in process of evolutionary development.[17]

It will be objected immediately that science finds no evidence of teleological or purposed order in this movement, that the most one can observe is simply a kind of natural evolution. With this I will not quibble: I am not claiming that the cosmic process provides *evidence* for believing in a God active through it; I am claiming merely that the evolutionary picture of nature and life currently painted in our scientific knowledge is not inconsistent with such belief. The purpose that informs an act is an interior connection between the various phases of events known to the agent who is performing it, and it is seldom directly visible to external observers, especially to those who can see only a tiny fraction of the total act in question. If God is acting through the process of nature's development over billions of years to accomplish some ultimate objective, this would hardly be apparent in the observations of lowly men, with a life-span of a mere three score years and ten and careful scientific observations and records going back at most only a few hundred years. To use a geometrical figure: one could hardly expect man to discern the teleological curvature of the movement of world history as a whole when he has accessible to his direct inspection scarcely more than an infinitesimal arc of that curve. Such teleological activity by a cosmic agent could be known only if he should in some way choose to reveal it to his creatures.[18]

---

[17] It is not consistent, of course, with the assumption that nature is not grounded in anything beyond herself, but that is a different point from the one I am making in this paper, one deserving full discussion in its own right, though it cannot be pursued here.

[18] I cannot here go into the complicated question of whether God has revealed himself, and, if so, how this is to be understood. [See Chapter 7, below.] Suffice it to recall that precisely this is the Christian claim: the knowledge of God and of his purposive activity in and for the world is not attained primarily through

Thus, to conceive the entire movement of nature and history as the expression of one overarching act of God is consistent both with the meaning of the term "act" and with the modern understanding of the cosmos as in evolutionary development. True, no evidence has been offered here to sustain such a view of an ultimate teleology working in nature, and I do not propose in this paper to offer any. That would involve us in an examination of the psychological, historical, and logical grounds for belief in God, and it would require sketching out doctrines of God and of revelation.[19] In short, it would lead far beyond the scope of the present inquiry. We are concerned here with the very restricted objective of clarifying and reinterpreting the notion of God's act in such a way that it will be intelligible in the light of current scientific and historical assumptions about the interconnectedness of all events. Unless this can be done, all speech about God as "Lord" of the world, as providentially guiding history, as loving and merciful father of mankind, as active agent in any significant sense at all— speech that is essential for Christian and Jewish faith—is hollow and empty, whatever be one's grounds for believing in God. Both the present sort of analysis (dealing with God's relation to the world) and exploration of the wider question of the grounds for speaking of God at all will be required if the highly problematic status that all such talk presently has is to be overcome.

V

Having proposed an interpretation of "act of God" in its primary and widest meaning, as designating the overall movement of nature and history toward God's ultimate goal, I must return in conclusion to the more customary understanding of the phrase as referring to particular events in which God does

---

observation of nature but rather through his self-disclosure. "For he has made known to us in all wisdom and insight the mystery of his will, according to his purpose which he set forth in Christ as a plan for the fullness of time, to unite all things in him, things in heaven and things on earth" (Eph. 1:9–10).

[19] [See Chapters 5, 7, and 10.]

something "unusual" or "special" in history. Is this ordinary meaning of the phrase to be ignored or dispensed with entirely? Is it not such *particular acts* in which faith believes and for which prayer cries rather than a cosmological overview? Have we not so transformed—and, some might say, "watered down" —the meaning of God's activity as to render it religiously irrelevant or empty?

To these questions two remarks may be addressed. (1) The question whether the phrase "act of God" can have any referential meaning at all is primarily intellectual or theoretical. In saying this I do not mean to ignore or disparage religious or existential aspects of this problem, for they are also there, but the principal difficulty here is that our understanding of the world, of experience, of history, has become such that there seems no way to conceive or imagine cosmic purposive activity working in events. That is, it is the *theory* informing all our experience and thought that appears radically inconsistent with that older personalistic (or anthropomorphic) theory of the world, which everywhere informs the biblical literature and our most fundamental theological conceptions. Unless this problem of theory, of conceptualization, of the basic categories of experience can be resolved, we are condemned either to live in an intolerable tension between our religious language and life and the rest of experience—a tension always threatening to disintegrate and destroy both the self and its faith—or to give up Christian faith and talk as outmoded and no longer relevant to the actual structures of our lives and world. It is a problem in theory, then, that we must address here, and it should not be surprising if the treatment of that problem will be, in the first instance, theoretical. We must find some way to *think* about the world once again with the categories of act and purpose if we wish to continue using these categories to speak of God and his relations to men. I freely admit, therefore, that I am proposing here a rather theoretical understanding of the notion of God's act.

The principal point I have tried to emphasize in this paper is that it is no longer possible for us to view the events in nature and history as relatively independent occurrences, each to be perceived and interpreted more or less in its own terms; for us the world has become a unified whole such that particular events are always experienced and understood in terms of their structural connections with the rest of experience, as described and clarified by scientist and historian. The order or structure of the whole thus has a kind of precedence, with us, over any particular happening, and we are inclined to discount even our own immediate experience—for example, to regard it as hallucinatory—if it cannot be understood in terms of that underlying and omnipresent order. In the more loosely textured world of earlier generations particular "acts of God" could be experienced and accepted more or less in their own terms, no matter how extraordinary they might appear, for who could say what character a new event might have? In our tightly structured world it is necessary to find place for God's activity in the fundamental order of things before it is even possible to speak meaningfully of his acting in particular events, for the conception of the latter and the very criteria with the aid of which we perceive and interpret them is derivative from and dependent upon our understanding of the basic order. Hence, if we are to speak of particular acts of God at all, we must first learn to speak of his act in and through the structure and movement of the whole. It is precisely a way of conceiving that act which is proposed in this paper.

(2) This proposal of theory, however, opens up once again a way to understand the notion of particular acts of God of more limited scope. These are not to be regarded (as in the traditional mythology) as more or less impulsive decisions in which God does something in history in quite unexpected and inexplicable fashion: they should be understood (quite consistently with the eschatological orientation of much biblical, and all New Testament, thought) as functions of and subordinate steps toward God's ultimate goal. The master act of God (which he has not yet completed) is the temporal movement of all nature and history toward the realization of his original intention in creation. This complex act comprises many events and processes of all sorts as its constituent phases and elements. Some of these, themselves teleologically ordered

toward certain subordinate ends or goals which are necessary steps toward the master end, may quite properly be regarded as (subordinate) acts or subacts performed by God as he works out his purpose.

Assuming (on the basis of Christian claims) that God has revealed something of his purposes for man and the world, one finds it possible to discern, with the help of modern knowledge of nature and history, some of the stages(subacts) through which the created order has moved as God has gradually been performing his master act.[20] The creation of the solar system, the emergence of life on earth, the evolution of higher forms of life and finally man—each of these (as well as many other natural processes and events) represents an indispensable step toward the realization of God's ultimate objectives for creation. Furthermore, the crucial phases of the actual movement of human history, and the emergence of *Heilsgeschichte* within that history, can be regarded as further subordinate acts of God: the beginnings of agriculture and later of civilization, the development of increasingly complex and interdependent modes of social, political, and economic organization making possible differentiation and specialization in sociocultural life, the emergence of primitive religious cultus and conceptions (especially in the Near East) providing a background against which faith in Yahweh could appear. Specific events of quite limited scope such as the remarkable escape of a few Hebrew tribes from Egyptian slavery, the creation of the Israelite kingdom under Saul and David, and the later exile and return of the inhabitants of Judah are acts through which God moved human history and consciousness toward a fuller awareness of who he is and what his purposes for creation are. Within this sequence, the ministry and death of Jesus Christ can quite properly be understood as the supreme act through which God at once made himself known to man and began a radical transformation of man according to his ulti-

[20] [A much fuller treatment of this history of God's activity will be found in my *Systematic Theology* (New York: Scribner's, 1968), Pts. II and III. Further elaboration of certain features of it also appears in the present volume, Chapters 7 and 8.]

mate purposes for man. Events in other cultural histories and the more recent events in Western history may all be seen in this way as governed or guided by the activity through which God is moving the whole of creation toward the eschaton, as subordinate acts within God's master act.[21] Thus, the whole course of history (including the history of nature and the evolution of life) can be apprehended once again as under God's providential control.

This does not mean, of course, that every natural or historical event need be or should be regarded as a distinct subact of God; only those events which move the creation forward a further step toward the realization of God's purposes could properly be so designated. There are many natural processes, for example, which, though originally set in motion by God's creative activity, now function as fundamental rhythms or orders that support and sustain the more complex processes of the teleological movement, thus giving the world a certain constancy and structure. It would hardly be appropriate to

[21] It will be evident from this description that God's act must not be conceived under only one image of activity, such as the carpenter making a table or the farmer cultivating a field or the parent educating his child. Within the schema of God's act we are including: first, his creation and maintenance of the material orders of nature, and also his ordering them in such a way that life can emerge from them; second, his creation of life and his ordering it through an evolutionary process in which higher and more complex forms gradually emerge from lower and simpler forms, ultimately producing self-conscious life; and third, his creation of the culture-producing being, man, his guidance of man's historical development so as to make possible the emergence of a genuinely free and responsible being, and his dealing with free (and sinful) man in such a way as to redeem him from his self-imposed bondage and enable him to become what had been originally intended. Obviously the forms of "act" appropriate to all the diverse forms of finite being here represented—ranging from bare matter to free spirits—and appropriate to the objectives God is seeking to accomplish with each will be quite various, and it would be a gross error in our theological construction if we attempted to assimilate them all to one form of (human) act, for example, that of man the maker. It is essential that we develop our analogies from the full range of human activities if we are going to render God's relation to his world intelligible by means of the basic schema, *act*.

regard the continuing steady functioning of such processes as new "acts of God"; they are, rather, the product of his earlier (creative) work, still sustained by him no doubt, but now serving as the (relatively completed) foundation on which he can build as yet unrealized superstructures. Furthermore, when certain finite processes evolved through the various stages of life to the level of conscious and free behavior, the purposive activity of finite agents began to appear within the historical process. Inasmuch as these acts in and of themselves, even though teleological in form, had (and have) their sources and goals within the finite order itself, they are not necessarily to be considered as direct subacts of God. Indeed, they could and often did (and do) go counter to God's purposes and acts, as with man's falling into cumulating patterns of sin. On the Christian view, perhaps only once in history—the march of Jesus to the cross—has there been a direct one-to-one correspondence and coincidence of human activity with divine. Only those natural and historical events which directly advance God's ultimate purposes—those which are essential constituent phases or steps of God's master act—may properly be regarded as (subordinate) acts of God within nature and history.[22]

This understanding of God's subordinate acts does not in any way undermine or threaten the unified and structural character of experience, or the methods or conclusions of science and history. For between particular events and overarching

[22] [It might be objected by some that this interpretation of God's act as including subacts actually performed by human agents requires us to think in terms of two agents for the same act, and this is at least paradoxical and quite possibly unintelligible (see Michael McLain, "On Theological Models," *Harvard Theological Review*, 62:183 [1969]). I would point out, however, that whatever the difficulties confronting full philosophical conception of such a notion, it is clearly in accord with our ordinary speech about actions and deeds. For example, when we say, "Hitler killed six million Jews" (or "Christopher Wren built St. Paul's Cathedral" or "Columbus discovered America"), we do not mean he personally performed every murder; indeed, he may not have pulled the trigger on a single person. Nevertheless, we regard a large measure of the responsibility for this horrendous crime as his, and we clearly think of it as his *deed*, however much the acts and responsibility of other agents of lower rank were also involved.]

structures and continuities, the same formal relationship obtains in the theological interpretation as in that of modern history or science: in all these cases the particular is seen in the context of, or as a phase of, a more comprehensive whole. Of course, the theological view posits a teleological movement in that whole which is not discernible to the naked scientific eye, but this eschatological goal in which faith believes does not itself disclose to faith the complex of particular historical steps through which God must move to achieve his end; man becomes aware of these only a posteriori, as creation gradually moves onward through its historical course and man learns to discern the several phases of that movement in his science and history. There is here, then, place both for the most rigorous application of scientific and historical methods to the analysis and interpretation of (past) experience and also for faith that the temporal movement of the whole, including the particular developments of our individual lives, is under God's providential care. *Putatively. Much crossfire*

It must be admitted that the doctrine of providence here entailed is more austere than the pietistic views often found in Christian circles. God's subordinate acts here are governed largely by his overarching purposes and ultimate objectives, not simply by the immediate needs or the prayerful pleas of his children. This is no God who "walks with me and talks with me" in close interpersonal communion, giving his full attention to my complaints, miraculously extracting me from difficulties into which I have gotten myself by invading nature and history with *ad hoc* rescue operations from on high. This is the Lord of heaven and earth, whose purposes we cannot fully fathom and whose ways are past finding out (Rom. 11:33). "It is he who sits above the circle of the earth, and its inhabitants are like grasshoppers" (Isa. 40:22). His thoughts are not ours, and our ways are not his (Isa. 55:8). He has brought this world into being for his own reasons, he is moving it through a history in accordance with his own objectives, and he shall accomplish his purposes when the eschaton comes. Doubtless we men, both as species and individuals, have place within those purposes, and certain of his subacts are responsive to our acts; in this we can rejoice, finding meaning for our lives and comfort for our souls. But the place we have is his to determine and assign, not ours; at the very most our lives are but almost infinitesimal constituents in his all-comprehending act, and his responsiveness to the particularities of our activity must be understood as a function and phase of his master act ordering all human and cosmic history. Though faith grounded on the conviction that in Christ God has disclosed his true will and nature may trust confidently until the end that he will deal with us justly and with love, we should hardly expect that he can or will bend his cosmic activity much to meet our private and peculiar needs or wishes. Indeed, it is precisely this steadfastness in his own purposes that makes him the faithful God: who could entrust himself to one who changed course with every turn in the breeze? *dig 2 samuel 24?*

Christian piety has too long been nurtured largely on those psalms and other biblical materials which portray God as a kind of genie who will extricate the faithful from the difficulties into which they fall; it is this erratic and fickle God who cannot be reconciled with the modern understanding of the order in nature and history. Far better would it be to nourish our piety on the paradigmatic Christian story: a man praying that this cup might pass from him, but submitting his will to God's, no matter what the consequences; that prayer answered not with legions of angels to rescue him but with lonely suffering on a cross, culminating in a cry of despair before the moment of death—and then a resurrection of new life, new faith, new hope, new love, in a new community born after his death. The God who works in this fashion to turn the darkest despairs and defeats into further steps toward the realization of his beneficent ultimate objectives, without violently ripping into the fabric of history or arbitrarily upsetting the momentum of its powers, is one who can also be conceived as working within and through the closely textured natural and historical processes of our modern experience: he is a God who acts, a living God, the adequate object for a profound faith, and his action is not completely unintelligible to a mind instructed and informed by modern science and history.

7

Revelation and Cultural History

The available God—the God spoken of in scripture and tradition, worshiped in church and synagogue, conceived in the minds of the faithful—is, as we have seen,[1] a cultural construct. But he has come to have great power and meaningfulness in Western history because he has been taken to be not only that but more: a symbol for the ultimate reality with which men have to do, a clue to what really matters in life, the center with reference to which all human existence should be oriented. However much it was admitted that the real referent of "God" was a mysterious transcendent X, inaccessible to man, it was simultaneously believed that the available referent was the appropriate symbolization for this real God, and therefore could quite properly guide and focus the actions and beliefs of men.

Important consequences follow from this for our understanding of how God comes to be known by men. If there is a God—or, more precisely, if the available God significantly symbolizes that ultimate reality with which men have to do and which should, therefore, orient human life—then it is necessary to conceive the real God as an Agent (according to the model of the available God), as One actively and purposively at work, and man's awareness or knowledge of him will be conceived as (at least in part) the consequence of this activity, that is, of God's own revelation of himself.

[1] Chapter 5, above.

I

Two considerations are involved here, and they fit together as two parts of a puzzle. In the first place, there is (as just noted) the imagery involved in the notion of (the available) God. In the Bible and the teaching of church and synagogue God is portrayed in anthropomorphic or personalistic terms as fundamentally an agent. He creates a world for his own ends. He places creatures of all sorts in his world, and he strives long and hard with the highest of his creatures, men, that they might realize his objectives for them. Toward this end, he communicates to men through prophets and other messengers, and according to the Christian story he even enters into human history in the form of a man that he might finally bring about the reconcilation and communion with men that he sought from the beginning. At all points the available God of Western tradition is conceived as actively at work in his world; in his relations with mankind he takes the initiative, leading and guiding men to forms of life and fulfillment of which originally they did not even dream. If this image is deemed at all appropriate for grasping the ultimate reality with which men have to do, that reality will itself have to be understood as in some sense active, not only in the creation and sustenance of the world but in directing the course of cosmic and human history. And the appearance and growth in culture and consciousness of awareness and understanding of God and his work will have to be regarded as something more than a merely autonomous development: they must be attributed (at least in part) to God's own intentions and work.

All of this, of course, is completely in keeping with the personalistic imagery suggested by the word "God." For our knowledge of other persons depends heavily, whenever it is significant and profound, on their disclosures of intentions and character through word and deed.[2] If I "speak my mind" to you, you can come to know what I am thinking; otherwise you

[2] See Chapter 4, above; see also my *Systematic Theology* (New York: Scribner's, 1968), pp. 32–40.

can only conjecture it. Unless I choose to reveal to you the "innermost secrets of my heart," it is unlikely you will ever guess them. However important may be our external observation of other persons in coming to know them, and however valuable are various theories of human behavior in helping us to understand why others think and act as they do, we come to know the other as one whom we can love and trust and respect primarily through the words and acts through which he discloses his character and intentions. If God is a (quasi-) personal being, it would be expected that he would be known—if he is known significantly or profoundly at all—in a (quasi-) personal way: through his own act(s) of disclosure and communication. The concept of God's *revelation,* as the basis of our knowledge of God, is bound up directly with the concept of God (as a personal being) itself.

In the second place, the fact of human finitude implies that if there is to be knowledge of a transcendent God at all, it can only be on the basis of his self-revelation. In experience and available knowledge man is confined to this world and its contents. He can learn much about the world and about himself through the systematic reflection of science and philosophy and through the insights and intuitions of poets and artists, but all of this remains knowledge confined within the limits of human experience. Prophets can criticize the present order of life or state of society by reference to dreams and visions of more glorious possibilities, thus opening up new futures for men, but these all remain creations of the human imagination, tied to human experience and capacity, hardly disclosures of some transcendent world of ultimate perfection and reality. There is no possible way for men to leap out of their skins into heaven where they can see God "face to face." What is ultimately real remains always a mysterious and unfathomable X.

This point I have tried to clarify and express theologically through distinguishing the "available" from the "real" God. That distinction implies that no sacred book, no religious experience, no holy tradition, no authoritative institution is a sufficient basis for speaking, finally, about the real God. However important any or all of these may be, their very accessibility shows them to be this-worldly and thus highly problematical as a basis for our knowledge of that which transcends this world. For there is no defensible way of moving from what is fully and totally given or experienced *in* the world—what is thus confined to the world—to that which is "beyond." Even such a movement in thought or imagination is little more than a projection or extrapolation from elements given in experience. The most exalted idea of God, as well as the most abstract and formal metaphysical conception of reality, is in this respect always earthbound. Man is finite and cannot exceed his own limits, whatever those limits may be and however difficult it may be precisely to specify them. barring John 14:12?

This means, then, that if God—the real God—is to be known, if man is actually to gain some accurate or true awareness or understanding of ultimate reality, it will only be because that reality has in some sense "come to" man. Ultimate reality conceived as passive structure or dead matter, of course, could not be thought capable of such a movement.[3] To speak of God, however, is at once to affirm the reality of that which transcends this world and to affirm that the structure of that reality is agential or personal, able to act and to communicate himself. As we have seen, our finite experience per se, confined as it is to this world, could never justify such affirmations; unless there were an activity from beyond the world disclosing to us—at the limits of the world, as it were—the transcendent God, there would be no ground at all for speaking of him. That is to say, it is inconceivable (by virtue of the very meaning of the idea of God) that men should

[3] For this reason it might be argued that were ultimate reality thus passive in character, we could never come to know it (with any kind of metaphysical assurance): our knowledge would be confined to the appearances and phenomena of experience, interpreted through our own powers of conception and imagination. This may, of course, be the way the world in fact is, and we may simply have to rest content with the flickering shadows and images that our finite experience reveals. There is much to be said for the "secular" posture that accepts with humility and grace our being limited to this world. But if ultimate reality is God, there is the possibility of disclosure to man of that which transcends experience and the world.

become aware of or come to know him unless God were himself
acting to make himself known. Or, put otherwise: only if ultimate reality is *God*, one who can act and can communicate
himself, could that which transcends experience become
known to men.

The personalistic or anthropomorphic imagery that underlies the conception of God thus fits together precisely with a
radical doctrine of human finitude.[4] In our interpersonal relations we encounter others at the very "limits" of that world
which is directly accessible through our senses, deliberately
and intentionally breaking in upon our experience from centers
of activity themselves beyond our reach. Mediated through
word, gesture, and action (all of which are open to our direct
observation in their purely physical aspects), another self
reveals to me his (more than merely physical) purposes and
character. Within my consciousness, then, I construct an
image of this other agent who, in his agency as such, transcends
my direct perception. Analogously, a doctrine of divine revela-

---

[4] See Chapter 3, above. It is no accident that the (modern) sense
of man's finitude grew up in close correlation with faith in the
transcendent creator God. Ancient man, for example in Greece,
thought of every reality, including the gods, as determinate and
limited. This was no restriction or deficiency: it was, on the contrary, just this determinateness that enabled them to be something
rather than nothing. To be boundless, unlimited, unformed was to
be at the opposite pole from real. It was the Christian awareness
of God's otherness from man as omnipotent Creator that led to
thought of him as *in*finite, *un*limited, a qualitatively different
order of being from this world or anything in it. But this conception
of God as Infinite redounded back on the notion of the finite,
which now in contrast could be seen only as radically defective
metaphysically, as insubstantial, as unable to maintain or sustain
itself. The modern understanding of man (since Hume and Kant)
as finite in such a way as to be restricted to the phenomena of experience, unable to penetrate through appearances to ultimate metaphysical reality, is a direct descendant and secularized variant
of the earlier theological conception of finitude. In this respect
the positivistic skepticism about metaphysics, so characteristic
of the contemporary world, is not really so antitheological as often
supposed, but in fact expresses a secularized form of the theological
understanding of human creatureliness. Far more threatening to
faith in (a genuinely transcendent) God is the (more ancient)
view that man has direct access in his own experience and knowledge to ultimate reality or God. That way lies paganism.

tion is simply an elaboration of the insight that God (cosmic purposive activity) could hardly be known simply on the basis of observation of the patterns of order in the (physical or organic) world. That world, or certain dimensions of it, would have to become mediators of *purpose* and *character,* but these transcend the limits of the merely physical and organic and live only in the qualitatively different order of *meaning.* Though the world in all its aspects may be open to our observation, experience, and manipulation, God as moral and purposive Agent is beyond our reach. He, however, could be known if he acted to communicate himself in such a way that men, from within their consciousness and culture, would be enabled imaginatively to construct images or conceptions representing him in his transcendence. Failing that, men must remain locked in the world, the only personal, purposive, and moral beings of which we know in a vast impersonal, amoral, and uncaring—however magnificent and impressive—universe.

II

How can divine revelation be conceived? How are we to think of cosmic purposive activity communicating itself to us? We know well what we mean when we speak of a friend revealing his innermost thoughts to us in intimate dialogue, but surely the cosmic Agent cannot be conceived as thus literally speaking and gesturing to us. What language does God speak that we might understand? Are thunderclap, fire, and windstorm to be grasped as his voice, or is it the "still small voice" of conscience (1 Kings 19:12)? What criteria may be offered for deciding such a question? Even if God exists—if there actually is cosmic moral purposiveness—is it really possible to conceive of him, the almighty Creator of the heavens and the earth, as somehow "communicating" with lowly, finite men, mere specks of cosmic dust?

We can begin to explore the complexities of this problem by considering the way one person becomes acquainted with another. I may sit down beside a stranger in a bus or plane and casually strike up a conversation with him. Gradually, as we talk, we discover mutual concerns, and our conversation quickens. Perhaps by the end of the ride we have become sufficiently interested in each other to agree to keep in touch. Eventually, with several future encounters, we become fast friends. It all seems a quite simple process: what begins as an accidental encounter and develops in *ad hoc* fashion flowers into full and close acquaintance.

We must observe here, however, that even in as simple an example as this, knowledge of the other is not gained immediately and directly in encounter with him: we are not friends when we first say, "Hello." We become friends through a process of mutual sharing and revealing, and only in, and in consequence of, such a development can I eventually come to say, "I know John very well." Personal knowledge is something that emerges in and through a *history*, a history of mutual self-disclosures. It is thus not to be understood either as a kind of immediate insight or intuition (as some writers on "I-thou" encounters seem to suggest) or as the product of mere observation and inference (as some empiricist philosophers claim). Rather it must be understood as in large part a gradually cumulating *historical knowledge*.[5] Knowledge of another person in his uniqueness, autonomy, and individuality—knowledge of him as just *that* particular person—is always a precipitate from acquaintance with (at least some moments of) his history.

If we look a little closer now, we will see that the birth and growth of a friendship are considerably more complex than has thus far been suggested. The easy development portrayed in my example of a moment ago is possible only if my potential friend and I already share in significant ways a common history at the moment we meet. Thus, we both speak English and are able to communicate with each other relatively easily. But to speak English is not merely to have learned a set of arbitrary noises that stand for meanings or concepts we would

---

[5] For detailed, careful, experimental study of the way in which interpersonal knowledge develops in a common history, see R. D. Laing, H. Phillipson, and A. R. Lee, *Interpersonal Perception* (London: Tavistock Publications, 1966).

have in any case. To speak English is to have our very experience structured by a particular set of symbols in particular
ways, enabling us to focus attention on this feature rather than
that, to see as significant and valuable this sort of activity and
to regard as pointless that other. That we both speak English
thus means that we grasp our experience in essentially the
same fundamental terms, assess it with reference to commonly
known norms and values, understand ourselves and our world
in terms of commonly accepted and appreciated categories.
The long history stored up in English vocabulary and usage
is common to us, and therefore when one of us speaks a word
to the other it is immediately understood. Moreover, since each
of us is a twentieth-century American, we share a common
cultural history. We have some of the same ideals about
"life, liberty, and the pursuit of happiness," "equality of op-
portunity," and the like, and we are both aware how far short
American society falls of realizing those ideals. We may differ
sharply on our interpretation of any or all of these matters,
and we may disagree about their meaning and their significance; one of us may be disillusioned and cynical and the other
innocent and naïve. But our common language and culture—
and thus what is in fact our common history—provide us with
a frame of discourse within which we can speak to and readily
understand each other, whatever difficulties, barriers, and misunderstandings may arise in the course of our dialogue.

The importance of this common background for our developing friendship can easily be seen if we alter the example
slightly. Suppose it is a Chinese Red Guard beside whom I sit
down. He speaks only broken English and I no Chinese; he is
an outspoken Maoist, committed to fomenting revolution wher-
ever he can, and I am a Christian and a liberal who abhors all
violence. It is not necessary to go on in great detail. Obviously
it will be much more difficult for any kind of intimacy or friendship to develop here. Even the simplest and most superficial
understanding on the bare linguistic level will be hard to
achieve. We will misinterpret each other's words and miss
nuances of meaning; we will disagree sharply about what is
valuable, good, or right, and probably neither of us will be able

to grasp the contentions of the other, to say nothing of understanding or appreciating why he holds those convictions; it will be very hard for us to avoid distrusting each other profoundly from first sight and being highly judgmental.

Yet, despite all, we might become friends. If we find something of significance that we share—perhaps we are both students of theoretical physics, or are deeply interested in the problems of agriculture, or simply love to travel—we may find a base upon which a friendship could gradually grow. As a Marxist, he participates in certain moral and philosophical currents that grew up in the Western history that I also share; as one who has sought in some small measure to inform himself about China and its problems, I participate—in however distant and poorly informed fashion—in the past that has been so fundamental in shaping his selfhood. Though unlikely, it is thus possible that friendship might develop between us. But it is a much less casual and simple process for men of sharply different cultural traditions and with little common language to become acquainted than that suggested in my original example.

Our knowledge of other persons comes through their self-revelation, their making external in word and gesture what is within. This is possible only if both speaker and hearer understand in similar ways the gestures and words that are the media of such self-disclosures. It is on the basis of a common language and a common history—and thus in a sense an already present common experience—that the mutual experience we call friendship develops.

III

Let us turn back now to the question of how God could communicate himself to man and man thus become aware of him. Obviously this will be a far more difficult and complex project than one person's striking up acquaintance with another. We can begin to sense something of the immensity of the problem when we remember that this God whom we are considering is not just any quasi-personal being worshiped by men: he is

supposedly the Creator of a universe believed to be hundreds
of millions of light years in diameter and billions of years old.

It is hard to see how our ordinary category *person* can be
applied very meaningfully to such a reality or being and how
one can think clearly of "personal" relations with it (him).
Obviously God cannot be thought of as a "person" in the usual
physical or bodily sense: approximately six feet tall, weighing
180 pounds, having two arms and two legs, and the like. But
(though this has not always been noticed) to interpret "person"
as referring primarily to man's "spirit" is hardly any more apt
in this case: every human person (spirit) has emerged and
developed within the context of a community of persons already there, a community that provided him with a culture
(already formed through a long history) including language,
institutions, social patterns, ideals, values, and the like. The
entire "spiritual" side of our personal existence is inconceivable
apart from the context provided by the already existing "spiritual" realities of history and culture and in every case presupposes these. To think of God as a "mind" or "spirit" or "will"
(in anything like the human sense) seems just as difficult as
to imagine him a physically human being. How then can God
be viewed as one who "communicates" himself to man?

In the conception of God's revealing himself the notion that
God is "personal" is used only in a highly formal or abstract
sense. It provides an image for grasping that and how a being
"beyond the limits" of our world could encounter us and disclose himself to us at and through those limits. It gives us a
structural model, so to speak, with the help of which we can
imagine or conceive a significant relation to that which transcends our experience—but no more may be made of the conception than that. The various other physical and spiritual
characteristics of persons as we know them in their concreteness cannot be uncritically applied to God. We can, of course,
elaborate the conception of God as personal by referring to him
as "Creator," "Lord," "Father," and the like, and speaking of
his "will" or his "love." But it must be understood that these
terms are all being used in a similar, highly formal way. They
express certain (otherwise inexpressible) dimensions of the

relationship between finite men and that which transcends them and their world, when ultimate reality is taken to be agential in character—to be God—and the world is understood to be structured by and expressive of purposive, historical activity. However, because of the radical otherness of God's order of being (as the very Creator of the heavens and the earth) from ours (as mere creatures), they should not be thought to convey knowledge of God in his concreteness, as they do with finite persons. But this formal interpersonal structure of the interrelationship with God in his transcendence is after all what is of religious importance. For it is the basis for our thinking of ourselves as in personal relation with him, able to address him in speech and to "hear" his "word" to us, he and we each capable of binding himself to the other in moral covenant and working together in community. And this would seem to bring us near to the central meaning of "God," both religiously and morally.

If we remember that the personal image provides only the principal *formal* basis for conceiving our relation to God and his relation to us, then the claim to know God in his transcendence of our world and its limits does not imply a break in the wall of our finitude through which we directly view that which is "beyond the limits" of experience, God becoming open, as it were, to our inspection and examination. What sort of structure or being God is in himself, outside his self-revelatory activity and beyond the world of our experience, we have no possible way of knowing or conjecturing. We cannot even know or guess what might be the means—from God's side—through which he communicates with men and otherwise acts in and on the world.[6] All this lies on the other side, so to speak, of the limiting point where man encounters God. Thus, whatever in God corresponds to our bodies, the vehicles through which we express and expose ourselves to each other, is in principle unknowable by us. To speak highly metaphorically: the most

[6] Austin Farrer has worked out the reasons for this inaccessibility of God's activity on God's side in very nice detail in his recent book, *Faith and Speculation* (London: A. and C. Black, 1967).

we can say is that we hear the sound of God's voice; we never see the movement of his lips or the expression on his face. Although the instrumentalities *within* the world through which God is known may be specified in some detail (as we shall see below), the instrumentalities through which God qua his transcendence acts are by definition completely inaccessible to us.

We always have some access to finite persons, even when they choose not to be communicative. Their bodies, after all, are available to our direct observation (though their personal center or will is not), and since the body is the personal center's medium of expression, it is often possible to infer or guess —or even, in one sense of the word, directly to "see"[7] what another is doing or thinking. Though such knowledge is far from adequate or complete, it teaches us much about another, and it is always useful, indeed indispensable, as a supplement and qualification of what is learned through personal intercourse. But we have no access to God's "body": we cannot directly observe his "behavior." He is not part of the universe open to our immediate experience and available to our observation. Unlike the case of finite persons, therefore, we would know nothing about God—even that he exists—did he not choose to reveal himself, and we have no basis whatsoever for speculating about his "nature."[8] We are in a position to speak only of his "character" and "will": what he has manifested to us through those experiences which have become the media for his revelatory activity. But of course according to the Chris-

[7] See Preface.

[8] In this respect Karl Barth was certainly right in insisting that there is no simply natural or experiential knowledge of God, and there can be no merely natural theology. Those contentions are entirely consistent with the personalistic imagery involved in the conception of God, and it is only slipshod thinking that leads us sometimes to want to hold that God is personal, but is nevertheless known through direct observation or experience. It is unfortunate that Barth's theological positivism precluded him from understanding and framing his insight here in terms of a philosophical interpretation of the nature of personal knowledge and confined him instead to a largely dogmatic restatement of what he took to be the biblical claim.

tian tradition these are the experiences of fatherliness, love, righteousness, and the like, and that is all that is necessary to know of God.

How, now, are we to conceive the process through which man becomes aware of or acquainted with God, as he reveals or manifests himself? If we go back to our example of learning to know a new friend whom we casually meet, we will see immediately how complicated is the problem. As between God and man when they first begin to become acquainted—unlike the relation between two strangers on a bus—we can presuppose no prior common language or history as the basis on which conversation can begin. God, the Creator of a universe billions of years old, has an untold history behind him; man is a relatively recent product of a long evolutionary process within that world, with no memory at all of the previous stages of life from which he evolved and little remembrance of the earlier generations of his own conscious experience. God and man cannot even directly encounter each other, looking each other in the eye, so to speak; for God is the source of all being and not to be identified with any of the beings man experiences or observes or encounters. It is not possible, then, even though both God and man are personal, to imagine them as simply beginning to talk together one day when they happen to meet: they never happen to meet, and they have no common language with which they could converse. Obviously, if man becomes acquainted with God, it will be through a much more complex process than the developing friendship of two persons on a bus.

IV

Personal revelation as the basis for growing personal acquaintance occurs only within and presupposes, as we noted, a common history, a structure of meaning or symbolical system within which the other is grasped as personal, and his speaking and acting can be understood as speaking and acting. The development of an appropriate context will, then, be the first requisite for the emergence of man's awareness of God.

A historicocultural setting must appear within which it is possible for men to apprehend some events as not merely ordinary intramundane happenings but as the act(s) of superhistorical, supercultural being(s). Until and unless man has the possibility of conceiving what occurs within his world as the work of power(s) transcending his experience, he will not be able to conceive either of God(s) or of divine revelation.

This is not the place—nor am I competent—to trace the rise and evolution of primitive religion.[9] Its earliest stages, perhaps, were characterized by a vague awareness of an all-pervasive power or mana in which men participated through ritual and which found symbolization in myth; eventually, however, sufficient differentiation and objectification took place to make possible the personification of various natural powers as superpersonal supernatural beings or gods who determined the destinies of men, and thus the conception of another order or other world, distinct from and transcending the world immediately experienced, was made possible. Some such development was essential if superpersonal reality beyond the limits of human experience were ever to make itself (or himself) known. As men became conscious of the world around them, in a way no lower animal had been aware of his world, as they began to develop language for differentiating and conceiving their experience, and tools and techniques for manipulating and transforming various features of their world, they also began to think in terms of realities *beyond* experience and not susceptible to their control, realities that controlled them. It is indifferent for our purposes how or why they came to think in terms of these two dimensions: the present and accessible, and the transcendent and mysterious. Doubtless their experience of overwhelming natural powers like earthquake and thunderstorm, their obvious powerlessness before the ravages of disease, their dreams of the grotesque and the horrible, their encounters with the uncanny and numinous were all of im-

[9] For an elaboration of the earliest phases of religious evolution, in the context of a general theory of religious development in history, see Robert Bellah, "Religious Evolution," *American Sociological Review*, 29:358-374 (1964).

portance here. The point is that a particular sort of conceptual framework—a mythology, if you please—had to appear if any revelation of God to man were to be possible. Modes of symbolization that refer *beyond* direct human experience and its world to a transcendent order had to appear *within* human culture and human consciousness, and just such modes did appear in the earliest stages of primitive culture. Thus categories were created for apprehending and interpreting experience with reference to that which transcends it. Doubtless these categories were often crude and misleading and inadequate, but they were the basis for later refinements and developments. According to the doctrine of divine providence, God "foresees" and "provides" for men's needs even before men are aware of them: such a historical development in primitive culture, then, is precisely what might be expected if there really were a God (beyond the limits of human experience) guiding the development of man's culture in a direction that would ultimately make it possible for him to reveal himself more fully.

The mere consistency of such a theological interpretation of these primitive beginnings of religious consciousness with the empirical facts does not, of course, prove it true. For fully naturalistic psychological and historical interpretations of these same data are also persuasive. Indeed, the theological interpretation I am proposing does not differ materially from a naturalistic view (as far as the latter goes), but rather maintains that precisely this "natural" cultural development must— or at least may—be understood to have a deeper dimension of meaning than appears on the surface. While a strictly humanistic or naturalistic interpretation sees this development in primitive thought as spontaneous and natural, perhaps almost accidental, the theological view suggests that it was purposeful: God was beginning to accomplish his intention of revealing himself to man. Hence, this process, far from being accidental or meaningless, was in fact an essential step in a meaningful history moving toward a definite goal intended from the beginning by God. Whereas in the one view the various developments in human culture and history evince no overall unity and significance, in the other the entire historical process is bound together as a meaningful progress of the long-standing purposes of God, the early stages being essential steps toward the eventual working out of his objectives.[10] Both views are compatible with the sequence of events as they actually happened: one sees this sequence as meaningful (as meant, intended); the other as simply fortuitous.

Once a fairly complex mythology emerged (and this must have taken some thousands of years from the first appearance of *Homo sapiens*), the self-disclosure of God could move forward more rapidly. It was now necessary (a) to develop criteria (in man's consciousness and culture) for discriminating those sorts of events or those qualities of experience to be attributed to the transcendent powers now believed in, and (b) to refine men's sense of the transcendent until it gradually came to focus in the conception of one God, Creator and Lord of the universe. Such developments occurred in a variety of ways and with varying degrees of effectiveness in many cultures around the earth. In the Near East (in the pre-Mosaic period) an especially favorable evolution occurred, culminating in the appearance of a group of tribes who bound themselves in covenant to the one God Yahweh: he would in a special way be their God whom alone they would worship and serve; they would be his people. Doubtless this was a sort of henotheism at first, other groups or tribes or nations similarly having their special gods. But eventually, in and through the historical struggles between the Israelite tribes and the Canaanites and other surrounding peoples, and especially in connection with a series of traumatic events that destroyed the independent political and cultural life of Israel, a wider and deeper understanding of Yahweh began to emerge. Imaginative interpretation of Israel's past by historians like the "Yahwist," and creative insight by the great prophets into tragic contemporary events, made it possible to see Yahweh as not only Israel's special God, but the God of the universe, Creator of the heavens and the earth and Lord of all history. He became understood as the supreme historical Actor, working continuously in history to establish his perfect king-

[10] See Chapter 6, above.

dom. This vision of a single unifying activity working through the entire cosmic and historical process made it possible for the first time to see all history, both cosmic and human, as a unified and meaningful whole moving forward through time toward an ultimate goal.

Once again, this development can obviously be understood in fully naturalistic or humanistic terms, as an immanent movement within general human history, and contemporary biblical scholarship provides us with just such interpretation. But also once again, some movement very like this would be required if there really were a quasi-personal God seeking to make himself known to man. If God is beyond the limits of man's experiencable world, if he is so different from man as to be the very Creator of the universe, and if he is not to destroy man's spontaneity, freedom, and cultural creativity—those very characteristics that make man *man*—in the process, is it possible to conceive his self-disclosure in any other way than through such an immanently developing cultural tradition, within which men gradually become aware who he is and what his character and will are? Knowledge of other persons, we have noted, always comes about through a slowly deepening historical process of mutual intercourse. God's self-revelation will (from the human side) be seen as a similar, though much more complex, historical process developing between him and his people, as they increasingly recognize the signs of his activity in the events of their lives and increasingly respond with devotion and revelation of themselves to him. The Old Testament is the principal extant record of the tumultuous and painful history of a growing consciousness, unparalleled elsewhere, of one God sovereign over the entire universe.

One further indispensable step was necessary if God were to succeed in making himself known. In the Old Testament period, and particularly after the exile, the consciousness *that* God is and *who* he is was establishing itself as a distinctive motif in one particular culture. But there still remained much ambiguity about God's purposes, character, and modes of action, and the knowledge of God remained parochial in one

relatively insignificant cultural stream. It was necessary, therefore, for God to show more decisively and clearly just what his
character and purposes were, so that men could discriminate
better his action in history, and misunderstandings and mis-
conceptions could gradually be overcome. Further, it was important that the awareness of God move out from the beach-
head established in Hebrew culture to other cultural traditions,
if ultimately God were to succeed in making himself known
to all nations and peoples. The Christian claim, of course, is
that precisely these two things happened in and with the events
centered upon the ministry, death, and resurrection of Jesus
Christ: here, in and through the character and actions of the
man Jesus, was the definitive revelation of God; here, in the
theological reinterpretations and missionary activity that followed upon his death, Jewish faith was universalized.

This climactic moment of the growing consciousness of
God, like those preceding it, is also susceptible of a fully humanistic interpretation. But here no more than there is such
an understanding in competition with the theological view,
threatening to undermine it; rather it is itself indispensable for
the full meaning of the theological conception. For if there is
a God beyond the limits of human experience, and if man is
immersed in history and enclosed within the world as he appears to be, then the only way God could become known to man
would be through revealing himself in such a way that within
human history itself consciousness of him would gradually
emerge. The fact that the Old Testament and New Testament
taken together provide us with just such a history of the growing awareness of God's self-disclosure is no proof of their truth.
But it is striking that they, when interpreted by even the most
humanistic modern historical methods, present a picture very
like what would be expected were there in fact a God seeking
to make himself known.

Knowledge of another person on the finite level comes about
only as an image of the character and intentions of the other
is formed within my consciousness, enabling me to think of
him as just this particular man with just these particular char-

acteristics. Similarly, awareness of God can come about only as a cultural image is formed over many generations, enabling participants in that culture to think of him as just this particular (though universal) being, distinct from all the particularities of their experience, the Creator of the heavens and the earth and the Lord of their lives. The partner in the dialogue with God is not the individual man but the human species as a whole; and the complex of memories out of which the image or conception of God is formed is not grounded simply in the private experience of the lonely individual: it is, rather, the precipitate of a long cultural history and a gradually cumulating tradition.

V

We moderns can describe the growth of this tradition (like any other) as an immanent historical development, to be understood in strictly psychological and sociological terms and by reference to the contingencies of a particular history and the possibilities of human creativity. There is no need to refer beyond the finite level to give an adequate account of it. But if the orientation in and meaning of life, as apprehended within this perspective, are experienced by us as authentic and true, and if life lived in its terms is appropriated as fundamentally right and good, it will hardly be possible for us to regard this development in human culture and consciousness as simply one more historical emergent, neither more nor less significant than any other. Rather this particular history will be conceived in such a way as to make evident and clear its peculiar function as that cultural development through which the ultimately Real and True and Good became known to us: it will be seen as the medium of divine revelation. And thus the conception of God as "living" (to use the biblical word), as a cosmic Agent actively at work in and upon his world and in actual interpersonal relation with men, will be brought into sharp focus. The "scandal of particularity" which is here implied is essentially bound up with the notion that God does in fact reveal himself; it belongs thus to the very conception of God as a truly active agent.[11]

To regard the history of man's growing consciousness of God as the history through which God has been revealing himself to man is no merely honorific or titular change of what in substance remains the same. These events must now be grasped in a unique two-dimensional way. So far as they are a process of growing human institutions, practices, beliefs, and customs, they are to be appropriated like other historical events: appreciated for the meanings and values that they created and that may still feed our spirits and help order our lives and communities; studied, criticized, and learned from, in respect of the failures and defects they manifest. So far, however, as the movement of this history is viewed as intended by God and the expression of his activity, it must be given a status qualitatively distinct from ordinary cultural processes. It now becomes the historical stream through which the ultimate Reality, toward which and in terms of which life is to be oriented, is encountered; here are given (in some sense) the very criteria by which our notions of real/unreal, true/false, good/bad, right/wrong, and the like, are to be measured, criticized, and reconstructed. Here there appears, then, an ultimate *authority* over against our autonomy.

This history, invested now with the authority of God's reve-

[11] It should be observed in passing that it is not only those who believe in God who give a particular tradition a special importance in this way. Every cultural perspective that provides significant orientation for individuals or communities inevitably gives preference to and treats as especially important the particular historical stream(s) that produced it. Since, however, few nontheological traditions have been as aware of their historical rootedness as Christian faith, philosophical interpretations of the significance of this fact—corresponding to the theological doctrine of divine revelation in history—have not often appeared. This has led some to conclude that the historical contingency of norms and values is peculiarly a problem for theistic faith, but that is certainly an error, as even a cursory study of cultural anthropology and the sociology of knowledge should make clear. (For further discussion of the general philosophical importance of the concept of revelation in the light of historical relativity, see my *Systematic Theology*, Chap. 2.)

even dangerously

lation, will necessarily be studied and appropriated in a different and distinctly more serious way than other stretches of the human past. It will be analyzed with a view to gaining clearer vision of the ultimate norms or criteria in terms of which life is to be lived; it will be critically scrutinized with the objective of pruning out misleading implications, reducing or overcoming ambiguities and inconsistencies, and eliminating irrelevancies and nonessentials; it will be reconstructed with the intention of bringing into sharp focus the norms revealed therein, so that their relevance to and impact on contemporary life and its problems can be seen more plainly. In the Christian case it is believed that this revelatory history comes to a climactic point in the ministry, death, and resurrection of Jesus Christ. It becomes of the greatest importance, then, to get as clear as possible how and in what respects this man and his career can and ought to be viewed as the very manifestation of God and thus as normative for human life, and how the norms given in and through this person-event impinge on contemporary life and thought, calling for its reordering and reconstruction.

It is the task of Christian theology in its various branches—biblical and historical, systematic and moral—to appropriate historically and sketch out imaginatively in this way the image of Jesus Christ in its normative significance for contemporary man.[12] Thus a vision of what authentic human existence may

+ skips lightly over a lot?

[12] For this reason Christian theology always involves a double movement, and it cannot be sophisticated unless there is careful attention to both dimensions. On the one hand, there must be the attempt to grasp from the theologian's own standpoint and historical situation the revelatory history and climactic revelatory event in their normativeness. This requires not only careful historical study of biblical and other materials, but also considerable self-consciousness about one's own perspective and presuppositions and the way these influence what one perceives and reconstructs historically. On the other hand, there must be the sustained effort to grapple with the social, cultural, intellectual, and personal problems of contemporary life in all their complexity and with the aid of whatever insight and theory modern science and art can contribute, in order to discern in just what way the divine revelation bears on contemporary life, diagnosing its deepest ills and suggesting directions in which healing can be sought.

be is glimpsed and in some degree articulated in terms relevant to and meaningful for contemporary social, cultural, intellectual, and personal life. And it becomes possible for individual Christians, and the church as the community of believers, consciously to attempt ordering their existence in accord with the will of the God whom they acknowledge as Lord.[13] *Fl Schism?*

[13] In the minds of some readers there may be a question about the relation between Chapter 5 on the one hand, and Chapters 6 and 7 on the other. In the former I appear to treat God as a construct of the human imagination; in the latter as an objective reality over against man. Which position do I intend? I am contending that the positions taken in these chapters are not inconsistent with each other, but rather express together the highly dialectical character of the notion of God. I stand by the position of Chapter 5 that all content that the notion of God has, everything that can be specified, is humanly constructed; we never have access to God in himself, so to speak, in such a way as to enable us to compare him (the "real" God) with our ideas of him (the "available" God) and to criticize and reformulate them in the light of that comparison. But at the same time it must be contended that our construct, God, is intended to be a symbolization of the ultimate reality with which we men have to do; it is supposed to represent with some measure of adequacy "how things really are." (Similar sorts of dialectical problems arise with all other ultimate metaphysical models or constructs, for example, conceptions of reality as "being-itself," or "power," or "matter," or "energy.") It is appropriate and necessary, therefore, in thinking through the structure of the concept of God, to work out interpretations of the way in which he is related to us and comes to be known by us (something similar is also necessary with other metaphysical interpretations). Chapters 6 and 7 are attempts to do precisely this. In order to undertake these moves one does not need to deny or forget the constructive character of the whole enterprise; on the contrary, they are simply a further working-through of just that construction: they enable us to see more fully just what is meant or intended by the construct, God. Or, to say the same thing in other words, these further elaborations enable us to see more precisely what it is like to apprehend human life and experience as "under God," that is, from the point of view of faith in him. To claim (the "available") God is a construct of the human imagination is not to deny that those who live and think in terms of him perceive him as the Real, the ultimate reality with which we have to do, the One in terms of whom all life and experience must be ordered; and contrariwise, to claim all experience and life should be ordered in terms of faith in a God believed "objectively real" does not involve the denial that everything we know or experience or can say about him is humanly constructed. Each of these must be affirmed if one is to make sense of the highly dia-

lectical notion of God as transcendent reality, as not to be identified with any of the particulars of experience or even with the world as a whole. Thus my interpretation of God as a symbolic construction of the human imagination is not intended to represent a more "skeptical" understanding than my interpretation of his acts and his self-revelation: each expresses an indispensable dimension of the structure of the concept of God, a dimension that that concept must have whether one speaks from the perspective of faith or the perspective of skepticism.

8

God and Evil

There are a number of serious logical, semantic, and epistemological issues rendering the notion of God problematical for contemporary men. Other essays in this volume address some of the more important of these. But even granting that the notion of God can be made fully intelligible—certainly a considerable concession—a major stumbling block for contemporary faith in God remains: If there is a God, and if he is loving, why is there such horrendous evil in the world? Do not the facts of terror, pain, and unjustifiable suffering demonstrate either that God is not good—and therefore not worthy of our adoration and worship—or that there is no God at all? A succession of sobering events symbolized by such names as Auschwitz, Hiroshima, and Vietnam have inscribed deeply into the contemporary consciousness both awareness of the appalling malignancy and destructiveness of evil in human life and also a sense of man's utter aloneness in combatting the powers that make it impossible for so many men to find fulfillment or meaning in their existence. A Doctor Rieux,[1] who courageously fights for human life and well-being in the face of an utterly unintelligible and meaningless (in the existentialist sense) plague, and who knows he can depend on no cosmic or divine powers to assist him in his struggle—indeed, who would have to despise a God who could create such a world, if he could believe in him at all—is representative of the feelings of a great many contemporaries. Exploration and examination of the varieties, subtleties, and enormities of evil in human life has

[1] Albert Camus, *The Plague* (New York: Knopf, 1957).

become perhaps the principal theme of literature, art, and drama since World War II.

The problem of evil is of course far from new. Its existential roots go deep into the suffering and struggle experienced by all living creatures, and it must have weighed upon man from the dawn of consciousness. The antiquity of the problem is to be seen not only in great literary documents such as Job and the Gilgamesh Epic, which make man's consciousness of and struggle against evil an explicit theme; the beginnings of human culture, with the invention of tools and language and the mastery of fire, must be understood as deliberate grappling with the evils continuously confronting humankind. The religious rites and practices, which were an important feature of human life as far back as we can trace it and which are found in every culture, witness to man's primordial awareness that his destiny is beyond his control, in the hands of unseen powers that may well be malevolent if not properly appeased. It can be argued that the deepest root of religious faith is the sense of man's ultimate helplessness in the universe and his need, therefore, to postulate power(s) who can and will protect and care for him. "God is our refuge and strength, a very present help in trouble" (Ps. 46:1 KJ). It is because belief in God is so intimately connected with the experience of evil that the problem of evil is peculiarly a problem for faith.

Despite its antiquity and universality, the problem of evil has a special poignancy and urgency for contemporary men. Not only are disease and natural calamity, as well as hatred, treachery, and warfare, still very much with us, in spite of great technological advances meliorating the former and profound moral insight as well as complex social and political institutions addressed to the latter. In addition, this generation is aware as no other that man's very prolificity as a species now threatens him with new problems of famine, disease, and other horrors, and his success technologically has resulted in his inadvertent poisoning of the environment in ways that could ultimately destroy many species of life including his own, if he does not earlier obliterate himself and his civilization with weapons of mass destruction. Man's very biological and technological success in the struggle against evil, compounded with his all too apparent moral callousness and political failures, as dramatized by death camps and napalm, now threatens to undo him completely. Little wonder that contemporary men feel the weight of the problem of evil profoundly and that this should raise with doubled urgency once again the question of the meaningfulness and appropriateness of faith in God.

I

The problem of evil (in the general sense just described) is clearly an important issue for every world-view or interpretation of life. All men are deeply involved in the struggle against evil, and all must develop categories of understanding and interpretation that enable them to identify and combat it. No one denies the existence of pain and suffering, moral perversity and depravity, social and political failure, and all would like to ameliorate or overcome them. Since that has not thus far proved possible, we all search for categoreal and interpretive schemes by means of which to make these unhappy realities intelligible to ourselves, thus counteracting their purely negative character and even enabling them, in their perverse way, to contribute something to such meaning as life can have. In thus relating the raw and painful dimensions of experience, perceived as evil, to broader categories of meaning and interpretation, all perspectives are on a level.

But a theistic understanding of life confronts a problem not felt by strictly naturalistic or humanistic views. Belief in God as Creator and Governor of the world implies that both the fundamental order of the universe and the basic course of (cosmic) history have been in some sense purposed by God and brought about through his work. Unlike naturalistic conceptions of the universe, which posit no underlying intentionality working in and through cosmic processes, here there is One who bears basic responsibility for both the fact *that* things are and *how* they are. Had God not created at all, there would be no world within which the evils we know could have appeared; had God chosen to create a different kind of world, then also these evils might have been avoided; even granting the world as God originally created it, had he guided the course of history in different ways, and possibly toward different ends, the world might have developed into a better place than it now is. In all these respects, the traditional conception of God implies that God had both freedom of choice and the power to effect his will. But the consequence of his work, at least with respect to man, is a world filled with appalling horrors. How can God be justified in the face of such a botched performance? Though every perspective must deal with the question of evil, the problem of theodicy (the justification of God) is peculiar to a theistic point of view. It doubles and reinforces—and deepens—the magnitude and complexity of the problem of evil, for now the very One who is claimed to be worthy of man's unconditional confidence and trust in face of all the evils of life himself appears as their principal author.[2]

It should be noted that the mere postulate of a basic intentionality in cosmic process—belief in the existence of God, any God—taken by itself, would not create the problem. God could be a malevolent demon, and the purposive movement of history would then be expected to manifest evils of all sorts—the cleverer the demon, the more subtle and morally outrageous the existential horrors. But none except the most perverted of men would deliberately worship and serve such a God, or expect others to do so. Men would be united in their despite of him and their opposition to him. As the source of misery in life, he would rightly be fought bitterly at every point, and the great heroes of the race would be those Promethean figures

---

[2] George D. O'Brien ("Prolegomena to a Dissolution to the Problem of Suffering," *Harvard Theological Review*, 57:301–323 [1964] argues that the problem of theodicy is really a pseudoproblem that dissolves when it is realized that the logical difference between God and man (Creator/creature) is such that man cannot (logically cannot) apply standards to God assessing or criticizing his character or activity. Although there certainly are confusions in the way in which the problem is usually formulated that call for dissolution— in some respects the present paper may be regarded as an attempt to show just that—this way of putting the matter, far from actually clarifying these fundamental issues, leads into an obscurantism that conceals them.

who stood up to him and spat in his face. As in the ancient gnostic systems, the creator and lord of this world would be universally recognized as man's chief enemy, and there would be no need or desire to "justify" him in any way at all. The problem of theodicy arises, then, from a combination of belief in cosmic purposiveness with belief that that intentionality is good, indeed, is the source of all goodness. If God were conceived principally or primarily under the image of *power*— even personal purposive power—men might well fear him, and they could probably be induced to serve him, but they would hardly be inclined to love and worship him, and there would be no reason whatsoever for anyone to attempt to justify him morally. It is because God is conceived as power *and* goodness, especially moral goodness, that the problem of theodicy is so poignant and difficult. How could a righteous and just and loving being, who was also all-powerful and thus capable of doing as he willed, create such a world as this and people it with creatures capable of the atrocities against each other characteristic of men?

We should not understand the difficulties here superficially, as simply a kind of complaint that men are heir to pain and suffering. That in itself would scarcely be a significant indictment of God or his love because it could well be the case that precisely such experience is necessary for the education and development of the human race. We might object that God made men into creatures who need to grow and develop instead of creating them perfect and complete from the beginning— as we shall see below this is in fact a rather superficial and thoughtless objection—but given such beings, it is hardly surprising that they may need considerable carrot-and-stick treatment. ". . . whom the Lord loveth he chasteneth" (Heb. 12:6 KJ). As with human parents, punishment for educative purposes is fully consistent with, even follows from, belief in God's care for and love of his children. Moreover, granted man's limited experience and perspective and God's cosmic vision and responsibilities, we should not be surprised that much in this world is beyond human comprehension or appreciation: what now appears to us evil and unjustifiable might, did we but realize the high purposes it actually serves, be accepted and even applauded by us. It is superficial, then, simply to complain, as is often done in discussions of the problem of theodicy, that evil—or rather, what appears to us as "evil"—exists at all. The serious problems do not arise with the bare existence of what we call evil, but rather when the quality of evil (such as the meaningless suffering of innocent children) and the enormity of evil (Auschwitz) seem completely incompatible with any purposes or activity we can recognize as righteous, good, or redemptive and cannot be balanced or justified by any conceivable consequences or ultimate goals. Evils of such an order do call into question God's goodness or power or both and make faith in him seem irrational and probably immoral. I shall not here debate the question whether there are indeed evils of such enormity and moral repugnance: this hardly seems to require argument in our time.

A naturalism that knows of no intentionality in the cosmos apart from man's own purposiveness need not face the question *why* there are beings like us, who perpetrate such horrors on each other, any more than it need give a kind of cosmic justification for typhoid germs or volcanic eruptions, electrons or spiral nebulas: all of these simply *are,* and men must deal with them as best they can in accordance with their own needs and desires. If a theistic view—the belief that the ultimate foundation of all that exists is loving purposiveness—is to be intelligible, however, and not mere sentimentality, it must be able to say something to the question why there is a world of the sort there is, and why men of the kind we are are to be found within it.[3]

[3] It is not satisfactory for a believer to claim that such questions are beyond human ken and that all we dare say here is that God so willed things. That answer is completely empty unless it is known on other grounds (as always turns out to be the case for faith) that God is good and loving and righteous and that thus his creation and sustenance of the world and man must also—despite all evidence to the contrary—be understood as expressions of his love and goodness. But in that case: first, we know more than we had admitted about the reasons why there is a world and men, namely, to express God's love and to be objects on which he can bestow his love (as virtually every orthodox theology has maintained); second,

II

My principal contention in this paper shall be that the existence of serious evil in the world and in man poses special problems for theism largely because the issues are framed and stated abstractly—and, in fact, unintelligibly—instead of grasped in their full concrete significance. I shall argue this point with reference particularly to the conceptions of God and of man, but we shall also see implications for the doctrines of creation and providence.[4] Let us begin with the conception of God.

Often God's "omnipotence" is understood to imply that God can, whenever he chooses and with no restriction or limitation whatsoever, will and accomplish whatever he pleases. Moreover, this power of God is conceived to be, as it were, instantaneous: God need not and does not "take time" to accomplish his objectives; as with the original creation depicted in Genesis, he speaks his word, and it is done. The traditional conception of miracle, in which God intervenes in history at critical moments to alter the course of events regardless of the natural and historical causative factors already at work, also presup-

---

we are back again to the problem of theodicy, for that problem is precisely the question of how a good and loving God is to be understood and justified in view of the experienced fact that his creatures are evil in the way they are. It still remains necessary, then, to justify (that is, explain or make reasonable or intelligible) God's creation and sustenance of just this sort of world and just these sorts of men. Without this, claims about God's love are put into serious question and perhaps emptied of meaning, and thus the very point of the theistic position—as over against every bare naturalism or humanism, for example—dissolves.

[4] I cannot, of course, in this short space discuss all aspects of the classical problem of evil. I shall hardly touch, for example, on the important distinction between "natural" and "moral" evil, with all its ramifications, and I shall not be able to discuss the problem of the ontological status of evil. I think, however, that this essay will suggest a basic point of view on the problems of theodicy that could be worked out consistently over the full range of issues. For a recent full treatment of the problem of evil, which includes excellent discussion of the relevant history of Christian thought, see John Hick, *Evil and the God of Love* (London: Macmillan, 1966).

poses this abstract notion of God's power as unconditional and absolute. Although it has often been allowed that God has given men a kind of power over against him by means of which they can resist his will, disobey him, and the like, the biblical suggestion that God not only can convert men to his cause when he chooses but even "hardens" their hearts when they are rebellious (see, for example, Exod. 7:3ff.; Rom. 9:17) has led to hard doctrines of divine determinism where God appears to be the immediate cause of every event, psychological as well as physical, evil as well as good. With views such as this, of course, there is no absolving God of responsibility for every detail of every event. He could have done anything and everything differently than he has; yet he has chosen to make things precisely as they are. He could even now, at the snap of a finger, transform the present world and its evils into a heavenly paradise should he but elect so to do, but for his own inscrutable reasons he has preferred to create and maintain the world as it is and man as he is.

When the doctrine of God's power is developed thus abstractly, out of relation to other features of the concept of God, a picture of a divine demon is painted before whom one might expect only the most uncritical to bow wholeheartedly. Yet just such an extreme view of the divine power seems implied not only by those atheistic critics who find it morally abhorrent that God should have "allowed" an Auschwitz to occur,[5] but also by the faithful in their pious belief in God's omnipotence. The presupposition of both these positions is that God—if there is a God—has a kind of absolute power enabling him to alter events in the world at will. The pious appear willing to accept, or overlook, the damning implications of this doctrine; the morally sensitive impious, revolted by those implications, must reject the God of whom such power is predicated.

The conception of God just outlined is deficient by virtue of its extreme abstractness. Despite the fact that the special problem of evil for faith arises only because God is conceived as

---

[5] See, e.g., Richard Rubenstein, *After Auschwitz* (Indianapolis: Bobbs-Merrill, 1966).

morally good as well as omnipotent, this view interprets God almost entirely in terms of the notion of power, absolute, unqualified, infinite. Such a view is neither biblical (despite suggestions of it in the Bible),[6] nor is it finally intelligible; and it

[6] That biblical writers speak upon occasion as though God's power were absolute and unqualified is not difficult to understand. Their thought is mythopoetic rather than critically systematic in form. Their faith expresses itself in the vivid imagery of the mighty divine warrior, Yahweh, vanquishing his foes and working his will with men and events. (See G. Ernest Wright, *The Old Testament and Theology* [New York: Harper and Row, 1969], Chap. 5.) Although in the development of Hebrew religion moral and other criticism was brought to bear on the image of Yahweh, and in consequence the conception of God as a moral being became highly refined by the latter part of the Old Testament period and the beginning of the Christian era, to the end Yahweh remains essentially a creation of the poetic imagination, undisciplined by systematic critical analysis. It should occasion no surprise, then, that in the myths and hymns and prayers and prophecies and histories of the Bible we find excesses and extravagances and inconsistencies of many sorts; surprise is more appropriately called for when such highly metaphorical speech is taken to be literal description of a divine being in whom we are asked to believe.

The development of theology in the West is indebted not only to the poetry of Hebrew faith, however. Its forms and methods have been decisively influenced by the Greek conceptual and analytical thought to which Western man is also heir. Its principal problem, therefore, has been the responsible reconstruction and reconception of the mythopoetic Yahweh into a conception of God intelligible and believable to men living in a world the fundamental order of which was conceived in terms of metaphysical principle or scientific law. To accomplish this it has been necessary systematically to work through the conception of God, developing criteria by means of which different views or interpretations could be analyzed and criticized, searching for the most appropriate concepts to express what was essential to the notion, and carefully distinguishing this from what was accidental or peripheral or simply an idiosyncratic manner of speaking. This process, in which genuinely systematic and critical thinking about God gradually developed, took many centuries and cannot be traced here. In its course a number of different fundamental conceptions or images have been proposed as the basis for unifying and ordering the notion of God and thus developing a disciplined and intelligible concept: the One, Being, the Whole, Mind, Power, the Absolute, and so forth. It goes without saying that some such explicit unifying idea is required if we are to hold together the various diverse strands to be attributed to God (as expressed, for example, in the so-called attributes of God) in a way that is comprehensible, that is, if we are to know what we are

has intolerable moral consequences, as we have been observing. The more concrete and fuller notion of agent (or person) appears, as we have noted,[7] to epitomize most precisely the dominant idea underlying biblical talk about God as one who acts, decides, purposes, works toward objectives, and makes covenants, and something at least close to the notion of agency seems essential if one is to make sense of the principal Christian claims about God's love for man, his forgiveness of man's sin, his active involvement in the historical process at all points and preeminently in and through the man Jesus.

If the conception of agent (rather than power or unity or being or any of the other possible paradigmatic notions) is to be given preeminence in thinking through what we mean by God, then everything else that we predicate of him will have to be qualified in whatever ways are required to make it predicable of an agent. Thus, God's power (to take the example with which we are here especially concerned) may not be thought of simply independently and abstractly, according to whatever meaning the term "power" taken simply by itself has: God's power will be thought of as the power of an agent and as power appropriate to an agent. It will be conceived as purposive, intentional, deliberate power, the model of which is human action, not simply blind brute force.

It may be supposed that it is just this thought of God's power as like that of an agent that gives rise to the problem of theodicy: for is not the difficulty precisely that God does not seem to *act* to rescue men, at least some men, from the torment and suffering into which they have fallen? I think, however, if we examine our paradigmatic notion of agency more closely, we will see that this is a serious oversimplification: it fails to take

trying to say when we say "God." In the present essays we are exploring the notion of *agent* (or person) as the fundamental unifying image or model for conceiving God.

[7] See esp. Chapter 6 (also Chapter 5), above. Further discussion of the propriety and even indispensability of the notion of agent or person as the unifying motif in the Christian doctrine of God will be found in my *Systematic Theology* (New York: Scribners, 1968), esp. Chaps. 2, 3, 5, 8.

account of what is involved in action; and it presumes to know, without further investigation, both what God's ends in acting are (evidently to keep man from unpleasantness or discomfort) and how he could best realize those objectives.

The concept of action is drawn from human experience, and anything we say about it must ultimately be based on that model. A deliberate act is a movement through time in which the agent is seeking to realize some objective. Moreover, prior to the achievement of his goal, when the disequilibrium driving him to act is relaxed and peace is experienced, the agent may have to engage in considerable struggle to overcome difficulties or obstacles along the way. Thus an act is inherently temporal: it takes place during a span of time that begins with the (at least implicit) positing of an objective and is concluded only when the goal is achieved, sometimes after many difficult and painful intermediary steps.[8]

This inherent temporality of action must be taken seriously when we develop our conception of God's action. It means that the notion that God acts, or can act, instantaneously will have to be repudiated. This is not because God does not have sufficient power to act instantaneously, but rather because temporal duration belongs to the very concept of *act*, and the idea of a strictly instantaneous act is therefore not consistent with itself. If we wish to speak of God as *acting*, then, we must be prepared to conceive him as achieving his ends through time. He is a cosmic Agent, sometimes working through aeons of history toward his objectives, not a cosmic Magician whose

[8] Even the simplest of acts, such as waggling my little finger, is teleologically ordered and takes time. It is an *act* (and not an involuntary movement, reflex, tic, or something of the sort) only if I am (at least implicitly) intentionally doing it (or something of which it is the consequence or side effect) and could have done otherwise. The problem of defining clearly just what action is currently is under much discussion in philosophical literature. Of the many articles discussing various aspects of this issue, I might mention the following, all conveniently collected in *Readings in the Theory of Action*, ed. N. S. Care and Charles Landesman (Bloomington: Indiana University Press, 1968): A. I. Melden, "Action"; D. W. Hamlyn, "Causality and Human Behavior"; A. C. Danto, "Basic Actions"; James Bogen, "Physical Determinism"; P. J. Fitzgerald, "Voluntary and Involuntary Acts."

every arbitrary wish is fulfilled instantaneously and effortlessly.

Though there are suggestions in the biblical literature of the cosmic Magician, the dominant image is surely of the cosmic Agent, working slowly and painfully and often with much difficulty through cosmic and human history to achieve his goals. There is no suggestion that God's creatures—certainly not mankind—are presently what he wills them to be. Although, as the creation stories suggest, God has completed certain phases of his work and pronounced them good, it is clear that much still remains to be done both in the cosmic order itself[9] and with sinful, rebellious, miserable men. And there is no expectation that these matters can or will be accomplished by simply wishing them done: they involve struggle, confusion, and pain in the whole created order[10] and great effort and profound sacrifice on the part of God.[11] The world is the arena of God's activity, within which he is working toward objectives not yet attained; it is to be expected, therefore, that it will be caught up in tensions of incompleteness and struggle. Men also, living within that world and themselves far from perfected, will experience confusion, ambiguity, and difficulty. Since the thrust of the whole process toward an ultimate goal is not clearly visible to those living within it, history may be apprehended as disordered, purposeless, even fundamentally evil. Our experience of the world as incomplete, in process of development, even chaotic, is completely consistent with the notion that God is fundamentally an agent, and his mode of relation to the world is through his action in and upon it.

The question, then, of why God allows all this evil—as if he could do away with it simply by magical fiat—does not properly arise. God is an agent hard at work in his world, striving to realize certain goals that he long since posited. We might, of course, wish to take exception to his objectives or to his methods for achieving them: these are the proper issues to

[9] ". . . behold, I create new heavens and a new earth" (Isa. 65: 17).

[10] " . . . the whole creation has been groaning in travail together until now" (Rom. 8:22).

[11] "For God so loved the world that he gave his only Son" (John 3:16).

raise with an agent at work. But it is hardly to be expected that there will be no difficulties, struggle, and even misery involved in carrying through God's program; these arise in the course of almost any serious and significant task. The biblical God is always portrayed as seeking to overcome evils of all sorts in his world; in the Christian story it is even said that he sacrifices himself without limit for the sake of suffering and sinful man. There is no question here of God's goodness, power, and concern. But these are conceived not in a way appropriate to a cosmic Magician but rather to an Agent at work in and on his world.

The conception of the cosmic Magician and Miracle-worker is based on abstracting certain elements from the model of agency and ignoring others; it is in fact not fully intelligible. For it presupposes the idea of agent—one who can posit an end and then appropriately act to achieve it—but it does not carry through this idea consistently. An agent is not one who erratically and impulsively performs first one instantaneous act and then another, without either plan or goal. On the contrary, an agent posits objectives to be worked out in systematic and orderly fashion through time, his minor or subordinate acts being steps directed toward the realization of his ultimate ends.[12] His power of agency, then, is his power to bring *order into time*, to create and carry through programs of historical development. If he is successful and powerful as an agent, it is because he anticipates what is required to carry through his programs and works effectively and efficiently toward their realization. To the degree, however, that much of his activity is dictated by momentary impulse or unanticipated crisis, he betrays his weakness of will or his lack of foresight; and it is clear that there is a point beyond which his activity will have become so erratic and random as to vitiate his agency completely. The more we push the conception of God in the direction of the cosmic Magician—one who performs arbitrary and irregular works—the more we undercut the conception of him as a powerful and effective Agent who is advancing steadily toward his ultimate objectives and can be depended upon un-

[12] See Chapter 6, above.

conditionally. It is surely the latter notion that must inform
the doctrine of God, not the former. But this means we may not
analyze the problem of evil in terms of disconnected atomic
events or circumstances that we wish God had not allowed to
happen: if God is indeed an effective Agent and the world is
the product and arena of his activity, there are no such isolated
and independent events.[13] We must see all events in the context of God's purposes for the world and the way in which he
is carrying them through.

III

What then are we to say about God's purposes for the world
and for man? The Jewish and Christian expectation which is a

[13] See Chapter 6, above. An "event" has elastic limits. It is
always defined in terms of the interests or purposes of the speaker.
Thus, we may regard the "decline of the West" as one overarching
event within the history of Western civilization, and we may
equally well regard the striking of five by the clock on the mantel
as an event, particularly if something momentous happens at that
moment. What we call an event, then, is always somewhat arbitrary: the temporal sequence could have been divided up in some
other way, had we other purposes or interests in mind. It is not
self-evident that the boundaries we men are spontaneously inclined to draw around such events as Auschwitz or Hiroshima,
and in terms of which we declare them irredeemably and in-
excusably evil, are necessarily the most appropriate for understanding the so-called problem of evil. It may be—in fact it is
the case, as I shall argue below—that these "events," like all
others, must be seen in wider context if they are to be understood at all. At any rate, it is certainly not appropriate to understand events circumscribed and defined in this fashion as in any
significant sense "acts of God," thus raising almost unanswerable
problems for theodicy. God's acts, like those of any other agent,
must be defined and circumscribed in terms of his purposes not
simply our perceptions; not even the most vivid perceptions of
external observers can be relied upon to discern correctly what an
agent is doing. At most, such events would have to be considered
unfortunate and deplorable side effects of God's activity. But it
may be that, when we have thought through more fully the meaning of what is claimed about God's purposes, we will be able to
understand why even such events might occur within the context
of his overarching activity without thereby proving that he is
monstrous, despicable, or blundering. I shall argue precisely this
point below.

corollary of the Western notion of God has generally conceived the goal of the historical process in terms of the symbol of the "kingdom of God," a community of free and loving beings ordered by and to God's own sovereign love. Certain eschatological symbols used to amplify this notion, such as "last judgment" and "hell," have, to be sure, sometimes been developed in quite unfortunate directions in the Christian tradition; nevertheless we can say that in general the intention of the whole set of eschatological symbols has been to express the expectation that God's purpose for men is that they realize and fulfill themselves as free and creative persons in a community of love and peace.[14] There are even suggestions that the present cosmic order, which often fails to sustain and enhance the life of free and responsible moral agents, must finally give way to a "new heaven and a new earth," which will be the proper context for the "New Jerusalem" within which human life will find completion and happiness (Rev. 21). The whole natural and historical order, thus, is seen to be moving toward the fulfillment of God's high purposes for his creatures, in particular for men.

We need not concern ourselves here with the plausibility of this vision of the goal of history; our interest is in its implications for the problem of theodicy. It should be clear that, from the point of view of human aspirations at least, God's intentions or objectives for the historical process and for man are blameless; they are, indeed, praiseworthy in the highest degree. God wills nothing less or other than human fulfillment and ultimate happiness—a community of love in which free and creative agents find their perfect realization. This is the goal toward which he is working in human history. It should not surprise us that God, as he is believed in in Western religious traditions, cannot be faulted with respect to his intentions: after all, the preeminent images under which he has

[14] We cannot here explore the full repertoire of symbols that have been used to amplify and fill out the conception of the goal of history, including "resurrection of the dead," "last judgment," "heaven," "hell," "second coming of Christ," "New Jerusalem," and others. For a fuller treatment of eschatology, see my *Systematic Theology*, Chaps. 22 and 30.

been conceived have been righteousness, love, fatherliness, forgiveness, and the like, and he has always been spoken of as One to whom men could look for succor in an hour of need, as the ground of hope for the future in the most despairing present.

Perhaps, then, the horrible suffering and other evil in history are to be set down against God's ineffective blundering procedures for realizing his objectives? Like "the evil that good men do" because of their incompetence and naïveté, God has badly botched his work? To deal with this question we must examine carefully the conditions that are logically required in order for there to be free and responsible and loving beings. We shall find, I think, that just as inadequate attention to the meaning of agency led to unwarranted expectations of God as a kind of cosmic Magician, so here the implications of conceiving man as a free and responsible being have not been carefully enough considered.

It has often been supposed that the conception of God's omnipotence implies that if he had only chosen to do so he could have directly created perfectly free, loving, spontaneous, responsible men, instead of persons who had to develop and acquire such characteristics through long and painful historical experience. But this, like the general notion of God's instantaneous magical acts, is in fact an incoherent conception. Dispositions such as trust or love or responsibility cannot be conceived as absent one moment, present the next. When we speak of a man's character, we are not referring to some momentary position he has taken up, or some stance he may drop a few moments—or even days or weeks—later: we are indicating, rather, the more or less permanent complex of attitudes, beliefs, and other traits, which define him as this particular self in relation to, but over against, other persons. It is not that character never changes through time. But the changes are relatively slow and for the most part unintended (though a man can modify his own, or others', character[s] over a long period by certain kinds of deliberate action).

The long-term dispositions, attitudes, and habits of a man grow up only through a considerable experience of relation and interrelation with other persons, use and manipulation of environmental objects, and training and practice of muscles, receptors, and the like. By "habit" and "attitude" we mean precisely such slowly developing, long-term, deep-seated dispositions, which are formed in and through a man's own experience and action, not ephemeral or superficial expressions or postures. If I do not now smoke cigarettes, it is not possible for me today, by decision, to acquire the habit of smoking two packs daily. Doubtless I can begin today to smoke two packs daily (however difficult it might be to carry through such a resolution), and after a while it might be appropriate to say that I am in the habit of smoking that much. But this practice does not become a habit instantaneously.

It is the same with dispositions like love or trust. Though we speak of "love at first sight," and it is proverbial that one should "never trust a stranger," thus implying the possibility of responding with love or trust virtually instantaneously in some situations, it is clear that in referring to someone as a "loving person" or a "trusting person" we are not speaking of a sudden or momentary stance or action. Rather, we are indicating attitudes that have developed over a long period, have manifested themselves in a variety of ways in the past, and can be depended upon to express themselves on appropriate occasions in the future. Though a person's basic character comes into being in and through a process in time—an infant does not yet have a "character" any more than he has "habits," though he may have a "temperament"—it is a slow development, a matter of one's whole life, at least up to the present moment. As with (at least some of) one's habits and motor skills one's character, unlike his temperament, is not simply a given with which he has to deal; nor did it just happen to him: his own (deliberate) actions have played a significant part in its formation. (That is why we hold a man partially, but only partially, responsible for his own character.) It would not be consistent with what we mean by the word, therefore, and not a proper use of it, to refer to someone's "character" as having been instantaneously created and thrust upon him. To have a character is to have a history, to be oriented by memory and experience and striving toward a future envisioned at least partially in terms of one's own intentions and goals. The notion of a fully formed person with no past at all appearing suddenly on the scene, and then proceeding to think and feel and act meaningfully and responsibly, is as incoherent and inconceivable as a married bachelor.

This means, then, that if God's objective for men was to create a community of free and responsible and loving agents, it was not open to him to do so instantaneously: beings of this sort can be created only through a history in which they themselves gradually form certain habits, skills, and attitudes, and learn to take responsibility for themselves and others. Though we might wish to take exception to God's objectives here, given those objectives it is simply muddled thinking that leads us to be critical of him for not having created men fully formed and perfectly developed from the beginning. A being who is free, whose character has been formed in part by his own choices and actions in the past and who takes responsibility for what he has done and what he is, as well as for what he shall do and become, simply cannot be conceived as "fully formed and perfectly developed from the beginning."[15] If God's goal was the development of free and responsible and loving agents, then his mode of creation would necessarily be through historical process, not instantaneous magical act.

It might be thought that this logical precondition applies only to each human being as an individual: he must have a span of years within which to develop a set of attitudes, habits, and skills on the basis of which he can act with some measure of freedom. But this oversimplifies. Even had Adam been granted twenty years to grow to maturity, it is really not conceivable that he could have done so simply on his own, apart from any previously existing context of community, culture,

[15] This point was already grasped in the early church by Irenaeus, who laid a foundation for a theodicy based upon it (see Hick, *Evil and the God of Love*, pp. 217 ff.). Its logical aspects have been explored in considerable detail in contemporary philosophical discussions of the problem of theodicy (see, e.g., the essays collected by Nelson Pike in *God and Evil* [Englewood Cliffs, N.J.: Prentice-Hall, 1964]).

and language. Both language and action are preeminently social realities, depending for their possibility on the existence of elaborate systems of symbolization on the one hand and structures of roles, institutions, and customs on the other, and it is dubious that they can even be clearly conceived consistently as the exclusive creation and property of a solitary individual.[16] And of course love and trust in the full interpersonal sense presuppose the prior existence of other personal beings who evoke these attitudes and toward whom they can be directed. But this means that the time span required if it is to be plausible, even logically, to speak of agents capable of loving and trusting attitudes and free and responsible acts is of the order not of a few years but at the very least of some generations. Human existence in anything like the form in which we now conceive and cherish it—characterized by language and high-level consciousness and reflection, custom, communal interaction, values such as freedom and justice, and interpersonal relations of love, kindness, and trust—presupposes a complex historical context stretching back indefinitely into the past.

If we add to the logical considerations here mentioned the fact that human existence is biological as well as social and personal, and we recall the complexity of our modern conception of life as unified and evolutionary with higher and lower forms mutually interdependent, it will be evident that the order of time required for human or personal life as presently conceived to be created will have to be extended to

---

[16] The discussion of logical problems here stems largely from Ludwig Wittgenstein's doubts about the possibility of a "private language" (see *Philosophical Investigations* [Oxford: Blackwell, 1958], I, §§ 239 ff.). Several essays discussing the issues Wittgenstein raises will be found conveniently collected in the Modern Studies in Philosophy volume on *Wittgenstein*, ed. by George Pitcher (Garden City, N.Y.: Anchor Books, 1966); of these I might call special attention to John W. Cook, "Wittgenstein on Privacy," and Norman Malcolm, "Wittgenstein's *Philosophical Investigations*." On the logical problems associated with the concept of purely private *action*, see esp. Melden, "Action" (cited in note 8, above); and Stanley Cavell, *Must We Mean What We Say?* (New York: Scribner's, 1969), esp. pp. 12–31.

millions of years. It is difficult in matters of this sort to know where logical and grammatical consideration (those having to do with what is implied strictly by the *meanings* of our terms) leave off and empirical hypotheses and knowledge begin, and I do not wish to argue this vexed problem of contemporary philosophy. My point ought by now to be clear, however: if we are to conceive of God as creating men of the sort we are, with the possibilities of freedom and love and creative fulfillment which are significant to us, it will be difficult for us—whatever may have been the case with other generations of men who thought in other terms—to avoid thinking of him as doing so through and by means of an evolutionary and historical process of a sort similar to that which actually, so far as we know, transpired. To argue, on the ground of God's omnipotence, that he could have created man whole and complete directly from the clay of Eden, or even could have created him without any cosmic context at all—a man living simply face-to-face with the Almighty—is, as I hope we can now see, abstract and empty. The "man" of such arguments is an empty chimera, in no clear relationship to the flesh-and-blood, sociocultural man we know in our experience and life and to whom our word "man" properly applies.[17]

Doubtless God could have made entirely different sorts of beings than those he created, and he could have placed them in a world of quite different order and structure. But in that case he would not have been creating beings with possibilities of what we call love and responsibility and creativity, for these are characteristics and potentialities of *men,* immersed as they are in all the disorder, chaos, struggle, and aspiration of human history, and how they would have to be qualified in order meaningfully to apply to some other entirely different

[17] If I were to develop in this essay the distinction between "moral evil" (for which man is largely responsible) and "natural evil" (earthquakes, certain diseases, cosmic catastrophes, animal suffering, and the like), I would advance the argument along these same general lines and argue that the latter can be rationalized as the unavoidable by-product of a law-abiding and orderly world, the only sort of context in which it is conceivable that rational and moral beings like men could exist.

sorts of beings we can have no way of knowing.[18] To our question, then, whether God has badly botched things by attempting to produce a free and loving community through a cosmic and historical process of the sort he created, we must answer, "No." As far as we can see, just some such process as this would be required to realize that objective.

But one might still hold that though the general pattern of the intervening stages of God's great act realizing his intention seems reasonable and proper, still it should have been possible to avoid some of the grosser evils that have appeared in human history. This, however, is simply a rephrasing of the very question we have been considering. If God was trying to create free and responsible men, it was necessary that he give them scope within which to exercise their freedom and thus learn to become responsible. As every parent knows, it is only as a child is given some freedom, including the freedom to make and profit from his own mistakes, that he can grow into a mature human being, able to take responsibility for himself and his actions. Thus, man as a species could become genuinely free and responsible only if he learned—through whatever painful experience this might require—to create the social and cultural institutions that could provide a context within which upcoming generations of men could fruitfully grow and mature. Were God himself to have created directly the appropriate social and political institutions, linguistic and symbolical frameworks, complexes of value and meaning, and the like, for human life to find fulfillment and happiness, it would simply not have been the case that man was taking responsibil-

---

[18] Cf. Ninian Smart who presents a logical analysis of the concept "good" and maintains "that the concept *goodness* is applied to beings of a certain sort, beings who are liable to temptations, possess inclinations, have fears, tend to assert themselves and so forth; and that if they were to be immunized from evil they would have to be built in a different way. But it soon becomes apparent that to rebuild them would mean that the ascription of goodness would become unintelligible, for the reasons why men are called good and bad have a connection with human nature as it is empirically discovered to be. Moral utterance is embedded in the cosmic status quo" ("Omnipotence, Evil and Supermen," in *God and Evil,* ed. Pike, p. 106).

ity for himself. For it would have meant that the largest part of what we now take to be man's own creation and doing—namely, the production of culture and complex forms of social order—had been provided for him. Under such conditions it would be empty to talk of men as free and responsible agents in any significant sense at all. Thus, for God, as it were, to have directly placed men in heaven would have been to fail to create *men* at all. To create a loving community of free and finite agents, God had to give men in the process of their development the power to produce their own institutions and customs, gradually learning to modify and re-create them through the long struggles of history into forms that would sustain and support and enhance a fully humane existence.

Men have, unfortunately, all too often used in horribly cruel and destructive ways the powers gained in the historical process. The institutions they have created, though enhancing and enriching human life, have often been the instruments of degradation and misery. And the values and ideals in terms of which they ordered their existence have usually been self-centered and parochial ideologies by means of which individuals and classes gained and maintained their power over others. There is no need to recite here the long list of historical evils perpetrated by men against each other and themselves. The point is that only through such long and painful struggles to create a viable social order and a good life could men gradually dream the dreams and see the visions of new and richer personal and social possibilities, and these aspirations and values could in turn slowly come to impregnate man's social and cultural life, stimulating transformation (one hopes) toward more humane and meaningful forms. I make no claims here that over the centuries men have made great progress toward this goal, though I believe if one thinks in terms of units of several thousand years some progress can be claimed, despite such horrifying symbols of our contemporary degradation as Auschwitz and Hiroshima. But I do say that only through the gradual development of such humanly created social institutions and cultural patterns could men be conceived as coming to full freedom and responsibility; thus the chance of terrible misery and suffering in the course of human development was one that God simply had to take.

IV

Let us reflect for a moment on some general implications of the argument thus far. Part of the difficulty of the problem of theodicy as often conceived devolves from insufficient attention to the way in which eschatology must qualify the conceptions of creation and providence. It has been supposed that God could have made his creatures perfect from the beginning if he had only chosen to do so, or at least he could have governed his world more righteously or efficiently, not allowing things to get into such a frightful state of affairs. He is, therefore, to be held responsible for much of the evil in the world, even that evil which sinful men have wrought. But this kind of reasoning presupposes that creation was simply an isolated event in the past, which might as well have been some other event, and that God's providential governance could have led history any number of other ways than it in fact did. That is, it presupposes that we can understand and assess creation and providence in abstraction, without reference to anything beyond them. A doctrine of eschatology means, however, that history is a unified whole moving toward an end. Hence the bare existence and course of history may not be grasped or evaluated simply by inspection of what has been up to now, but only with reference to the final goal. "Creation" can no longer refer simply to a past and completed event or process that established the world: it must now be seen as the beginning of a history not yet complete, as the first steps or underlying stages of a process through which God has been and still is working toward the realization of his ultimate purposes. And "providence" can no longer be understood to refer simply to God's activity as a kind of "lord" or "governor" of the world concerned primarily with maintaining the existing order: eschatology means that God's governing is transformative and teleological, not simply conservative or maintenative; it directs the historical process toward its ultimate goal. Both creation and providence must be assessed, therefore, in the light of that end, not simply in consideration of the present condition of things.

This failure of traditional theology to see the full implications of its own eschatology for the doctrines of creation and providence has led to claims that the world is good simply as it is. It has been argued that since the good and omnipotent God created the heavens and the earth, they were complete and good just as originally made (as Genesis 1 suggests); as providential Lord, then, his work consisted in continuing to maintain things as they were. But as men gradually became morally aware of themselves and their world, they could see that the world and they themselves were not good in many respects; at best much was ambiguous, and much could be adjudged plainly evil. This in turn reflected seriously on the righteousness and goodness of the God who had created it all and continued to maintain it. How is such a God to be justified morally? In fact he cannot be. When the problem is posed in these terms there is too much that offends man's moral sensitivity. All man can do is rebel against God in the name of his own moral consciousness, as the ancient Job and many modern antitheists; or finally bow before God's sheer power, as the ancient Job and much traditional theology. The first alternative weakens man's moral commitments by implying that the power actually determining men's destinies is immoral (or at least amoral); the second undermines man's very moral sense by requiring him to honor that which he cannot respect. Either way man is left metaphysically defenseless against temptations to use his own power, likewise, without moral restraints. Thus piety itself can become responsible for the terrible evils of intolerance, fanaticism, and persecution.[19] But this whole problem arises, as we have seen, because God's world, and God himself, have been understood too much as static structures that must be justified morally as they now are, and this necessity simply contradicts too many facts of experience. If the historical eschatological implications of the Hebraic-Christian tradition are taken seriously, however, and

[19] See Chapter 5, note 31.

God is seen as an Agent actively at work leading the historical process toward the creation of genuinely free and responsible finite agents, the problem of evil in this form does not arise.

V

The problem must be stated otherwise: In the light of all the suffering and evil that this whole enterprise seems to involve or to have required, is it really worth the price? Can we morally approve God's great experiment with the world and man in view of all the misery and suffering it brings with it? Or would it have been better had God never undertaken to create free and responsible and loving beings? Here doubtless different persons will give different answers. We are being asked to imagine the complete nonexistence of ourselves and of everything human that we know and cherish and ultimately hope for and to decide whether such would be better than the existence of the human world as we know it, with all its suffering and misery but also with its dreams and visions of fulfillment and joy. Who can give an answer to a question like that, especially with its implication that it is right and ultimately good that some must suffer terribly so that others might enjoy a fuller and more significant existence? The most we can say is that some great goods have come out of this terrible suffering—goods (like love) we can hardly bring ourselves to wish had never existed, goods (like freedom) we could scarcely bear to dispense with, goods, moreover, that we really cannot imagine having come into being in any other way than through such suffering. In the light of these considerations we may well find ourselves affirming that it is indeed better that there are men and women, love and joy and trust, knowledge and beauty, value and meaning, rather than that none of these things should ever have been at all, despite the terrifying price that has been and apparently must be paid. If there is to be a real possibility of the kind of peace and joy for which we all long, and which, I suspect, is the highest vision of the good and meaningful life to which we men can come, if truly free and responsible and loving beings are to achieve realization and fulfillment, then the struggles and pain, suffering, terror and guilt so common in human affairs as men grow into responsible selfhood and orderly and creative forms of community life seem to have been almost unavoidable.

We can, of course, imagine and dream that it might have been different. Since the worst evils of history are men's own doing, their creations on the basis of their own freedom, the possibility of having done otherwise seems always to have been there also. It would seem that men *could* have created a better, more stable, more orderly, less unjust social order early in their history; they could have learned love and trust instead of self-centeredness and hatred; they could have entered into a much freer and happier world, had they only "chosen" to do so, had they only ordered their lives and their communities in more constructive and imaginative ways. But they did not, and great historical evils have been the consequence. It remains now for us to create, while there is still time, a better and more just social order, one that can be the context within which genuinely free and loving persons can emerge. The difficulties are enormous, especially because of the momentum of evil at work in our histories and in us, but we ourselves must tackle them and find some way to resolve them: God has granted man sufficient freedom to take responsibility for himself and the future of his race in just this way, and there is, therefore, no one else to whom we can turn—not even God—to get us off the hook.

Does this mean, then, that there is one last imputation of fault to be brought against God, namely, that having created men as beings who could get themselves into such difficulties, he has now deserted them, leaving them to find their own way out? It would seem that our theodicy is caught in a serious dilemma here. On the one hand, if we maintain that God is in real and continuous *control* of the course of history, then we must ascribe responsibility for its evils to him. On the other hand, if, in order to avoid this consequence, we suggest that God has granted man real freedom to set his own course and shape his own destiny, thus making man responsible for the way history has gone, then God appears to desert his children when the going gets rough, instead of seeing his frail and sinful creatures through to happiness and peace.

The dilemma is false, at least for the conception of God posited by Christian faith. For the alternatives in bringing about man's freedom are not either complete divine determination on the one hand, or total absence of all divine guidance on the other, so that God is either completely responsible for all that happens in history or man has no assistance at all in gaining his freedom. In neither of those alternative sorts of situations could free and responsible and loving selves emerge: mature and healthy persons do not develop either in a family dominated completely by autocratic parents who refuse to allow their children any freedom or in a situation where the children must fend for themselves from their earliest years with no parental help or guidance. Free selves emerge only in a context of loving care, where new and unexpected possibilities are prepared and promoted by the parents, where the child's mistakes and failures are turned to good use by the parents' imagination and ingenuity, where the child's guilt and despair are overcome by the psychological security created by the parents' forgiveness and love. Similarly God's relation to man—if the divine Parent is seeking to grant his children freedom—must not be conceived either as a kind of divine determinism or as an absence of all care and assistance. It must be thought of as providing a context of love and guidance—the very opposite of desertion—which gradually evokes new dimensions of freedom and responsibility while creatively transforming and redeeming men's blunders, failures, and sin, without undercutting their responsibility through miraculously lifting them out of historical difficulties.

The biblical history can be interpreted as presenting just such a portrait of God in relation to man. Though there are frequent suggestions that God intervenes compulsively in human history, accomplishing his own purposes quite without regard to human decision, desire, or action, this, as we have observed, is because the biblical mythopoetic portrait has not been critically analyzed and purged with reference to the logical requirements of its own central contentions about God's agency and his historical work leading men into responsible agency. When the biblical history, as reconstructed by modern historical-critical scholarship, is examined in the light of these theological-critical considerations, the clouds begin to lift. The long processes of cosmic development and biological evolution can now be seen as God's preparatory work: through the further movement of history, from the most primitive human beginnings to the time of Christ, God was, step by step, making himself known to man as ultimately righteous and loving, and simultaneously leading men to see that they also must become loving and just if they are to gain true freedom and fulfillment.[20]

Throughout this whole movement human spontaneity in the creation of culture and history is never violated. For this reason this entire historical development can be understood in the ordinary psychological and sociological terms applicable to any stretch of history, as every modern critical interpretation makes clear. And yet, out of this whole development emerges a community so deeply aware of God's continuous love and care and guidance that its members are able and willing to commit themselves in similar love and care for their fellowmen, even for enemies. Although it is man himself who is acting throughout this historical development, and man therefore who must bear the consequence whether evil or good, God's intention that men move toward a community of profound love and thus to deeper and more authentic freedom and responsibility is simultaneously being realized. God's mode of action vis-à-vis man as emerging agent thus proves to be—as with all love—primarily evocative rather than coercive. His purposes are not achieved through a divine determinism of human events, but rather only as he succeeds in leading men into increasing human spontaneity and creativity. Conversely, because of this same dialectical relation between God and man, God's giving men genuine responsibility for them-

[20] For fuller elaboration of this view of history as God's creative and loving activity, see Chapters 6 and 7, above. A much fuller and more detailed treatment will be found in my *Systematic Theology,* Pts. II and III.

selves and their destinies must be regarded not as evidence of his desertion but of his profound love and care for them.

With this understanding, the last charge against God that the facts of evil raise is shown to be mistaken. It is true that God does not invade history with power and miracle, lifting men bodily out of their misery: that in fact would be to destroy the tender plant of freedom and responsibility that had begun to grow within them. Thus he quite properly takes the course of involving himself intimately and profoundly in every movement and development in this historicocultural process from within, sacrificing his cosmic power and allowing himself to be subjected to man's every whim and will, that ultimately he might win men to him in love and freedom (cf. Phil. 2). In this way—and this is at the very heart of the Christian claim—God is continuously at work in the most profoundly relevant way possible: seeking to overcome the sufferings and other evils in human history as he gradually and painfully brings men into maturity.

Faith in God is the stance that appropriates this movement of cosmic and human history toward man's freedom and maturity not as the consequence merely of cosmic determinism or biological mutation or historical chance but as willed and purposed, a movement under God. Even though God's providential care is not directly perceived and is not something that can be expected to do for men what only they can do for themselves, faith enables men to hope and believe there is a genuine possibility of their reaching responsibility and freedom without destroying themselves. Unfaith, however—believing man to be fundamentally alone in the world as a purposive being—can live with no such confidence and can face the evils and difficulties of existence with no such hopes. For it knows of no cosmic intentionality that wills man's existence and is working for his successful emergence into full humanity and humaneness.

How can there be, and why should there be, evil in a world in which God is absolutely good and ultimately sovereign? There can be because God's absolute goodness is love —the love that wills genuine freedom and profound personal communion with those whom it creates and to whom it is subsequently in relation—and his power is his capacity to create and sustain cosmic and historical processes within which finite love and freedom can be born. God's absolute goodness and power on the one hand and our experience of suffering and evil on the other are irreconcilable only if we do not realize what it is for God to be an Agent who creates and works with his creatures out of genuine love for them, and if we fail to understand what is required for men to become truly free and responsible and loving themselves.

It was out of the depths of terrible suffering—passion, crucifixion, death—that the profoundest community and deepest love and freedom known to men were born. The principal symbol of these is still a cross, because they are seldom if ever created among men without unrequited suffering. When we remember this, we may perhaps also dare to believe and expect that out of the passion, crucifixion, death of even an Auschwitz meaning and humanizing power are flowing.

Part IV. Belief and Unbelief

9

Secular, Religious, and Theistic World-Views*

"World-view" is a third-order concept invented by philosophers
and analysts of culture for specific technical purposes. (It is
a term not found in most English dictionaries.) We may consider the uncriticized view of "world"—as that structured
totality which provides the context within which men live and
which contains all possible objects of knowledge and experience—as a first-order position. The "critical" conception
(Kant), which understands the "world" as not simply an object
that is what it is independently of any human knowers or ex-
periencers but as a construct to which the experiencing subject
contributes quite as significantly as the objective "other," then
involves moving to a second-order position. The concept of
world-view requires one further remove (not envisioned by
Kant): to a position from which it can be seen that the constructed worlds of different subjects (or different communities,
or different epochs) are not one and identical—an "objective"
world (in either an uncritical or a Kantian sense)—but themselves differ significantly. One's "world" is in some sense a
function of one's "view" and is thus relative to his psychological
and historical situation. Once this third-order consciousness of
the complexity of man's situation and experience has developed, it is no longer possible to speak simply and straightfor-

* This chapter was originally prepared (in a slightly different
version) for a conference on "World-Views: Their Nature and
Their Role in Culture," convened by the Wenner-Gren Foundation
for Anthropological Research in August 1968.

wardly of "the world" as a common stable object of knowledge, open and available to all men everywhere to live in and to observe; now one must first ask about the "world-view" a man has. For it will be his "view" of "the world" more than "the world as it is in itself" (whatever that might mean) that determines in most significant ways his experience, his attitudes, and his knowing.

In this essay I do not intend to argue either the propriety of this concept or the philosophical problems which it raises or difficulties in which it is involved.[1] The concept of "world-view," as well as related ones such as "absolute presuppositions" (Collingwood), cultural style, *Zeitgeist,* has proved sufficiently useful in cultural and historical analysis to justify its introduction, at least for heuristic purposes. It is a notion that enables a cultural analyst or historian to discern, relate, and hold together in significant unity certain common features of the most diverse artifacts or cultural expressions of a given community or epoch, all of them understood as expressive of the world-view there prevailing; it also facilitates distinguishing and comparing certain comprehensive features of the experience, attitudes, and stance in life of one community (or individual, or period) with another, in a way not otherwise possible. When we examine a man's or a community's world-view, we come to understand something of the overall character of the experience undergone and the life lived from that perspective. This in turn enables grasping more adequately the profound differences between men and appreciating more fully the infinite variety in human life and experience. Seeing both the diversity of the world-views within which men have their experience, think their thoughts, and make their decisions, and the reasons for these differing perspectives, may make possible

[1] Many of the philosophical problems connected with the psychological and historical "relativism" that the concept of "world-view" presupposes and suggests have been discussed in my book, *Relativism, Knowledge and Faith* (Chicago: University of Chicago Press, 1960). Though I now regard many of the details of the argument presented there as unsophisticated and unconvincing, I still think its main contentions are substantially correct.

greater sympathy for and understanding of those with whom one sharply disagrees. The concept of "world-view" thus has many uses and potential benefits.

In this essay I would like to put the concept to a different use than any of those just suggested. As a third-order concept —one standing beyond, but in a special relation to, both the object(s) of experience (the "world") and the subjects who have that experience (the "viewers")—this notion can facilitate understanding of ourselves (as subjects) and the contemporary cultural strains and tensions in which we participate. We can gain a certain distance from ourselves and see some things about ourselves that we might not otherwise note by asking about our own world-view(s), that is, about the perspective(s) on the world and stance(s) in life that inform and significantly shape our experience and our actions. In this way we may gain a measure of understanding and knowledge of our selves and our culture that would not otherwise be available to us. For we can learn something not only of the standpoint we occupy in living out our lives, but of the tensions and stresses within that standpoint—or, perhaps better put, of the stresses among the several standpoints we take up successively and sometimes attempt to take up simultaneously. Such fuller understanding of our own world-views may make it possible more rationally to deal with these stresses and strains.

I

There are many levels or degrees of self-awareness to which we might profitably apply the concept of world-view. We might, for example, distinguish a Western world-view from an Eastern outlook; we could characterize a technological perspective in contrast with an aesthetic; it might be useful to seek to clarify the "generation gap" by distinguishing a teen-ager's world-view from that of persons over thirty or to illuminate America's racial problem by distinguishing the world-view of black Americans from white. All such analyses would doubtless be instructive as we gained some insight into our own standpoint as well as those of contemporaries. All, however, with the possible exception of the first, would be limited and less than universal in significance, for they deal with "worlds" or "subworlds" that are but dimensions or features of our experience. That is, they set forth aspects of our world, but they do not attempt to set forth the all-embracing concept of "world" itself in some distinctive form. They provide ways of perceiving certain characteristics within our world, but not diverse ways of considering the very category of "world." Hence they do not grapple with the problem of world-view on the deepest level, which is the question of how *world* is itself grasped and conceived.

Should we then turn to the metaphysicians for analysis of the several different options for conceiving the world? Perhaps it should be viewed as process or structure or matter, or under some other category. Analysis of such "world hypotheses"[2] would be profitable for some purposes, including the deepening of insight into certain implications or presuppositions of some world-views, but here we would be dealing with *theories* about the world and its structure rather than with the basic form or category in and through which one's experience (of the world) is itself had. For the latter, phenomenological description of experience in its most universal dimensions is more appropriate than metaphysical construction. One's world-view is not so much an explanation of the world as it is his basic apprehension or feeling of the world in which he lives and acts. Doubtless this fundamental experience of world will have its appropriate conceptual or theoretical expression, and this should not be ignored, but it is not the proper place to begin.

We are seeking, then, to isolate and delineate fundamental intuitions or apprehensions of world—the structured or unified totality of all that is—which are important or significant for modern Westerners, for ourselves. How shall we approach this problem? We may begin by considering the purpose or function of the concept "world." The term appears to come from Germanic roots meaning literally "man-era," that is, this human age or period, human existence; from this the identification of

[2] See the book of that title by Stephen C. Pepper (Berkeley: University of California Press, 1942).

world with the earth, and subsequently with the universe, developed secondarily.[3] The world, then, is the context (in the
broadest sense) of human life. It is that within which all our
experience falls and all our activities occur. Its order or structure is what we seek to know in all our cognitive activities (including science); its value and meaning (or the value and
meaning of its constituents) are what we feel and appreciate
in moments of joy and well-being; it provides the setting
within which the tasks and problems of life are confronted and
the goals and objectives of our striving are posited. All our
feeling, willing, and knowing occur within the world and are
oriented in terms of our apprehension of the world. For this
reason our world-view, our sense or intuition of what the world
ultimately is or means, will color and shape every aspect of our
experience and activity.

What different sorts of world-view are open to us? We may
rephrase this question in this way: How are we related to the
world? In what different kinds of relation to the world do we
stand? Is there any convenient way of classifying this infinity
of relations so as to make it manageable? The common analysis
of experience into three distinctive moments—thinking, feeling, and willing—will serve our purpose well here. We can be
said to relate to the world in three ways or modes: through
feeling what is present to us here and now, impinging on us
through sensory receptors and emotions; through constructing
the order or structure of the world in our *thinking,* as we reflect
on experience had in the past and relate various features of
that experience to each other with concepts, conceptual systems, and theories; through *acting* in and on the world, that is,
through that driving forward and outward in which we set
objectives for ourselves and, through testing and experiment-
ing, learn how to achieve them—a thrust which originated in
the blind inner dynamism of life but which ultimately evolved
into deliberate volitional activity. Clearly these are not separate
sorts of relation in which we stand at different times and inde-

[3] See *A New English Dictionary on Historical Principles,* ed.
J. A. H. Murray *et al.* (10 vols., Oxford: Clarendon Press, 1888–
1928), X, Pt. 2, 2d Half, 300, 302.

pendently of each other; they are all complexly involved with each other in the living experience and activity of the self. But they are distinguishable as different moments of life and different modes of our relation to the world, and they suggest, therefore, different ways in which the world serves as context for our existence: it is something felt (immediately in the present), something thought about (in reflection on past experience), and something acted in and upon (as we drive into the future). Every world-view, if it is to provide the all-embracing context of experience and activity, must make room for, and make possible significant interpretation of, each of these moments of experience and modes of time. Distinctively different world-views are generated, however, if one of these moments or modes is given the dominant place in determining the intuition of the world, and the others are subordinated to it.[4] The world—the overall context of human existence—will then be seen and interpreted in terms of feeling-tones and categories especially appropriate to that mode, and human life will be apprehended as having a corresponding cast and character. In this way the world and life will gain unity, consistency, and order, and it will be possible both to feel and to see how the world provides the proper context for life, but this will be to some extent at the expense of the other two modes.[5] I shall

[4] Wilhelm Dilthey's suggestive typology of world-views appears based on these threefold classifications, though he does not stress this anthropological rootedness as much as I shall do. (See "Das Wesen der Philosophie," in *Gesammelte Schriften* [12 vols. Leipzig: Teubner, 1923–1936], V, esp. 400–406, and "Die Typen der Weltanschauung und ihre Ausbildung in den metaphysischen Systemen," *ibid.*, VIII, 75–118.) Although I am dependent on Dilthey here in broad outlines, I have worked out the individual types somewhat differently than he, paying more particular attention to theological issues. His analysis, it seems to me, seriously distorts the theological considerations involved in the conception of world-views.

[5] I am doubtful that any world-view could be based on all three of these moments of experience and activity kept in some sort of perfect equilibrium with each other. (Indeed, it is not even clear what "perfect equilibrium" might be when such distinct dimensions of experience are being balanced against each other). Three principles could never give unity simply of themselves, and the world in the sense in which we are using the term here is un-

suggest that "secular," "religious," and "theistic" world-views develop in accord with emphases, respectively, on thinking, feeling, and willing.[6]

I must make clear immediately that in developing this three-fold typology, I shall be using the terms "religion" and "religious" in a more restricted sense than is often done. Belief in God is ordinarily taken to be a "religious" stance, and some may even hold that it is of the very essence of religion. As we shall see, however, there are good reasons for rather sharply distinguishing "religion" from "theistic belief" for some purposes, and even for holding that they may, under some circumstances, be opposed to each other. At any rate, in this essay I shall argue that they have clearly distinguishable roots in the experience of the self and therefore are not necessarily inter-dependent. (This, however, does not mean that I hold it no longer appropriate to use the term "religion" in the wider and more customary sense, as inclusive of theistic belief as well as other positions. That use is too well ingrained in the language and too useful in its own right to make it possible—or even desirable—simply to eradicate it because of the particular sorts of theoretical issues raised in this essay. Indeed, when it was convenient to do so, I have not hesitated to use the term in this ordinary sense in many of the preceding essays of this volume.)

---

deniably one (the one all-embracing or overarching context of human existence).

[6] I am not committed to arguing here that this threefold classification is absolutely fundamental to the self and that other classifications of moments of experience or modes of relation to the world are inconceivable or false. There may well be other classifications with equal right to our attention. If there are, they could, I would expect, provide the basis for different typologies of world-views than the threefold one I will present. It would be instructive, I think, to attempt to produce such alternative typologies and to see what could be learned from each and from their relation to each other. (It may be noted that in previous writing with somewhat different objectives in view I have suggested other possible classifications of world-views. See *The Context of Decision* [New York: Abingdon Press, 1961], Chap. 1, and Chapter 3, above.) In this essay I will be able to consider only the one typology, based on the common-sense division of the functions of the self into feeling, thinking, and willing.

II

A naturalistic or secular world-view results when man's reflective activities are given a dominant role in determining the understanding of human existence and the environment in which it is found.[7] By a secular view, I mean to indicate any position that understands man's existence simply in terms of *this world* as it is given to our experience and especially as it is known in our science and philosophy. There are, of course, many degrees and sorts of secularism, but they all share a high valuation of scientific knowledge as the most appropriate basis for understanding the world, and they generally take a hard-nosed attitude toward the "sentimentality" of the "sympathetic fallacy" by which men too easily find value and meaning lodged directly in the nature of things: however important to us men, these belong to human culture and are an expression of human need and desire.

On this view man is understood primarily biologically and secondarily sociologically and psychologically. He is an animal who has evolved from lower forms of life to a position where, through the invention of language and the increasing use of tools and ultimately technology, he has gained an amazing degree of control over his environment and himself. Through the development of complex social institutions he has found ways of dividing responsibilities and reordering his life so that a whole new order of reality—culture—could be produced, sustained, and developed in many directions. He has worked out mythologies and ideologies to give himself orientation in the world; he has imaginatively created values and ideals to guide his animal striving and his deliberate labors; he has painfully developed methods for testing and reformulating the symbolical schemes through which he has gained knowledge of his world and powerful mastery over the forces, without him and

[7] Cf. Dilthey *Gesammelte Schriften,* VIII, 100–107, for a discussion of the perspective of naturalism as it has developed historically. Although I am posing questions here from a somewhat different angle than Dilthey, his interpretation of naturalism corresponds fairly well to my conception of secularism.

within him, which would otherwise fully determine his being and his destiny. In short, he has become a *historical,* not merely a natural, being, whose proper home is the culture he has himself created. Through this process he has transformed himself into a being with considerable freedom and rationality, one with both consciousness and self-consciousness and with deep appreciations of value and meaning, one able to set deliberate purposes for himself and to make the decisions and perform the actions necessary to realize these objectives. Through all of this, though he has had to superimpose social and cultural patterns on his animal nature, thus reforming and sublimating his animal drives and instincts, he has nevertheless found it possible to meet his basic physical needs and in addition to secure for himself a measure of physical comfort and a variety of physical satisfactions unknown to any other species.

Secular stances can manifest great variety, attracting adherents from virtually every position or status in society: the sensitive humanist and pacifist working for the universal brotherhood of man; the crude sensualist and egoist seeking only his own physical pleasure and comfort; democratic politicians, bending all their efforts and political power toward the development of a good society; tyrannical dictators or coldly realistic ecclesiastical bureaucrats; sophisticated philosophers; ordinary day laborers; unhappy lovers; well-fed businessmen. The one thing all have in common is their tendency to see human existence in terms of what is given in *this* life and *this* world, as that is open and available in whatever knowledge— or supposed knowledge—they may each possess, whether it be the understanding borne of common sense and hard experience or the sophisticated and elaborate theories of science or philosophy. The world is, in some real sense, as we apprehend it in our thought, and we had best adapt and adjust ourselves to it. It is foolish to depend upon or otherwise take seriously a "God" —some superhuman will who cares for man and who has given the cosmos a fundamental order and meaning and value independent of man and in terms of which men ought to orient their lives. It is equally foolish to suppose that the kind of value and meaning of significance to men inheres in the world "naturally"; these were created in and by human culture, and they are acquired and maintained only through human striving. Man is basically alone in the world, and he had best make the most of his brief time here. The position is beautifully expressed in Bertrand Russell's "A Free Man's Worship":

> Brief and powerless is Man's life; on him and all his race the slow, sure doom falls pitiless and dark. Blind to good and evil, reckless of destruction, omnipotent matter rolls on its relentless way; for Man, condemned to-day to lose his dearest, to-morrow himself to pass through the gate of darkness, it remains only to cherish, ere yet the blow falls, the lofty thoughts that ennoble his little day; disdaining the coward terrors of the slave of Fate, to worship at the shrine that his own hands have built; undismayed by the empire of chance, to preserve a mind free from the wanton tyranny that rules his outward life; proudly defiant of the irresistible forces that tolerate, for a moment, his knowledge and his condemnation, to sustain alone, a weary but unyielding Atlas, the world that his own ideals have fashioned despite the trampling march of unconscious power.[8]

A view such as this, though rooted in "thinking," does not by any means ignore human feeling or willing. It understands well that such meaning and value as we experience in life is related closely to our feelings of joy and contentment and physical satisfaction, and it recognizes that the conditions productive of such fulfillment are in some measure under our control and can be gained by human striving. It usually involves, therefore, a eudaemonistic ethic, but this can be of a very high and sensitive sort, appreciative of aesthetic, intellectual, and moral values and devoted to cultivating them. Indeed, religious and quasi-religious values, emphasizing a sense of harmony with the All or the Universe and the well-being or fulfillment of the individual, may also be given signifi-

---

[8] *Mysticism and Logic* (New York: Longmans Green and Co., 1918), pp. 56–57.

cant place here. And the awareness that human society and culture are the product of man's vision and man's labors, and that men's problems will have to be solved by human ingenuity and devotion, can furnish ethical motivation of a high order, leading to well-disciplined, morally directed action. A secular world-view can thus provide a way of seeing the world and human existence that gives a measure of fulfillment to all sides and activities of the self.

It is clear, however, that its greatest strength derives from its attempt to shape an understanding of the world as closely in accord with the deliverances of human reflective activity as possible; its claim to objective truth, its claim to see the world and human life as they are, unembroidered by fancy or desire, is what most strongly commends it. A secular world-view is less able to do full justice to man's need and desire to feel at one with the world, in harmonious relation to all that is, aware of a glorious depth of meaning in reality, which overflows everything and gives profundity and significance to even the most commonplace experiences of life. This sort of fulfillment of the feeling dimension of human selfhood is better achieved by a religious world-view. Nor can the secular position fully accommodate the demands of the human will: with all our thinking, we know little about the future into which we are moving— whether it will be cosmic or human disaster or whether there will long continue a natural and historical context within which men can live and find some measure of fulfillment; accordingly it is difficult to know whether hard striving after distant goals is really worth the personal and social effort and sacrifice involved. Certainly there seems no good reason to suppose that our purposive activity has as its context an intentionality or purposiveness in the universe itself, working toward similar goals and giving some promise of their ultimate attainment. Belief in God could give our volitional activity this kind of setting,[9] but such belief characterizes a theistic position, not a secular one.

[9] See esp. Chapter 5, above. It was Kant, with his "moral postulate" of God, who first clearly expressed this point.

III

When *feeling* is given a dominant place in shaping the interpretation of reality or the world, a religious world-view results.[10] There has been an intimate interrelation and association of religious with theistic perspectives in Western history, which has led many to assume that these positions belong together or are perhaps even identical with each other. The theological renaissance during the last generation called this assumption into question, however, and it is becoming increasingly apparent, in my opinion, that these perspectives are sharply different at certain crucial points and that they rest on differing anthropological bases. In this analysis I shall try to show that religion draws especially on the affectional side of the self while theism is rooted more particularly in the volitional.

Perhaps the point can be made most clearly and directly, and also somewhat oversimply, by reminding ourselves that the noun "religion" signifies a domain of human culture to be contrasted with, say, politics and science, and the adjective "religious" is used to qualify certain experiences or feelings, ideas or customs, institutions or communities—in short, these terms apply to human or cultural realities. But the proper name "God" designates "the Creator and Ruler of the Universe," "the One object of supreme adoration,"[11] that is, it intends a reality *over against* man (and even the entire world) and certainly to be distinguished from all merely human or cultural creations or artifacts. In the one case we are speaking of a sphere of

[10] Here my position must be distinguished sharply from Dilthey's. He believes religious world-views to be intrinsically connected with the supernatural or the invisible and seems to think religion is especially appropriate to more primitive stages of society than our own (see *Gesammelte Schriften,* V, 381–392; VIII, 88–9). What I here describe as the religious world-view is in many respects similar to what Dilthey has called "objective idealism" (VIII, 112–118). The reader may refer to his discussion for an exposition of the historical and philosophical development of this position.

[11] *A New English Dictionary on Historical Principles,* ed. Murray *et al.,* IV, 2d Half, 268.

the human; in the other, of an independent reality who has his being from himself alone (aseity). These sharp distinctions would have to be qualified carefully in any full analysis, but certainly they characterize correctly the different intensions of the words "God" and "religion." This distinction is confirmed, I think, by our increasing willingness to say such things as, "A man can be deeply religious even though he does not believe in God," and by such developments as the Supreme Court's accepting the claims of conscientious objectors to war as "religious" even though no belief in a "Supreme Being" is professed. It can be argued that many of the post-Freudian developments in psychoanalysis are really religious in character and emphasis[12] —though they are hardly theistic—and this accounts for their wide popular appeal. Theologically the distinction between "faith in God" and "religiousness" appears in Karl Barth's interpretation of "the revelation of God as the abolition of religion"[13] as well as in the widespread interest in Dietrich Bonhoeffer's notion of "religionless Christianity."[14]

What now is a religious world-view? Perhaps the leading spokesman for such a position in recent times has been Paul Tillich. Tillich has been especially concerned to emphasize the dimension of "depth" in all experience, pointing to the inexhaustibility of the "ground of being" in overcoming the "threat of nonbeing" which we as finite creatures experience.[15] Awareness of and reliance upon the infinite resources of the "power of being" will give us sufficient "courage" to face the various difficulties of life and to live productively with the "anxiety" that characterizes our existence;[16] indeed, in some

[12] See, e.g., Philip Rieff, *The Triumph of the Therapeutic* (New York: Harper and Row, 1966). Certainly Norman O. Brown's works would fall into this category.

[13] See the section with that title in *Church Dogmatics* (Edinburgh: T. and T. Clark, 1956) I/2, pp. 280–361, as well as Barth's much earlier *Epistle to the Romans* (London: Oxford University Press, 1933).

[14] See esp. *Letters and Papers from Prison* (London: SCM Press, 1953), pp. 121 ff.

[15] *Systematic Theology* (3 vols., Chicago: University of Chicago Press, 1951–1963), I, Pt. II.

[16] *The Courage To Be* (London: Nisbet, 1952).

moments of exaltation or "ecstasy"[17] it will veritably lift us out of ourselves into a fuller participation in that which is "ultimately real." Despite our "alienation" from each other and from the "ground of being," Tillich holds out hope for fulfillment of our existence in "reunion" and "love."[18]

Tillich uses much evocative language. It speaks to men's sense of loneliness, meaninglessness, emptiness, estrangement, and promises unity, love, harmony, peace. But Tillich is not merely attempting to manipulate feelings. He takes himself to be presenting a description or interpretation of the way things "really are"; indeed, "being-itself" is his most fundamental concern. We have here, then, a world-view, but not one based primarily or directly on the results of the positive sciences; its ultimate root is not in man's cognitive endeavors but rather in his deep "feeling" about both his present estrangement from the world and his ultimate harmony with reality. And this feeling (or these feelings) about man's place in the world becomes the source of insight into and understanding of both the world itself and man. Following his great predecessor Schleiermacher, who directly and openly made *Gefühl* the ground of all consciousness and experience,[19] Tillich sees our ordinary thinking about things in the world, as well as our scientific knowledge, to be a highly restricted product of our limited "technical reason," and not to be trusted as an adequate basis for overall orientation in life. Such reason is abstracted from the full "ontological reason" which includes feeling as well as structure,[20] and which is our fundamental link with reality.

It is not possible to develop Tillich's views further here, nor to compare them with others. His position is typical of those who look for and sense hidden depths of meaning in life, who feel even the most ordinary experiences to be somehow extraor-

[17] *Systematic Theology*, I, 111 ff.

[18] *Ibid.*, II and III; *Love, Power and Justice* (London: Oxford University Press, 1954).

[19] See *The Christian Faith*, tr. H. R. Mackintosh and J. S. Stewart (Edinburgh: T. and T. Clark, 1928), §§ 3–5; *On Religion: Speeches to Its Cultured Despisers*, tr. John Oman (London: K. Paul, Trench, Trübner and Co., 1893), Second Speech.

[20] *Systematic Theology*, I, 71–79, 89–94.

dinary, who experience feelings of absolute dependence on resources beyond themselves or have a sense for the infinite
either in the daily occasions of this life or somehow transcending them, who rejoice in the glory and power of Being as they
apprehend it. In short, it expresses well specifically *religious*
experience and articulates it as a religious world-view. We
should not suppose, of course, that all religious positions will
take on the intellectual and philosophical garb characteristic
of Tillich's. The humblest man may feel deep piety and express
it in very simple terms. Again—one thinks of Dag Hammarskjöld—the deep religious orientation of a man's life may be
expressed only in moments of solitude or to a secret diary, the
religious interior being covered over and concealed by active
political and social involvement. Immoral knaves, drug addicts,
and fanatical and demonic monsters, as well as "saintly" men,
"flower children," and highly disciplined "mystics," may all be
driven by deep religious motivation and feeling. Feeling has
many forms and permutations: it becomes "religious" when it
serves as the basis for life and the key to orientation in the
world. Virtually any of its forms or species can play this role
(and have at one time or another in human history). Hence
though religious world-views can be the source of great meaning in life, they can also manifest demonic powers of terror and
destructiveness: feeling—and thus religion—has almost infinite variety.

A religious world-view, of course, is not constructed simply
and solely of feeling: it also has place for the cognitive and
the volitional sides of life. We have already observed in Tillich
the drive toward system and ontological claim, and we have
noted the way in which religious feeling may motivate behavior. Although the dominant and ordering principles of a
religious perspective may be drawn from the affections, it is
evident that significant roles can be given to man's cognitive
powers and his ability to act. However, in this perspective they
are not given their full autonomy, but are subjected to the
affectional. Religious philosophies (as with Tillich, Heidegger,
Nietzsche, the Romantics, and others) are notoriously vague
and imprecise in their use of language, heavily dependent on

evocative meaning, and often critical and scornful of the precision and careful definition of logician or scientist. Seldom are such positions developed in close relation to the exact sciences, and no science has been directly fathered by man's religiousness per se: theistic world-views, with their emphasis on purposiveness and disciplined volitional activity, gave birth to the attempt to master the world in science and technology, and secular world-views, with their predilection for positive factual knowledge, are much better fitted than religious positions to sustain and further scientific endeavors. Nor does the moral dimension of man's volitional activity gain its full autonomy in a religious perspective. In his phenomenology of religious experience, Rudolf Otto made clear the amoral character of the primitive experience of the "holy,"[21] and it is well known that religious history is black with horror and fanaticism. The power of will to posit constructive goals to be realized in the future and to act deliberately and creatively to bring about the realization of those goals often becomes subordinated here to the demands of present immediate feeling. Thus the joy and pain and ecstasy and emptiness of present experience become the basis of life, at the expense both of the possibilities for meaning latent in an open (though divinely purposed) future, which will be at least partially constructed by our deliberate volitional activity, and of the well-ordered, closely textured world gained through our reflection on the structure of past experience and articulated in our scientific descriptions and theories. But for many the satisfaction and fulfillment gained through a world-view oriented most fundamentally on feeling are sufficiently powerful that the corresponding subordination of intellect and will seems small price to pay; indeed, religious thinkers such as Schleiermacher may argue that feeling is the very ground out of which the other two emerge and in which they are always rooted.

[21] *The Idea of the Holy* (London: Oxford University Press, 1923). See also Gerardus van der Leeuw, *Religion in Essence and Manifestation* (London: George Allen and Unwin, 1938), Chap. 78.

IV

With a theistic world-view we move to a quite different sort of orientation than either of the other two.[22] Where the latter define and describe their worlds in terms of that which is directly accessible (to feeling or thinking), theism speaks of a being or reality other than both man and the world—"God"—in terms of which the world and man must themselves be understood; where secularism and religion grasp their worlds more simply in terms of inherent order or structure (known in man's reflection) or meaning and value (apprehended in feeling), theism takes the world to be ordered from beyond itself by intentional or purposive activity rooted in the "will of God." The ultimate reality is thus not directly accessible to us at all, but knowable only through a "self-disclosure" or "communication" by God, as the purposes and objectives of a finite self may be "revealed" to another through deliberate speech.[23] Precisely because it speaks in this way of a reality or being in some significant sense "transcending" the world, theism has seemed highly dubious to many moderns: how could we ever come to know of such a God?

I cannot here argue these issues;[24] nor would it be to our immediate purpose to do so. We are seeking now to grasp the distinctiveness of the theistic world-view and its anthropological rootedness in the volitional side of the self. It is necessary for us to note briefly certain features of human purposive activity in order to make clear how this perspective is generated. To carry through from start to finish even relatively simple intentions—such as to plant a garden, or to learn to play the piano, or even to write a letter—a considerable variety of activities may be required. One must obtain the necessary materials, secure certain kinds of information, make various plans,

[22] My discussion in this section may be compared with what Dilthey calls the "idealism of freedom" (*Gesammelte Schriften,* VIII, 107–112). But similar qualifications hold here, as indicated in note 10, above.

[23] See Chapter 7, above.

[24] For some discussion, see Chapter 7, above, and Chapter 10, below.

and carry out the several steps of the project in proper order. Many of these actions, under other circumstances, could just as well be done for other reasons, but they are given an inner unity and order in each particular case by the particular purpose governing them. This purpose has its origins in motives, desires, and decisions of the agent and is not itself directly perceptible; until externalized in some beginning action, it remains subjective tendency or intention. Moreover, as the action begins, the purpose being served will hardly be immediately apparent to an external observer; even when the objective has been achieved, we may not be certain just what intention the agent was seeking to realize, unless he has chosen to disclose it openly. Decision and purpose as such are not directly open to the view of external observers; in some sense "lying beyond" or "transcending" their direct experience, these "inner springs" of action become known only (often quite indefinitely) through observation of behavior or (more definitely and specifically) through the agent's own disclosure of his intentions in deliberate communication. Yet it is decision and purpose that order the activity that is observable, and they effect significant physical changes (the ground gets spaded, vegetables appear where before there had been weeds, and so forth). Intentional or volitional activity thus creates objects with ordering principles and springs that transcend them and that may remain concealed even when the object itself is (apparently) fully present and visible; nevertheless, precisely these (hidden) purposes in-form the object, giving it its distinctive character.

We can see now why a world-view generated on the model of human purposive activity will involve not only a conception of the world but a conception of God as well. If the world is to be understood as ordered by *intentional activity,* as the expression of *purposes* working toward certain *objectives,* there must be some sort of quasi-will transcending the given world itself as the locus in which those intentions are lodged and as the center promoting the realization of those purposes: in short, in addition to the experienced world itself, there must be a transcendent Agent working in and on and through the world. In contrast to world-views based primarily on feeling or cognition, a doctrine of God belongs necessarily and intrinsically to a world-view rooted in the human experience of intentionality and purposiveness.

It is not difficult now to understand some of the other features of a theistic world-view. First and foremost will be the conception of God's ontological independence from the world as its creator and purposer: the world, including man, will be understood as in some significant sense derivative from God and his purposes, both of which, in turn, will be knowable perhaps in part by inference from the character of and directional development in the world, but most decisively only if God chooses deliberately to reveal himself. Thus the development of a historical tradition that speaks of the "act" or "acts" in which God has "revealed himself" is to be expected here. For anyone who stands within such a tradition and believes God has revealed (at least some of) his purposes for man and the world, an adequate understanding of human life and its context will have to be rooted primarily in that revelation rather than simply in man's feelings about existence (religion) or his scientific knowledge of the world (secularism). The norms of human action and the most appropriate goals for human striving will similarly be defined with reference to revelation. A theistic interpretation of the world thus differs decisively from religious and secular views not only formally (as involving doctrines of cosmic intentionality and God) but also materially: for the specific character of what is taken to be God's revelation will significantly shape the understanding of the world itself and of human life. This last point accounts for the wide variety of theistic positions, in many respects inconsistent with each other. The event or book or person or idea or value that is taken to be revelatory of God's inner nature and will is materially determinative of the conception both of the world and of authentic human existence.

In its emphasis on the transcendent God, theism differs sharply both from secularism, contented simply with life in this world, and religion, which perceives unusual depths and values and meanings in experience, but is not essentially committed to an independent transcendent God. Although it is well known that the line between theism and religion may often become vague—as when religious depth and meaning are interpreted as "divine" reality, or the voluntaristic core of God's ontological independence is played down—an important similarity between theistic and secular world-views in contrast to religion may not be so widely recognized. However, both theistic and secular world-views emphasize that the world is not to be confused with God or the divine in any way, that our lives are lived out in this world, and that—here there is a sharp contrast with religious positions—our experience is, thus, fully secular or worldly in all respects. From this point of view it is a mistake—indeed, for theism it is idolatry—to confuse anything in this world or in experience, even its "depths" of meaning and value, with the divine and eternal. Because of this common ground, an alliance can develop between Christian and secular perspectives (for example, in the contemporary movements toward "religionless Christianity" or "secular theology"), with a common emphasis on responsible work in the world and enjoyment of the goods of this life, in contrast with any sort of otherworldliness or religious sentimentality.

Theism, like the other world-views discussed, may be subscribed to by persons in any walk or station of life. Its greatest strength, and its greatest liability, is its anthropomorphism. Since it sees the world as informed at every point by quasi-personal purposive activity, the world is not alien to man's purposing and striving. For theistic positions that see God as a "loving Father" who cares for men and is seeking to transform their chaotic and destructive history into a community where love and creativity and freedom reign—the "kingdom of God" —the world is neither an impersonal process (secularism) nor simply the directly given locus of awesome power and value (religion); it is a dynamic history moving toward a goal of consuming importance to man, and it provides a precisely appropriate context for his own labors toward community and freedom. Such a world makes intelligible and reasonable the sacrifices of present generations of men for the sake of a more humane existence in the hidden future because it sees that future as secured in the continuing activity of God (whose humane objectives have been revealed), and thus not to be finally undermined by the happenstance contingency of cosmic or historical catastrophe. Man's temporal purposive activity gains profound meaning because it is a participation in and contribution to a meaningful historical movement in the world itself. Moreover, confidence in this purposive movement in history as a whole does not rest either on the fluctuations of feeling (religion) or the continually changing probabilities and hypotheses of our ordinary knowledge (secularism). Its ground is objective: the nature and will of the absolutely dependable God. Such a world-view, therefore, can provide stability, continuity, direction, and meaning for life almost without regard to the particular vicissitudes of experience or feeling tones of existence. It thus makes provision in its own distinctive way for man's feelings of anxiety and guilt, exaltation and fulfillment.

But the transcendent God, the source of theism's great strength, is also the ground of its most damaging weakness. For what good reasons, after all, can be given for believing in this God and in the related intentionality of the world? Our ordinary methods of knowledge lead us to an awareness of an orderly world, but they reveal no teleological movement nor any divine being; as we have seen, they tend toward a secular world-view. Even if we take our deep feelings as clue to the nature of reality and say that value and meaning have ontological place in the world, this is no ground for speaking of a cosmic purposive movement toward humane goals; at most it provides basis for a religious world-view. A theistic position involves the acceptance of the events of a particular history as revelatory of the transcendent will which has created and is governing the world, and this is a price that—whatever the power of tradition in the past—many seem increasingly unwilling to pay. In consequence, although the theistic world-view is as securely based anthropologically as either the religious or secular positions, and although it provides the fullest and most satisfying interpretation of the universe as man's proper "home," it is in serious jeopardy in contemporary life.

V

In this essay I have suggested that theistic, religious, and secular world-views are not simply speculative options open to philosophers seeking to develop theories about the world. On the contrary, they are interpretations of the world with deep roots in our common human nature (as perceived in the West), and they provide frameworks or interpretive contexts within which life as a whole is experienced and lived. Each of us sees the world in terms of one of these world-views, or, more likely, some combination of them. For what I have delineated here are ideal types that are realized in pure form only very rarely if at all. These idealizations, however, expressing leading tendencies or major thrusts, make possible distinguishing clearly the several different theological motifs that may be at work in the "mixed" world-views we find in philosophy and everyday life. The appearance of the word "God" in a man's speech or writing does not always indicate a theistic world-view: it may be the somewhat confused expression of what is otherwise a basically religious position, or it may be the simply perfunctory utterance of a fundamentally secular man. On the other hand, the professions of a robust secularist may upon close examination disclose underlying religious, or even theistic, buttresses (Marxism, for example, with its sense of a teleologically ordered history).

A typology of this sort may serve as a vehicle for deeper self-understanding. Each of us is a thinking/feeling/willing self, and each sees the world as the context within which these several sides of his being find expression. We will attain better understanding of the world-view within which we live and act, and we will achieve a more critical approach to our own conception of the world, if we recognize clearly its anthropological base and its one-sidedness, and if we are aware of the other principal alternatives with their strengths and weaknesses. Doubtless temperamental differences among individuals, and cultural and historical differences among communities, will affect our preferences for this or that world-view. These matters, too, the present analysis helps to make comprehensible, and we are thereby given some measure of critical distance and control over them. The stances in life of selves and communities affect every aspect of experience, thought, and action in subtle ways of which we are often unaware, and analysis and interpretation of the world-views related to these postures is essential to a full understanding of our existence.

10

The Foundations of Belief

Why believe in God? This issue has again become theologically problematic and controversial. One might expect it always to have that status among theologians, but the neo-orthodox period in recent theological history was dominated by the view that this is a matter of "faith," a faith that in itself is neither arguable nor the consequence of an intelligible process of human growth or development but simply the "gift of God." As an inexplicable divine given, it was the datum from which all theology proceeds and which it presupposes; it was not itself to be understood and explained in human terms, certainly not psychologically or sociologically. And all "arguments for the existence of God"—the form in which some members of earlier generations addressed this question—were despised as products of sinful hubris, on the one hand, and as totally unconvincing to "modern man," on the other. But the proclamation that "God is dead!" has made it apparent that the neo-orthodox emperor really had no clothes on and that, therefore, the question of the grounds for belief—whether psychological, sociological, historical, or metaphysical—must once again be openly addressed.

I

I do not propose here to attempt a reformulation of any of the traditional arguments for God's existence. These arguments appear to most men today (myself included) to have little cogency. Moreover, since they are hardly the route by which many persons have come to faith, it is not clear just what light they throw on its actual human grounds or bases; the relationship between the "God" they establish and the God of vital faith has always been obscure. The movement from unfaith to faith[1] is much more subtle and complex than any merely syllogistic argument could possibly reveal—involving matters of feeling and will as well as intellect—and it depends on certain historical and sociological presuppositions which a strictly logical analysis ignores. Yet it is this movement that is the motivating interest behind the arguments, and that, presumably, they were intended to illumine. At any rate, it is this movement to which we shall seek to attend in this paper.

This means that we cannot begin our investigation in the relatively neutral manner of the traditional arguments, simply examining the ordinary experience of the world had by everyman (whether believer or not) and then, through careful analysis, showing how God is presupposed or implied. Rather, we shall have to attend to the peculiarities of the *believer's* situation in the world and the believer's experience and ideas, and see if we can uncover the route through which the movement to that position has occurred. Then we will be in a position to query whether the several steps of that movement were justifiable and also to investigate what kind of justifica-

---

[1] I recognize, of course, that the term "faith" is used in many ways. It may be contended, for example, that all men live by some faith ("ultimate concern") and that, therefore, the question should be formulated so as to ask about the movement from one mode of faith to another, rather than from "unfaith" (with its implication of a complete absence of any faith at all) to "faith." I grant the legitimacy and significance of posing the question in that way for certain purposes. However, it is also important to focus attention directly on the peculiar character of what in the West has generally been regarded as normative or standard faith, namely, faith in "God." For analysis of this problem the dichotomy faith/unfaith is useful. Since it is this problem with which we are especially concerned in this essay, it is this polarity (and the particular meanings of the terms appropriate to it) with which we will be working. It should be understood, of course, that "faith" and "unfaith" in this usage represent "ideal types" or "limiting notions"; it is doubtful they ever appear in pure form in human beings—certainly they do not in the modern pluralistic world (see below).

tion is or would be appropriate for them. Only at that point will we be in a position to suggest the path on which an unbeliever might be expected to set out, if he were interested in moving toward faith in God, and to explore the grounds for such a movement and for the decisions that would be required along the way. This will be as near as we can come to setting forth the foundations of belief in God.

Since we are seeking here to analyze concrete living faith in God, and not some abstract notion of a God-in-general, our attention will necessarily be focused on a particular conception of God, and not on some least common denominator of the various God-ideas of different religions and philosophies. It is the God of Christian faith with which we shall be concerned, and the route to such faith that we shall attempt to explore. This involves no claim that such faith is better or truer than, say, Jewish faith or Hindu faith. Nor is it intended to suggest that what is said here will be of no relevance to understanding other kinds of faith in God (or faith in other gods); there would doubtless be significant similarities, as well as important differences, in the paths traversed by those of other communions and traditions. But these matters could be discussed only after similar concrete analyses of those other standpoints were available to compare with this one. Until such materials are at hand, we simply do not have the data on which to base an interpretation of why men-in-general come to believe in God-in-general; the most that can be done now is try to illumine the question of why some particular individuals and groups—in this case, Christians—have come to believe in (the Christian) God.

Both the nature of the self and the nature of (Christian) faith require this approach to the problem rather than the more traditional sorts of proof for God's existence. In Christian faith God is conceived as Creator and Lord of the world, all things in heaven and earth ultimately belonging to him and existing to serve his purposes. Faith in God, therefore, must be a stance taken up by the whole self, including and shaping its posture toward all the world, toward life, and toward itself: nothing with which the self is concerned is irrelevant to such faith, and no dimension or level of the self can remain unaffected by it. The reality denoted by the word "faith" thus involves far more than mere intellectual appropriation of ("believing") certain ideas, and for this reason no analysis of logical relations between mere ideas ("proofs") will throw much light on the real foundations of faith. Much more relevant will be exploration of how a self comes to acquire or take up the fundamental orientation or stance in life that characterizes it and all its activities. This is shaped not only by the explicit choices, conscious wishes and desires, direct personal experience and thought, and special aptitudes and training of the self; but by the character of the communities and institutions in which the self participates, by the distinctions and emphases of the language and the culture in which the self experiences and thinks, and thus by the history of the society in which the self finds itself, and in certain crucial respects by the significant antecedent histories that have helped shape that society. Selves are not simply self-forming; nor do they gain their structure simply as an autonomous evolution from the biological organism that is their base. They are social and historical realities, largely constituted by their relations to other selves and thus by the communities and histories in which they participate. To understand the orientation or stance of a self decisively determined by "faith in God," it will be necessary to see how the interpersonal and communal relations in which that self stands provide certain indispensable conditions for precisely this posture.

It is clear that "faith in God," or "believing in Jesus Christ," or being persuaded of "God's forgiveness of sins," and the like could happen only to a self in a culture or subculture where such words as "God," "faith," "Jesus Christ," "sin," had fairly distinct meanings and significant uses. Not everyone in a culture that has such words will find them particularly meaningful or significant, that is, appropriate to express or otherwise deal with important dimensions of his own experience, but they must at least be available in the culture as a necessary condition of experience with the particular specification and articulation and description they indicate. Speech about "God," that is to say, will occur only in a culture where "God" is a word

of fairly definite and distinct meaning. These facts provide us
with a beginning point for our investigation, and they suggest
two questions: First, why do those selves (living in such a culture), who in fact speak of "faith" in "God," do so? What
conditions in addition to an appropriate cultural context are
requisite for a self to "believe" in "God"? Second, what is the
specific character of this requisite cultural context? Why and
how did it arise and develop, and how is it sustained?

Since the second of these is presupposed by the first, let us
begin there. I shall not give a full historical description of some
particular period of church history here; that would go far
beyond the limits permissible in a paper of this sort, and in any
case I am not competent for such a task. I will attempt, rather,
to set out certain logical conditions, certain presuppositions
(Collingwood), that must obtain in a given cultural setting
for such words (with something like the meaning[s] they have
come to have in the Christian vocabulary) to have significant
use. These conditions were probably met in some form through
the better part of Western (and biblical) history; today the
matter has become much more complicated.

II

The first and most decisive presupposition of the use of the
term "God" (in the Christian sense) is a certain metaphysical
dualism or duality, an understanding of reality as distinguished
into two fundamental levels or dimensions or orders: "God"
and "the world," the "Creator" and "creation." Moreover, as the
second phrase just cited suggests, these two orders stand in a
quite specific relation to each other: the second depends on the
first for its reality or being, whereas the first has a kind of
independence or self-subsistence.[2] For the term "God" to be-

[2] I cannot take this matter up here, but it should be noted that
certain kinds of metaphysical dualism, such as infinite/finite,
reality/appearance, whole/part, clearly have somewhat different
implications than God/world and Creator/creation, and therefore
cannot be presumed to represent the same metaphysical apprehensions as the last two. A failure to note this and to make careful distinctions on this point has led to much confusion in Western

come usable at all there will have to appear in the language some means of distinguishing these two orders from each other, of giving the appropriate weight and dignity to the first and perceiving the essential dependence and contingency of the second, and of relating the two to each other in proper fashion. This in turn presupposes the development of some (accepted) views of how each order or level is perceived, experienced, or known. Since the whole being of man belongs to the created order (man is "in the world"), and this order also provides the principal content of his experience, the problem of its perception and knowledge is not particularly serious and may even be taken for granted. But for precisely the same reason, the problem of the perception and knowledge of God is acute. Hence theories of the way in which the Creator is known must be developed: God "sends" messengers or prophets to men; he sometimes "visits" men in trances or dreams or special ecstasies; a scripture may be treasured as God's "word" or "revelation" to man; it may be supposed that God was particularly intimate with or in some way present to the forefathers of the community, who have passed down traditions through which he is known. We need not consider at this point whether any of these supposed sources of knowledge of God are valid (or seem valid to us); it is sufficient to recognize that in varying degrees they have been accepted as appropriate bases for such knowledge in communities and cultures where "God" was

---

theological and philosophical thought (for example, the confusion of "religion" and "theism," discussed in Chapter 9). The special closeness of the God/world terminology to the Creator/creation terminology, and the semantic distance of both from other dualistic conceptions, is clearly apparent in our ordinary linguistic usage: it is quite natural to speak of God "creating" the world, but one would hardly say that the whole "creates" its parts, or reality "creates" appearances. The decisive significance of the notion of "creation" for the meaning of "God" in Hebraic-Christian thought was worked out early in the Christian era. See Georges Florovsky, "The Concept of Creation in Saint Athanasius," in *Studia Patristica*, VI, ed. F. L. Cross (Berlin: Akademie Verlag, 1962), 36–57; see also Hans Jonas, "Judaism, Christianity, and the Western Tradition," *Commentary*, 44:61–68 (Nov. 1967).

a living and significant word and where "faith in God" was a reality of everyday life.

Speech about "God," then, presupposes not only awareness of a basic metaphysical duality of a special sort, but also some sensitivity to the special or unusual epistemological problems involved in knowing the more fundamental of these two orders of reality. Indeed, in the traditions descendant from ancient Hebrew culture, it was believed that man, simply of himself and by his own powers, could never have come to know God, the Lord of the world; but that God had taken initiative in this matter, had "chosen" a people as his own, and had made himself known to them through the Torah, through his prophets, and through his "mighty acts" in Israel's history. God was thus seen consistently as a superpersonal Agent who had created the world for his own purposes, who acted in that world that those ends might be achieved, who revealed himself to some and concealed himself from others. In the Christian mythology these motifs were carried to a dramatic climax in the claim that God had come into the world in the form of the particular man, Jesus, and that here, above all, he made himself known. "No one has ever seen God; the only Son, who is in the bosom of the Father, he has made him known" (John 1:18).

This brief outline of certain metaphysical and epistemological presuppositions involved in the typical Christian use of the word "God"[3] helps to clarify some aspects of our question about

[3] I am not contending, of course, that the God/world duality has been a rigid and unchanging form throughout these thousands of years or that there are not real stresses and tensions between the various expressions of this duality. On the contrary, it has appeared in many modes—some vague and indistinct, others sharp and clear; some highly mythological, others metaphysical; some largely intellectual, others more moral or religious. Often it has been qualified by or interpreted in terms of other models of metaphysical duality (see note 2, above), but throughout its long and changing history it has resisted dissolution into any of them. One cannot predict the future history of language and culture with any finality, of course, but it is difficult to see how the word "God" could retain a meaning significantly continuous with its history up to the present, without implying as a central part of its meaning something of the fundamental metaphysical relationship of superordination/subordination as suggested by the Creator/crea-

how men come to believe in God. A cultural development will
have to occur which will make it possible for this particular
kind of metaphysical duality (with its epistemological consequences) to become a virtually unquestioned presupposition of
all experience. Particular experiences, then, will be apprehended as falling within a frame set by the acts of God: his
creative activity, his sustaining and governing activity, his
revelatory and redemptive activity. A person living within such
a setting would interpret his own experiences of a creative or
redemptive sort, particularly those of overwhelming personal
meaning and deep feeling, as manifestations of God's presence
and work, and thus of revelatory significance. Even the seeming counterevidences of natural disaster or historical defeat or
inexplicable suffering could be interpreted as expressing some
hidden or unknown purposes of God, thus also in an oblique
way revealing his presence, activity, and even solicitude. "For
the Lord disciplines him whom he loves" (Heb. 12:6). All life
would be received in anticipation that God was actively at work
there, would be inspected for signs of his presence, and would
be interpreted as evidencing his self-manifestation. Little wonder that the most ordinary men with little or no personal "religious experience" might nevertheless lead lives of genuine
piety and deep faith in God: this was the very form within
which they apprehended themselves and their daily experience
of the world. Much that they experienced, thus, would confirm
their faith to them, and it was only on those rare and unusual
occasions when the ordinary categories supplied by the language and culture did not quite seem to apply, or for certain
rare and unusual individuals, that faith could be seriously
called into question.

---

tion imagery. In this paper, therefore, this specification will be
taken as fundamental to the meaning of the term, although it is
recognized that this also, doubtless, will take forms and modes in
the future that cannot be presently foreseen. (For a full treatment
of the meaning of the notions of "Creator" and "creation," see my
Systematic Theology (New York: Scribner's, 1968), Chaps. 9,
20.)

III

Thus far we have considered faith or belief in God as a cultural pattern that developed in Western history, associated with the institutions and practices of the Christian church. It would be possible, of course, to trace the history behind these patterns and practices back into their Roman, Greek, and especially Hebraic roots, going back finally to primitive religious beliefs and practices; such analysis would give us an answer, on one level, to our question of why (some) men believe (or believed) in God. The outlines of this history are well known, however, and need not be rehearsed here. We shall presuppose them as we proceed to a more direct attack on the principal problem with which we are concerned in this paper: granted this is *how* Western men have come to what they have called "faith," what justification can be offered for such belief?

The way in which this question is to be understood depends on the context in which it arises. On the one hand, it is a question that can originate within the believing culture itself. In that case the question refers to the fact (mentioned above) that knowledge of God is understood to be of an unusual or peculiar character, not as directly available or accessible as knowledge of the world. The answer to the question when posed in this way will be given by referring to prophets or scriptures or visions or other special sources through which it is believed God's revelation has been mediated. Because the reliability of these epistemic sources is generally accepted within the community, they can serve as an ultimate court of appeal for settling disputes about particular claims to knowledge of God. Thus particular claims are "justified" by reference to such sources.

On the other hand, the request to justify a claim about God may arise from outside the community of faith. In such a case it is clearly not adequate simply to refer to the sources which the community itself regards as revelatory and on which it founds its own convictions, for these sources and what is being claimed for them are themselves being called into question. What is the justification for regarding the Bible as God's word?

What is the justification for regarding Amos and Isaiah as God's spokesmen? Why suppose what the Christian community calls "God" is significant or real at all? The request for justification in this sense ordinarily arises only in a pluralistic cultural situation in which two or more somewhat distinctive traditions are in contact with each other, making possible discernment and radical questioning of the fundamental presuppositions of each other. This kind of questioning of the Christian tradition has become most insistent in the modern world where a growing historical consciousness has made Western men aware of the diversity of their cultural roots, where the rapid evolution of culture has given rise to new patterns of socioeconomic order, technological achievement, and scientific theory, and where increasing contacts with other civilizations and societies have heightened sensitivity to and appreciation for religious and cultural traditions different from those dominant in the West.

It has usually been supposed that an answer to this second form of the request for justification will involve either recourse to some sort of rational "proof" of God's existence, comprehensible to and coercive of all rational beings regardless of their cultural tradition, or an attempt, on universal rational, moral, or other grounds, to establish the superiority of the Christian religion over those other religions or humanistic traditions making competing claims. Such procedures, however, ignore the fact (for which I have been contending here) that the fundamental orientation of a self is grounded in a cultural history, not in rational argument, and they fail to attend seriously to the self-awareness of Christian faith that its knowledge of God has in fact come to it through the special *Heilsgeschichte* that gave it birth. It is not surprising, therefore, that they have not been conspicuously successful. We shall attempt to deal here with this problem of justification in a way that is in closer touch both with the Christian self-understanding (and thus the sort of answer ordinarily given in the other context within which the request for justification arises) and with the modern sociopsychological understanding of the social and cultural rootedness of selves.

From this vantage point it would appear that a self justifies its stance in life always by reference to a set of accepted meanings and criteria of meaning made available to it through some tradition at hand in the culture.[4] In pluralistic cultures, however, the problem of justification is complicated because there are available to the self several, perhaps conflicting, traditions of meaning to which it might appeal. Which then should it choose in defining itself and the character of the world in which it takes itself to be living? What criteria for selection among the available alternatives can be constructed? We shall face this question later in this essay. For now it will suffice to note merely that the criteria to be used in such selection cannot be created by the self *de novo:* they also will in some way have to be made available to it through the historical traditions at hand. Meaning and the criteria of meaning are incorrigibly historical, and the justification of a point of view will always involve reference to and the use of some tradition of meaning, or combination of traditions, accessible to the self.

Our immediate problem, then, of the justification of talk about "God" involves two issues: First, what kind of justification for such talk can be provided by the (Christian) tradition at hand in the culture? This will involve examining once again the traditional Christian reference to God's revelation of himself in a particular historical sequence, to see whether indeed such a claim is coherent and in what sense it might be intelligible. Second, what reasons can be given for accepting this reassessed Christian interpretation in preference to other alternative interpretations available in the culture? This will involve some analysis of the sort of "decision" that the movement to faith involves and the bases on which such decision can or should be made.

[4] This is just as true for "rational" or "scientific" forms of justification which make appeal to the significance of "rational proof" and "experimental evidence"—criteria of meaning by no means universally recognized, but relatively recently developed in a particular historical tradition, and a very narrow basis on which to rest the whole structure of "meaning" within which a self can live and die—as for appeal to "the values of democracy," "the revolutionary spirit," patriotic loyalty to the "Fatherland," or any number of other traditions or partial traditions.

IV

The Christian community, we have noted, claims its understanding of God is based on his revelation of himself in the events of Israel's history and particularly in Jesus Christ. What can we make of this? One possible move would be to deny the metaphysical duality that we have seen the notion of "God" presupposes, maintain that "God" is really in some sense part of the world, and then develop a theory of experience and knowledge to explain how we know that part of the world which we have decided to call "God." But this way out (though not an uncommon one) is of course cheating, for it proposes to change the meanings of the terms with which it deals when the particularity and peculiarity of those meanings raises special problems, thus resolving difficulties by refusing to face them.

If it is justification for faith in the Christian God we are seeking, it is with the Christian conception of God that we must deal, and not secretly resort to conquest by redefinition. It is, then, within the framework of the special metaphysical duality indicated by the word "God" that we must work, with its implication that knowledge of God is not directly accessible to man like knowledge of the world. The problem is: how could man, situated within the world and within the historical process, come to know the One who is Creator of the world and Governor of that process, and in that sense "outside" or "beyond" them? It might be possible to "observe" God (so to speak) in his creative and historical work if we were outside the world, at some third point where we could "see" both God and the world on which he was working. This is one way we come to know about the creative and historical activities of finite agents: we observe the carpenter making his table or the painter at work on his canvas, and we see how the artifact is shaped as the agent works at his task. But there is no such third point outside both the world and God from which we can observe him at work; our location is within the world, within the reality which God has created and upon which he is supposed to be working. The question is: how, from this position, would it be possible to come to know him?

A second way in which we know agency, or better, a second dimension of our knowledge of agency, is through our own experience as agents. We are aware of setting purposes for ourselves, and then carrying them through; we have painted pictures and built benches, have read books and practiced scales on the piano, and through our efforts we have achieved goals previously posited. But this sort of knowledge of agency is of no help either in dealing with the problem of the knowledge of God: at best this might throw some light on God's knowledge of himself and his purposes, but surely not on man's knowledge of him.

The third dimension of our knowledge of agency is our awareness of the activity of other agents upon us. The child, hearing the father's reprimand and seeing the raised hand, easily associates the sudden pain in his behind with his father's act. From the mother's tender care during infancy to the complicated maneuverings in a chess game or a political or social process, we are the recipients or patients of the actions of others upon us. Here, it would seem, is our closest finite cognitive analogy to the knowledge of God's agency, for we are within, and a part of, that world upon which he is alleged to be acting; we are recipient of his activity. Yet, at precisely the crucial point, the analogy fails: for God, unlike our fellows, cannot be directly observed in his action upon us; at most, the consequences of his acts can be felt. But then, how are we to know that they are *his* acts, and not simply the pressures of those other creatures in whose midst we find ourselves and through whom he is said to be acting? We are left with the problem with which we have been struggling all along: by what criterion can any particular event be recognized as not merely an ordinary event but an act of *God*? How does one ever know that *God* is the agent behind the act? Or, to state the problem in terms of the traditional media through which God was alleged to "reveal" himself: How does one know that the prophet was sent by God, or that the scripture is his word? How does one know that the movements of Assyria are to be referred to Yahweh's anger (Isa. 10:5) and not merely to the imperialistic ambitions of the Assyrian emperor?

It is clear that the knowledge of God, whether for Isaiah, for Luther, or for us cannot arise simply and directly and completely out of some particular event or experience—some alleged epiphany or encounter—in which God is directly known. Visions, or messages of moral condemnation, or aggressive movements of military powers will be seen as the media through which God is working out his purposes *only if we bring the idea of God as Creator of the world and Lord of history to the experience of those media,* apprehending and interpreting the actual events of our experience in terms of that presupposition. That is, *the knowledge of God is given more in the presuppositions (the faith) with which experience is apprehended and interpreted than with the particularities or details of experience itself.* This agrees directly with our earlier conclusion (p. 233), except that now we can see this fact as not merely a historical or sociological explanation of faith, but as properly descriptive of the epistemic situation that must obtain if there is to be knowledge of God at all. If it is *God* who is to be known, he cannot be encountered simply as one of the objects in the world; though encountered through experience, he must be apprehended as the One behind all the objects in the world and transcending the world itself. Just as our knowledge of "world" or "universe" is not given in some particular experience of a particular object called "world," but is given in and through and with and behind all our particular experiences—it develops as one of the fundamental presuppositions with which we come to mature experience and by means of which we order it into a unified whole—so our apprehension of the One behind the world can only be in and through and with and behind all of the particularities, and identified with none. This reality also is more of the order of presupposition than direct object of knowledge. In particular (as I argued in Chapter 5), it is a *practical* presupposition that informs and makes intelligible certain forms of life or postures of the self or modes of action.

Thus men come to know God and to know of him only in the

indirect way of coming to presuppose his being and purposes in the interpretation of their experience, not through direct encounter. It is their possession of such categories as holy, divine, God's revelation, act of God, leading them to give "theological" interpretations to the particular feelings they have upon occasion—as well as to the momentous events of their lives and the turning points of their histories—that enables them to speak of God. Knowledge that arose simply and directly out of particular events or experiences would be knowledge of precisely those particularities, not of the God who transcends all events and experiences. From this we can conclude that the only way men could come to know God or to know of God would be for these presuppositions and categories to be formed in their consciousness. Stated from the side of God (as his problem in revealing himself to man): God must find a way, not of encountering man directly, but of developing a presuppositional framework in human consciousness that will make it possible for men to grasp their experience not only in worldly terms but as enclosed within God's activity; a society must develop within human history in whose culture reference to God begins to function as a fundamental presupposition by means of which the selves in that culture grasp and interpret all their experience. God's activity of revealing himself, then, will be nothing else than the appearance within human history of a society that sees life in these terms, and the history of revelation will be the history of these emerging categories. From this point of view the history—including the prehistory—of Israel can be understood as the development through which God gradually revealed himself, not because this is a history filled with epiphanies and miracles which no longer occur, but because this is a history in which faith in God became an effective presupposition for ordering and understanding all experience.[5]

This argument, of course, does not in any way *prove* that the God of the universe was making himself known through the events of Israel's history. What it does maintain is that if there is such a God, and if man is to come to know him, it would have to be through some such historicocultural develop-

[5] See Chapter 7, above, for elaboration of these points.

ment of faith as that which we find in Israel's history. Not through any and every sort of presuppositional development could God become known: only through a development in which the Creator/creation duality began to function significantly, and experience began to be articulated in its terms.

Once the basic categoreal scheme had emerged historically, then all that remained for God's revelation to be completed— for the knowledge of God (so far as that knowledge could be available to man at all) to reach some kind of definiteness and adequacy—was the occurrence of an event, or the appearance of a person, which could serve as the definitive image or paradigm giving specificity and definite content to the concept of God. With the appearance of such a paradigm the revelatory process proper would have reached its goal; what remained to be done would be the spreading of its effects to other cultural traditions and later historical periods (until this presupposition became effective in all cultures). To Christian faith the appearance of Jesus Christ marks both these developments: the emergence of a definitive paradigm in terms of which God himself is understood (this is the meaning of the claim that Christ was "the image of the invisible God" [Col. 1:15]),[6] and the beginning of the universalization of the parochial God of Jewish history to become a God worshiped by peoples of many nations and cultures and backgrounds. This, once again, no more establishes the truth of the Christian claim about the definitiveness of God's revelation in Christ than our earlier argument established the truth of Israel's claim to be God's "chosen people." It simply means that if men were ever to come to what could properly be called knowledge of God, some definitive event or person as paradigm for that knowledge would have to appear, since a direct encounter with and apprehension of God is not possible; that is, something like what Christian faith claims has happened would have to occur.

We have established then, not that Israel's or the church's

---

[6] Cf.: "He who has seen me has seen the Father . . . . I am in the Father and the Father in me" (John 14:9–10); "He [the Son] reflects the glory of God and bears the very stamp of his nature" (Heb. 1:3).

claims are true, but that they are at least intelligible; for the kind of history of which they speak would seem to be precisely the requisite, if knowledge of *God*—that which the word "God" designates—were to become possible to man. We must turn, now, to the second problem noted above: Why, among all the presuppositional frameworks presented us by our pluralistic culture, should this one be accepted as true or right? What kinds of decisions and steps would be involved in the movement from, for example, a secular stance to "belief" in the "God" spoken of in Christian faith?

V

It should be clear from the foregoing that an answer to these questions is not to be sought through some kind of "proof" that the Christian God exists. We are asking, now, about the validity or desirability of the fundamental orientation or stance of a self in the world, about the fundamental presupposition(s) with which a self approaches, apprehends, and interprets all its experience and thought; we are not dealing with the question whether one more object within the world or within experience exists. Accordingly it would not be appropriate to deal with this problem through, for example, analyzing certain sense data or other experiences and determining what sort of inferences might be made from them. Nor would it be proper to expect this problem to be soluble by reference to the so-called criterion of falsifiability: since (from within the Christian perspective) experience is framed and ordered by theological presuppositions, it is difficult to see how any particular experiences could be expected to refute those presuppositions.[7] Moreover, an attempt to move from an

[7] This is not a problem peculiar to theological presuppositions. No framework of presuppositions, giving experience the basic categories and forms through which the selves living within it apprehend, order, and interpret what happens to them, is subject to falsification or disconfirmation of any ordinary sort. For an interesting exposition and confirmation of this thesis, which shows how our scientific knowledge also is caught up in this problem of fundamental presuppositions or paradigms giving experience its

analysis of experience to a justification of the presuppositions that frame it (in the manner of the so-called arguments for the existence of God) begs the question: if A has experience in certain forms he will, of course, find those forms presupposed by it; but B, who has his experience in other categories, will not find A's basic forms presupposed at all.[8] If argument is to be given for the desirability or appropriateness of a particular configuration of fundamental presuppositions of experience, it will have to take a form different from any of those usually suggested.

We are confronted here with two issues: What is the nature of the transition from unfaith to faith, from one presuppositional framework to another? Why might a self wish to pass through such a transition? Some analogies illuminate the first question. We are dealing here with the movement of a self from one fundamental sort of orientation to another. In what sorts of situations does this occur? One example might be a radical change of vocation. A man, having prepared himself in college and professional school for a medical career and having become a successful surgeon, gives it all up for an entirely different form of life; for example, he decides to retreat into the woods to live an isolated life in a small cottage,

---

basic order and determining the very questions that can be put, see Thomas S. Kuhn, *The Structure of Scientific Revolutions* (Chicago: University of Chicago Press, 1962). Kuhn shows in detail how difficult it is to move from an accepted framework or paradigm to a new one, even though the older pattern has ceased functioning effectively. In many cases it has been difficult, even for brilliant scientific investigators, to see that many of their problems arose from the *framework within which they were operating* rather than their failure to grasp or understand or properly analyze the particular issues with which they were dealing. In this case a revolutionary (and almost inexplicable) leap to a new framework or basic paradigm was required before the proper issues could be clearly discerned and attacked.

[8] This is true whether one proceeds from a general analysis of "the contingency of finite being" (cosmological argument), from a consideration of the presuppositions of our thought (ontological argument), from an analysis of the types and presuppositions of order in experience (teleological arguments), or from a consideration of specific forms of value (for example, the so-called moral argument).

supporting himself by hunting, fishing, and gardening. Such sharp changes of vocation, though not common, certainly occur. When they do, the whole form of a man's life changes. The people he associates with, the objectives he strives for, the way he spends his time, the things he thinks about—all undergo radical transformation. If he takes up the new form of life permanently, the habits and daily patterns that give his self structure and order become re-formed, and he, very literally, becomes a considerably different man than he was before, though of course there remain significant continuities.

A similar, though perhaps more radical, sort of transformation occurs when one elects to leave his homeland and native culture to spend his life in the midst of another people of strange customs, beliefs, and practices, for example, the European colonists of the seventeenth and eighteenth centuries going out into a new world or the Christian missionaries of the nineteenth century making their homes with "heathen" whose forms of life and faith were radically different from their own. In cases like these it may become necessary to adapt oneself to new and peculiar economic and political practices, as well as to find a place for oneself in a strange social order. The new language teaches one to apprehend and appreciate different aspects of experience formerly unnoticed, and the roles one is called upon to play give him a new understanding of his self in relation to those with whom he is interacting. And so one comes to be a different person, leading a different life, cherishing different values, working toward different objectives, thinking different thoughts. The whole social and cultural matrix of life has changed, and since the self is in large measure shaped by its cultural setting and its patterns of social interaction, the self changes with it. One comes gradually to adopt a new presuppositional framework within which one has his experience.

From these examples we can see both *that* changes in the basic stance of a self occur and something of *how* they occur. They come about through the self's moving into a new socio-cultural setting, which, in the course of time, radically reforms or reshapes it. Deliberate decision by the self is often involved in such a movement, but usually this is not a decision to become a new self, or a decision to adopt a new presuppositional framework, but rather the decision to place oneself in a new geographical, vocational, social, or cultural setting. The transformation of the self and its framework of interpretation follows more or less unconsciously, arising almost automatically out of the new patterns of interaction that develop in the new environment. Moreover, the decision of the self to move into the new setting is seldom made on the basis of adequate or full knowledge of the life it will lead there; such knowledge could be acquired only after the self had already lived that life for some years and become accustomed to it. (Certainly this decision is not made on the basis of some rational assessment of the adequacy or validity of the presuppositional framework within which one will come eventually to have his experience in the new setting.) The decision is made, rather, on the basis of somewhat sketchy and fragmentary reports or intimations of the new possibilities that will open up, on the one hand, and because of dissatisfaction with the self's present situation, on the other. Like Abraham, the self moves away from its familiar environs, not really knowing into what kind of situation it is going (Heb. 11:8). In such movements the self acts more on the basis of hope than knowledge. For hope is that stance of the self toward a particular future which makes possible acceptance of its openness and unknownness as positive and inviting, rather than as so threatening or simply uninteresting as to forestall all movement toward it. The movement to a new setting arises more out of the self's hopes about that setting than it does out of concrete knowledge of the new life that can and will be lived there.

Let us return now to the problem of the movement from unfaith to faith. It is similar to the kinds of transition just sketched in the following respects: First, this movement will involve a fundamental reorienting of the self, giving it a different presuppositional framework through which it has its experience. Second, the full information or knowledge that might justify such a movement is not available to the self before the event, but can become available only after the self has become habituated to its new situation and apprehends in some significant degree its experience in the new categories; thus the movement is made possible more by hope than by knowledge. Third, for this reason it is grounded in certain respects in decisions of the self, the deliberate setting of the self to move into the unknown and unproven despite the ambiguity or absence of sufficient "rational evidence" (the so-called "leap of faith"). Fourth, deliberate decisions and actions of the self can, however, only move it into a new social context and cultural setting (such as the church, with its special ethos), within which the reordering of the self may occur; the self cannot directly produce such a fundamental reordering of its presuppositions simply by decision.

There is also an important difference between our examples and the movement to faith, at least for most of us in contemporary pluralistic Western society. The "new world" to which we are invited to move in this case is not entirely new to us. We already participate (in varying degrees) in different aspects of the Christian ethos, and we thus already possess in certain respects the presuppositional framework called faith. But at the same time, we participate in other traditions very much alive in our culture, which have taught us to apprehend and evaluate our experience without reference to what Christians call "God," which, indeed, stand in direct contradiction to and call into serious question the Christian presuppositions. We are not so much refugees from one society about to set sail for a new world of promise and hope as men with one foot—perhaps most of both feet—in a secular experiential order, and at the same time with a kind of slipping toehold in faith. Moreover, such experience as we have already had with the Christian presuppositions may have served more to dampen our hopes than to whet our appetites for the life available when experience is ordered by faith in God. Unlike pilgrims looking forward to their life in a new country, we may already know enough about the land of faith not to have very high expectations about what will be found there; indeed, we may find ourselves inclined to turn toward other traditions of meaning (in which we also participate) as more likely to be valid and significant contexts within which to lead our lives. The movement from unfaith to faith (or vice versa) involves more a shifting of emphasis within the self—from one internalized tradition of meaning to another coexisting but inconsistent tradition—than an external movement of the self as a whole from one environment to another.

Thus, this movement, though analogous to those examples given above, is somewhat more complex. This is not, however, as is often thought to be the case, because our examples have dealt with intramundane movements, while the appearance of faith in God involves a kind of movement away from this world. In both cases the self remains in the world, a part of the finite order. But in the one case it lives in this world aware, perhaps, that it is finite but not that it is a creature and thus under a Creator; in the other it leads its worldly life, has its experience, orients itself, with reference to God.

The movement to faith for the man immersed in a pluralistic culture, finding himself ordering his experience in diverse (and sometimes mutually contradictory) ways, will consist of a gradual but deliberate and increasing shifting of weight from one's "secular" foot toward the toehold in Christian tradition, a deliberate attempt to orient oneself increasingly with reference to the Christian framework for grasping the world and interpreting experience. As with any movement toward a new presuppositional framework, however, this can be accomplished only indirectly: one cannot simply decide to have faith in God, repressing by main force all tendencies toward unbelief, and it is psychologically disastrous to attempt this. What one can do—like any immigrant into a new society —is begin to learn the language of the Christian community by entering directly into discourse with those who find it useful and meaningful, participate increasingly in the memories and traditions of that community so that one begins to apprehend its history as one's own and begins to see one's own past in the wider context provided by that history, and enter into the activities and work of the community so that one comes to grasp and understand oneself and one's experience in terms

of the categories and roles of that society, in short, as a
"child of God" seeking to work in his "kingdom."

No one can promise that such deliberate participation in
the life, history, and work of the Christian community will
result in that reorientation of the self toward God which is
called "faith." The empirical Christian community into which
one seeks to move is no foreign land, isolated from the rest of
culture and uninfluenced by those secular traditions that
compete with faith within the individual. It too is confused
and at odds with itself; it too is a living process of change the
outcome of which is unclear. Indeed, the vitality and self-
consciousness of many actual Christian churches today is so
low that it is doubtful they can lay sufficiently powerful
demands on their participants effectively to reorient the presuppositional framework within which they have their experience. And that is certainly a main reason why faith seems so
dubious and problematical to many nominal Christians. Nevertheless, it is in the traditions specially borne by this community—if anywhere—that words like "faith," "Jesus Christ,"
and "God" have the use with which we are here concerned,
and it will be only within this community, therefore, or in
connection with some institution or outreach of it, that the
mode of existence they express and the presuppositional
framework they indicate can be acquired. Hence if our earlier
analysis of the historical and communal presuppositions of
faith was sociologically and psychologically correct, it is
important—if Christian faith is to survive—for the church to
become a more disciplined and responsible community in
which the members genuinely covenant with each other and
with God to speak the Christian language, participate in the
Christian history, and work responsibly at the task of the
Christian community in the world.

In a time when quasi-Christian presuppositions held more or
less universal sway in the culture of the West—so much so
that the culture could reasonably be called "Christendom"—
deliberate and self-conscious covenanting together to be Christian was perhaps not essential to ensure that the fundamental
Christian presuppositions would provide the framework in

which men apprehended and interpreted their experience. But in our pluralistic situation, where we live continually with many and contradictory demands upon us, such deliberate and self-conscious willing to be Christian would seem essential: this is the day, if ever there was one, for the church as a voluntary association of men and women who commit themselves to each other and to the God of Christian faith.

I am not calling here for a new pietism in which Christians seek to repress, in psychically unhealthy fashion, every tendency toward worldly thought, feeling, or action. On the contrary, I am suggesting that the tradition of meaning by which one's self and one's life are oriented should be consciously reflected upon, and the community and tradition one desires to be dominant should be chosen deliberately and responsibly. In such reflection and choice what is wanted is not an attempt heteronomously to repress or suppress the "secular" side of the self's experience and activity in the name of "religious" or "theistic" feeling and conviction, but rather a liberating movement of the self as it seeks to overcome the tensions between mutually inconsistent internalized presuppositional frameworks through a free activity of reeducating or re-forming itself into a more consistent and integral whole. Such a movement of the self toward integrity and wholeness may, of course, be in a direction opposite from theistic faith; the self may seek to overcome its internal tensions and contradictions through divesting itself, as far as possible, of the theistic presuppositional framework partially informing its experience, thus becoming more explicitly secular (or possible more "religious," in the sense explored in Chapter 9). But no matter which direction, the movement may well be deliberate and need not be repressive or unhealthy. The movement toward faith in God (as well as toward unfaith) is genuinely liberating for the self only when it expresses an honest search for integrity and wholeness in experience and life.

In a time when man is coming of age, it is only natural that he should be increasingly free to choose the community in which he will search for meaning and will give himself in his most fundamental loyalty. The pluralism of traditions of meaning makes available such freedom to us in a way seldom true in the past. But with this gain in human freedom and responsibility goes a corresponding price in the understanding of faith in God: in a pluralistic setting of this sort "faith" will not be so much knowledge of God—that he exists and what he is—as a deliberate and voluntary commitment to God (and the community that speaks of him) and hope for increasing reorientation of the self and its fundamental categories of experience, so that God will become the deepest and most fundamental presupposition of its existence and self-understanding. In this sense, as expressing more a life-policy than possession of an esoteric item of information, the phrase, "I believe in God," may still be affirmed.[9] Commitment, hope, loyalty: it is in these terms that faith can best be understood in our time.

VI

We have now characterized the stance of faith in God (for our own time as well as for earlier periods of a more integral Christendom); we have considered sociological and psychological dimensions of that stance, and we have said something about its metaphysical and epistemological presuppositions; and we have examined the sociopsychological movement involved in the transition from unfaith to faith. It remains to consider why anyone might embark on such a movement. (This is the proper form of our initial too rationalistically formulated question of why men do, or should, believe in God.)

We may ask ourselves: Why do men ever seek a new community as their home? Why do they search for a new form of life or a new understanding of themselves? As we noted earlier, it is because of dissatisfaction with their present situation and a certain attractiveness of the new possibility before them. Christian faith in God has always been introduced to men as a *gospel,* as good news about the possibility of a genuine, full, and meaningful human life. "I came that they may have life, and have it abundantly" (John 10:10). It is

[9] See Chapter 5, note 26.

this possibility that is held out to men caught in the dilemmas and contradictions and murderous struggles of existence. Hope that participation in this community and this history will lead to a reorientation of and a new life for the self is the real ground for those decisions taken by a self to associate more closely with the Christian community, to appropriate the Christian history, and to take responsibility for God's work in the world. Few, if any, become Christians by first asking, "Why believe in God?" and then, having been given convincing reasons, simply taking up the stance of faith. That is not how selves appropriate the contexts of meaning within which they live, and in terms of which they have such experience of the world and understanding of themselves as they come to have. Such appropriation occurs rather through deliberate association of oneself with a community and a frame of orientation in which one hopes to find his place in the world. This is the most fundamental kind of issue a self ever faces, and it can be resolved only through exercise of the full powers of the self—will and feeling, as well as reason—for it is the whole self, and not merely the mind, that must find its proper home here.

We can see without difficulty how attractive from this point of view Christian faith might be to moderns. It is not easy for the self to feel "at home" in the world we know today through science. The natural process seems almost completely indifferent to our specifically human concerns for justice, meaning, and freedom; it is an onrushing flow and complex order of material energies, which have, because of peculiarly fortunate circumstances on this planet, chanced to produce life and finally man. But neither man's being nor his projects seem to have any grounding in the ultimate foundations of things, so far as we know them scientifically. Man has been granted a small space of time on this earth to make for himself a world of meaning and value, and this order which he has created is that for which he lives, but it cannot be long before all his work will be carelessly wiped away as the cosmic process that has accidentally brought him into being proceeds just as accidentally to destroy him. In such a world man is a refugee and stranger with no proper and secure home. He can only make the best of things until the impersonal cosmic doom falls.

In contrast to this perspective we can see why the Christian claim that ultimate reality is *God*—creative, purposive, loving, personal being—can have profound meaning for selves. For it signifies that impersonal cosmic order is not in fact the most fundamental context within which we exist: that order itself exists for the realization of (God's) personal purpose and thus has meaning. And the appearance and life of man within that order is no mere cosmic accident or surd; it was itself purposed by the Creator of this world as a kind of climax or completion to his creative work (Gen. 1). For faith, then, this universe—earth, at any rate—is no strange and threatening place within which alien spirit can at best find only a temporary resting place before doom falls: it is, rather, man's proper home, the context purposed for him and his existence by the loving God. And the events of human life and history, in their "natural" just as much as in their "cultural" aspects, are expressions of the sovereign love of Father God. It is not difficult to feel the strong appeal that such a framework for self-understanding and the interpretation of experience can provide: in such a perspective the self can appropriate its life and world with great freedom and creativity, openness and love. A world under God does indeed offer the possibility of "abundant life."

This way of putting the matter, however, is misleading. For it suggests that the principal reason for believing in God is because one *wants* to, because it makes life more comfortable and pleasant than the cold impersonality of a nontheistic world. Thus, the fundamental problem of the self seems here to be resolved anthropocentrically, in terms of the wants and desires of man for self-fulfillment and emotional security. But faith in God means something quite different from that—and this is part of the profound importance of the Creator/creation duality which I earlier argued was an indispensable ingredient of the meaning of the word "God." To believe in God is to believe there is a basic intentionality at work in the cosmos quite independent of man's purposive activity, and that the world and man, in the last analysis, exist for and serve these purposes of God. The metaphysical duality preserves and underlines the fact (as faith sees it) that man cannot be understood and find fulfillment simply in terms of himself and his own needs and desires: he exists for purposes rooted beyond himself and beyond this world, and only in and through orientation to those purposes will he find the fulfillment for which he was created. "You are not your own" (1 Cor. 6:19). The movement of the self toward faith in God is thus not a simple one, like the movements toward a more integral selfhood involved in the appropriation of other (either "secular" or "religious") presuppositional frameworks. The sharp distinction between God and the world means that this movement will have to be highly dialectical: the self will find its fulfillment, not simply through seeking it for its own sake, but only through giving up its anthropo- and egocentrism and becoming centered on its Creator. "Whoever seeks to gain his life will lose it, but whoever loses his life will preserve it" (Luke 17:33). "But seek first his kingdom and his righteousness, and all these things shall be yours as well" (Matt. 6:33). In the perspective of faith man's freedom and purposiveness acquire the profoundest possible meaning, for here they do not exist as alien in a totally impersonal world but they fall within the context of God's own purposes and freedom. But precisely this implies that God has a freedom and purposiveness over against and independent of man, that he is Creator and Lord, that man is creature and servant. This essential duality, as we have seen, is intrinsic to the meaning of the word "God"; "faith in God" designates the orientation of selves and communities in a world that is determined and given its deepest meaning by it.

The movement to a new orientation is always motivated by the desire of the self to better its circumstances, that is, it is self-centered; but in this case the new orientation promises such fulfillment only on condition that the desires of the self be subordinated to purposes grounded completely independently of the self and its wishes, to the will of God. For this reason some Calvinists went so far as to say that we must be willing even to be damned for the glory of God: only in giving up completely desires for self-fulfillment is real fulfillment gained.

What can we say, now, on our initial question about the grounds of belief in this God? I have tried to show that this problem is ordinarily posed in an improper and misleading way. The "knowledge of God" is not given (even to those who have it) as is our knowledge of the ordinary objects of experience; it is given, rather, in the form of certain basic presuppositions (faith) about life and the world, with which experience is approached, apprehended, and interpreted. This being the case, to the extent that these presuppositions are our own they of course appear *true* (to life and to experience); indeed, "God" appears as the fundamental reality on which all existence is based and without which it would be inconceivable.[10] The self, its experience, its world are all apprehended as having their meaning on the ground of this most fundamental presupposition, and hence it is unthinkable to call this presupposition into radical question. There is no point within faith from which leverage for such questioning could be obtained. For faith, the "grounds of belief in God" are drawn from the widest reaches of experience and thought, and it is this that the so-called arguments for the existence of God seek to make explicit.

To the extent, however, that our actual experience is not ordered in terms of the presupposition about God, it being apprehended and interpreted in other ("secular" or "religious") categories, the various dimensions of life and the world have

[10] At this point I differ rather sharply with R. G. Collingwood. I have learned much from his doctrine of "absolute presuppositions," and the position stated in this paper has much in common with his view. I cannot, however, concur in his position that it is improper to inquire whether absolute presuppositions are true, since they are only "presupposed" (*Essay on Metaphysics* [Oxford: Clarendon Press, 1940], Chaps. 4–5). Insofar as we are conscious of our absolute presuppositions at all, it is hard to see why we would presuppose them unless we thought them in some significant sense true. Certainly that is the case with the presupposition about God, with which we are concerned in this paper, for here the self is not concerned simply with a heuristic device to deal with some aspect of experience; it is concerned with its true and proper home in the world.

their meaning essentially without reference to him. (Perhaps their meaning is thought to be intrinsic; perhaps it is thought to derive from some bare "ground of being" or "form of the Good" or other metaphysical resource.) Accordingly, there appear to be no clear grounds for belief in God, either in experience or in thought. That is, there appear to be no clear reasons given in this presuppositional framework of experience for holding "God" to be part of—indeed, the single indispensable feature of—one's way of apprehending all of life and the world. Since, in those regions of experience in which such presuppositional frameworks are dominant, they are the ones which appear "true," it also seems true here that there is no good reason for believing in God.

Those of us who, because of the pluralistic bases of the frameworks of meaning that orient our selves, stand with one foot in theistic faith and one in a-theism, will, it should be clear, simply be unable to deal with the truth of the God-presupposition in direct fashion. For that can be done only either from within faith or from without, and the answers one obtains from these differing vantage points will be opposite.[11] There is no merely intellectual or conceptual bridge

[11] J. J. C. Smart seems to be making a similar point when he suggests that the question of God's existence cannot properly arise either within the language of faith or without it. "The word 'God' gets its meaning from the part it plays in religious speech and literature, and in religious speech and literature the question of existence does not arise . . . any more than the question 'Do electrons exist?' arises within physics. Outside religion the question 'Does God exist?' has as little meaning as the question 'Do electrons exist?' as asked by the scientifically ignorant" ("The Existence of God," in Antony Flew and Alasdair MacIntyre, *New Essays in Philosophical Theology* [London: SCM Press, 1955], p. 41). From the fact that the question "Does God exist?" does not properly arise within either the language of faith or unfaith, Smart draws the conclusion, however, that it is not a "proper question" at all and presumably can be ignored. But this is a mistake. For, as I have been arguing, there are many today who speak both the language of faith (on some occasions or with reference to some aspects of experience) and of unfaith (in other connections). For such persons the question does arise as a highly personal and important issue that must in some way be resolved if they are to avoid schizophrenia. To realize that there is no

from one position to the other. The way in which such a movement is made, I have been contending, is not via argument or
proof, but rather by commitment of the self, movement into
a new sociocultural situation, and resolve to take up the stance
appropriate to that position. "Whoever has the will to do the
will of God shall know whether my teaching comes from him
or is merely my own" (John 7:17 NEB). Only from within a
stance subscribing to a given frame of presuppositions can
they be apprehended as "true."

The "foundations of belief in God" are, therefore, twofold:
first, the self's participation in and life as a member of the
believing community; and second, the whole meaningful experience of life and the world, apprehended and interpreted
within the frame of orientation the self has appropriated from
that community.

---

natural domain of our language within which this question can
properly arise does not dissolve it, as Smart seems to suppose.
Quite the contrary: it helps to explain the extreme poignancy and
urgency of this existential issue. For it now becomes clear that
every attempt even to frame this question linguistically or con-
ceptually will be artificial and imprecise and in many respects
unsatisfactory and unclear. The problem emerges from deeper
cleavages in the self than we can grasp in our conscious intro-
specting and intellectualizing, and its resolution, therefore, cannot be accomplished simply through logical analysis or argu-
mentation.

11

The Secular Utility of "God-Talk"

In previous chapters we have explored the conceptions of transcendence and God in some detail. We have been concerned particularly with discerning the meaning that these notions can have for contemporary faith, in face of the growing secularity of Western culture and the claims of some philosophers that they are simply unintelligible. In all this we have been trying to gain a clearer understanding of the bases for belief in God. I am far from claiming that these difficult problems have been dealt with thoroughly or completely, but perhaps enough has been said to make clear the basic outlines of a theistic position. In this concluding essay I wish to move away somewhat from the positions and problems of faith to a consideration of the significance of the word "God"—or the "available God"—for secular man living in a secular culture. What is to be argued here will not, of course, be without importance for faith, and in that respect this chapter will add certain emphases to what has been said up to this point about the meaning of "God-talk," but its main intention will be to show that the word "God" has significance as a cultural symbol and tool of self-understanding whether we are believers or not.

It is important that we be clear that it is the *secular* significance of "God" with which we are here concerned. It is of course true that the word "God" is both the highest and weightiest term of our several Western religious traditions and that it is especially under religious or theistic auspices that this word is most frequently solemnly pronounced. I do not in any way wish to deny the importance of these usages or disparage their significance. God is the supreme object of worship in church and synagogue and much—perhaps the deepest and most far-reaching meaning that this concept has in our culture—is to be discovered only in the attitude of devotion and prayer. But the word "God" has not only this private and parochial use in our society, and it does not have a merely parochial or private significance. It is a word in ordinary and everyday English, to be found in every dictionary and known and understood by every speaker of the language. It is imprinted on our coins and uttered as part of the pledge of allegiance;[1] it appears in casual oaths as well as desperate cries for help; it carries overtones of value and meaning and significance for ignorant and cultured, secular and believing, alike, whether it is thought to designate that reality most surely to be believed in, or that superstition most certainly to be repudiated. "God" is a word that all Westerners know and understand, one of the most momentous and weighty in our language; it is a word that has helped move men to the vilest of crimes as well as the most inspired acts of devotion and self-giving. As Martin Buber has remarked:

> . . . it is the most heavy-laden of all human words. None has become so soiled, so mutilated. Just for this reason I may not abandon it. Generations of men have laid the burden of their anxious lives upon this word and weighed it to the ground; it lies in the dust and bears their whole burden. The races of man with their religious factions have torn the word to pieces; they have killed for it and died for it, and it bears their finger-marks and their blood. Where might I find a word like it to describe the highest! If I took the purest, most sparkling concept from the inner treasure-chamber of the philosophers, I could only capture

[1] For analysis of the more than perfunctory significance of such references, see Robert Bellah's reflections in "Civil Religion in America," *Dædalus*, 96:1–21 (1967).

thereby an unbinding product of thought. I could not cap-
ture the presence of Him whom the generations of men
have honoured and degraded with their awesome living
and dying. I do indeed mean Him whom the hell-tormented
and heaven-storming generations of men mean. Certainly,
they draw caricatures and write "God" underneath; they
murder one another and say "in God's name". . . And just
for this reason is not the word "God," the word of appeal,
the word which has become a *name,* consecrated in all
human tongues for all times? We must esteem those who
interdict it because they rebel against the injustice and
wrong which are so readily referred to "God" for authoriza-
tion. But we may not give it up . . . We cannot cleanse the
word "God" and we cannot make it whole; but, defiled and
multilated as it is, we can raise it from the ground and set
it over an hour of great care.[2]

I

How, now, shall we lay hold of the secular significance of
the notion of God? A convenient place to begin is with the
meaning the word has simply as a part of the English language.
For here is the common ground on which all English-speaking
people meet, the common reservoir of meaning from which we
all draw, the common articulation of experience and reality
which we all use.

The word of course has a double use in English. On the one
hand there is the common noun "god" (spelled with a small g),
used to refer to the various deities of polytheistic pantheons or
of different religions. The Oxford English Dictionary defines
"god" in this sense as referring to "A superhuman person . . .
who is worshipped as having power over nature and the for-
tunes of mankind." On the other hand the word "God" (spelled
with a capital G) is a proper name designating, in Western
cultures which have been so heavily influenced by Judaeo-
Christian monotheistic traditions, "the One object of supreme

[2] *Eclipse of God* (London: Gollancz, 1953), pp. 17–18.

adoration; the Creator and Ruler of the Universe."[3] These two uses—as common noun and proper name—of course are not entirely separable: for Western men the only true god is *God,* and all the other gods are mere idols.

Analysis of these brief dictionary definitions will enable us to uncover some of the principal functions the notion of God has served, and can still serve, in Western culture. But before we turn to that I want to emphasize that these functions which we will be examining are not dependent on our "believing in God," or our "being religious," or anything of that sort. They rather define fundamental forms in which our thought and experience as Western men is cast, whether we are believers or not; and they can help us thus to isolate issues and questions with which we must deal in some way, willy-nilly, and which it is better, more rational, for us to face explicitly and openly, rather than allowing ourselves simply to be determined by them unconsciously. Although modern secular men have been able to cast doubt upon and to discard many of the beliefs to which their forefathers subscribed, and in terms of which they interpreted their experience, they have not been able to move completely beyond the theological questions that certain of those beliefs articulated and illuminated. The word "God," even in its diminished use and vitality in contemporary secular culture, still has sufficient force to help isolate and analyze these issues, and for this reason, as we shall see, theological analysis and conceptualization are still important secular tasks.

Upon what issues, now, does "God" help us to focus clearly? We may begin with the familiar identification of God as "the Creator and Ruler of the Universe." This commonplace signifies that whatever else may be meant by the word "God," he is at least to be regarded as the source and foundation of all that exists and the basis of the order we find in the world and in ourselves. The word thus refers us to the ultimate or fundamental reality with which we have to do, not some relatively superficial level of experience or parochial aspect of the world.

[3] *A New English Dictionary on Historical Principles,* ed. J. A. H. Murray *et al.* (Oxford: Clarendon Press, 1888–1928), IV, 2d Half, 267–268.

Whether one "believes" in God or not has nothing to do with the fact that this is what the word designates; nor does it in any way affect the seriousness of the question about the ultimately real. This question we must in some way face, whether we are Christians or atheists, positivists or metaphysicians, secular or religious men. For it is about the basis for distinguishing the important from the unimportant in life, the superficial from the significant, a distinction we must make in some way every time we make a decision, and which becomes of crucial importance whenever we seek to formulate policies and plans for the future, whether they be for ourselves and our families or for the larger social or political institutions for which we have some responsibility. I do not mean to say that every time we make a decision or formulate a policy we do so, or should do so, with "God" in mind; I do insist that on every such occasion we discriminate between the more and the less important, and such discriminations are always made in terms of some (perhaps often unconscious) scales of value or reality. The question about God is the question about the ultimately real, about that which is the source and basis of all else. It is, therefore, about what consitutes the real *as* real. To suppress this question is to fail to face clearly the basis on which we are making our choices, and thus to be all the more at the mercy of concealed powers and values rather than masters of our own decisions. In contrast, to ask this question openly and self-consciously—Who is God? What is God? What is the ultimate reality with which we have to do?—is to face up as clearly and as consciously and as rationally as we can to the issue of what is of lasting importance.

The word "God" more than any other in English brings us face to face with this issue. We have no other single words that so directly emphasize it, though some phrases can be used for this purpose. For example, we may ask ourselves what we regard as of "ultimate importance," or of "highest significance," or of "deepest meaning," or as "most real." But such phrases simply begin with a relatively commonplace distinction, of the important or the significant or the real, and with the aid of an adjective such as "highest" or "most" they focus our attention on this distinction raised to a superlative degree. In such phrases we are dealing simply with extensions of the ordinary, relatively superficial, discriminations that we make from day to day, and we are not forced to face directly the question whether there is one final or ultimate court of appeal to which all such distinctions are ordered. The word "God" on the other hand, being the proper name for that One who in the West has been regarded as the source and foundation of all else, directs us immediately away from the multiplicities and qualities of everyday experience—even raised to a superlative degree—and faces us with the question of the One ultimate or fundamental reality with which we have to do. In a unique way it thus orders all our distinctions and discriminations to itself and leads us to ask whether the ordering we have given the realities we experience is appropriate or false. Since "God" designates the Source of all else, if we use it seriously we never dare stop critically questioning our judgments about the real or the important until we have pushed back to the level of reality which unifies and gives order to all the rest, which assigns to every other dimension or level or quality its proper place, to that which can in some sense be properly regarded as "the Creator and Ruler of the Universe."

It is important to note again that our procedure here has not required us to "believe" in the Christian or the Jewish God; nor have we been asked to take up a "religious" position (in the sense of Chapter 9). We have not concerned ourselves at all with the *content* of a doctrine of God that had to be believed true before we could begin. We have looked rather at the *question* the word "God" poses for anyone who understands it (whether he is a believer or not), the question about the one ultimate Source of all that is. It could be said that we have been attending to the *formal* rather than the *material* aspects of the meaning of the word. Whether we will answer this question in terms of the Christian doctrine of God, or the Marxist doctrine of the dialectical process of history, or the materialist doctrine of atoms and the void, or by reference to some other metaphysical or theological conception remains at this point completely undetermined and open. But the term itself, when taken seriously, leads us to pose explicitly and openly the issues about what is genuinely important and real in a way and with a force we might otherwise overlook. To be concerned about God, as Paul Tillich has long insisted, is to be concerned about what it is that is ultimately worth being concerned about—and that is a question well worth raising, whatever the answer we might finally decide to give. Being about the fundamental principles and priorities that order all our activities, it is of prime significance for the conduct of our lives here and now in this world. It is a question, therefore, of genuinely *secular* importance. All of us, whether we count ourselves secular men or religious, recognize clearly that when someone uses the word "God" seriously, or asks about God with seriousness, it is precisely about the ultimate reality with which we have to do and the ultimate meaning of our lives as human beings that he is asking. Since the word "God" poses these issues for us more clearly than any other in the language, the possibilities for understanding ourselves and our experience are hampered if we deliberately avoid its use in our secular reflection and education.

II

The word "God" not only poses the question of ultimate reality or importance; it also raises the issue of value and worth. As we have seen, it designates "the One object of supreme adoration," that which is most attractive to us, the worth of which draws us and evokes a willingness to give ourselves in complete devotion. It suggests, as few other words in the language, an ultimate unity of being and value, what is and what ought to be. For Western traditions God has been understood as gracious, loving, just, in short, as good, and as the source of all goodness in life. It has undoubtedly been difficult to maintain these emphases in face of the manifest evil in the world and in consistency with the claims about eternal torment or hell visited upon those who disobey the divine will. But these matters have always been understood primarily as difficulties or problems that had to be interpreted in the light of God's goodness; they were not often held to call into question the goodness of God itself. The powerful monotheistic thrust in Judaeo-Christian faith has demanded that *all* reality, value as well as being, be rooted in the One ultimate reality, so all of life—life in its striving and aspiring as well as in its bare existence—could be centered in him.

Once again it is clear we need not be believers to sense this meaning in the word "God" as it has been handed down in the language, and we need not be believers to feel the question it poses. Perhaps the issue can be stated most easily if we recall briefly the humanistic interpretation of value that is frequently given. In this view it is acknowledged that our being—at least in its physical and organic aspects—is rooted in nature and must be continually sustained by natural physical and organic processes, but it is claimed that man himself creates the value and meaning of life, which belong to culture rather than nature. Man has created the cultural world in which justice and truth, beauty and goodness, as well as evil and error, have come into being; man, therefore, must maintain and enhance that which makes life worth living, which makes it uniquely human and good, and he is responsible to no one beyond himself. If he destroys himself through stupidity or imprudence, so much the worse for him; if he creates a heaven on earth, so much the better. Man is a more or less accidental product of a long and painful evolutionary process: he should make the most of his brief existence on earth and build as good a life for himself and his fellows as he can.

In contrast with such a view—common enough, especially in university circles—which sees human life rooted partly in natural process, partly in man's own creativity and culture, the concept of God poses the question whether there is not an ultimate unity behind our being, a unity in which both value and existence are rooted. If this is the case, human life is not simply ours to make what we will; to find fulfillment and meaning we must conform ourselves to an order from beyond the human sphere. Our intuitions of value and truth are not the ultimate court of appeal, but must themselves be judged and evaluated by reference to the source and ground of the worthful and true. The anthropocentric orientation of much that we are and much that we do is called into question.

It may seem that such a severe limiting of human autonomy in fact cripples and frustrates human life, that man should throw off bondage to a God who inhibits him, exercising his freedom and creativity with courage and passion. It is a popular claim made by Nietzsche, Hartmann, Sartre, and others that the idea of God is a threat to human freedom and that for precisely this reason it must be rejected if man is to come into his own. But that is of course just the question: is human fulfillment *created* by man *ex nihilo* out of his own freedom, or is it *discovered* as man orients himself in accord with an order of worth and meaning from beyond? I am not attempting here to prejudice the answer to that question in any way. I am simply concerned to emphasize that, whether we are believers or unbelievers, this issue is posed most sharply and clearly in serious contemplation of what is mediated by the idea of God— as the examples of Sartre and Nietzsche themselves show; this concept, therefore, enables us to face most directly the question whether human life should be oriented primarily on men's desires and value intuitions, or whether these must be relativized by something beyond them. In this respect the notion of God—a transcendent will conceived as the "Ruler of the Universe"—enables us to gain a certain distance from or perspective on ourselves and what we cherish. Instead of having to accept our intuitions of value and meaning simply as they are, thus in effect being subject to them rather than their master, it becomes possible to submit them to the most critical examination and appraisal. The variety of attractive goods and values may pull us in diverse directions as we sense now the claims of family responsibility, then the joys of bohemian freedom; now the unbending demands of truth and justice, then the plasticity and yielding of mercy and graciousness; now the grandeur of unswerving determination to achieve our goal no matter what the obstacles, then the glory of giving up ourselves and our desires without reservation for the sake of some cause —and this unending multiplicity of goods may threaten to pull us to pieces. In this situation it is the search for and sense of an ultimate Good behind all these penultimate values that can restore an integrity and unity to our lives that would otherwise be lacking. The monotheistic conception and quest help make possible integration of the self in face of the continuous conflict of values and goods.

I want to emphasize once more that what I am saying about the significance of the idea of God does not depend on our being believers in him. We are speaking here of a *question* that is raised for any and all of us simply by the meaning of the word: is there finally a unity of being and value in which both are grounded? This question, and its significance and ramifications, can scarcely be avoided once one considers seriously what is meant in all Western languages when one speaks of God. The word "God" requires us to reexamine critically our intuitions of value and meaning and to push on to see whether there is not some ultimate Good beyond them, by reference to which they should all be judged. In thus suggesting that the source of value and goodness is not in us but beyond us, "God" demands and makes possible a kind of self-criticism and self-transcendence that we otherwise simply could not attain. Its secular importance—its importance for self-understanding and self-criticism in *this* life—is therefore hard to overestimate. No other word in the language can put this kind of radical question mark beside our every deepest insight and highest ideal.

III

This brings us to the fundamental theological distinction posed in the word: the distinction between God and the idols, between "God" and "the gods." The claim of Western monotheism, which is encapsulated in the word "God" itself, is that our ultimate loyalty—that orientation which finally gives order and coherence to our lives—dare not be directed to any merely finite object, to any aspect of this world or this life; it must be directed to the Source of all being and life and value. To be oriented on power or money or sex, to give oneself without reservation to one's family or job or nation, to devote one's whole being to the pursuit even of such lofty (but limited) values as truth or beauty—or justice—is to develop one or another side of the self at the expense of other potentialities and aptitudes; it is thus to cripple, and in certain respects enslave, oneself. Only an orientation on the Source of all being and value will enable us to remain open to all that exists and all that is good, and thus free to develop and mature fully and creatively. Devoting oneself unconditionally to anything less than God—which is to say, devoting oneself unconditionally to anything other than God—is giving oneself to an idol and allowing oneself to be enslaved. The roots of evil in human life are to be found in just such bondage to the finite goods of life; for these are not able to meet our deepest needs, particularly the need to be free and open to the new and unanticipated. Genuine fulfillment can be found only in relation to that One who is the source of all goods that we now know or ever will encounter. As the name for that One who transcends all finite goods as their source and ground, "God" is thus used to designate that in relation to whom men can achieve genuine freedom and fulfillment; it is the name for that ultimate object of loyalty that can never be reduced to an idol and that shows all lesser objects of devotion to be idols when given a rank and loyalty they do not deserve.

In forcing us to face the distinction between God and the idols, the word "God" performs its greatest service. For this distinction gives us a critical lever on anything and everything in our world that might claim our attention and devotion. In providing a critical distance from all claims upon us—whether of family or vocation, nation or ideology—it makes possible some objective weighing of their merits. Thus it helps check our tendencies to fanaticism, on the one hand—that is, the too easy and too complete giving of ourselves to a finite cause—and our temptations to retreat into cold and barren aloofness on the other. We need not be "believers" in this or that idea of God in order to recognize and enjoy this secular service which understanding of the term itself confers. We need only grasp the formal meaning of the word: that the True God is never to be confused with any reality within our world or our experience, with anything finite; to give oneself without reservation in any finite relation is to be an idolater, and thus to have one's humanity crippled and frustrated. Understanding the significance of the question mark that the word "God" puts beside each of our finite loyalties and interests gives a leverage on life and the world that otherwise would simply not be available. Far from being of significance only to believers, or in the religious sphere of life, "God" thus enables our secular existence itself to be freer and more open and thus potentially fuller and more creative.

IV

We have devoted ourselves in this concluding chapter almost entirely to what I have called the formal meaning of the notion of God in Western culture, deliberately avoiding as far as possible its material content. However, it is never possible absolutely to separate formal from material dimensions of meaning, and it is necessary in conclusion to note briefly their connection here. The fundamental analogy or imagery that underlies Western thinking about God is personal or agential: God is grasped through such images as "lord," "father," "judge"; he is referred to with the personal pronoun "he"; he is said to love and forgive, to be faithful and just, to rule the world (which is likened in such an image to a political kingdom). The anthropomorphism of much of this biblical and Christian imagery has seemed crude and offensive to many, particularly to sensitive and sophisticated folk, and for this reason, in part, they have found it difficult to speak or think of God. I do not wish to argue these issues here, but only to observe that there is an important connection between this personalistic language and the formal problems to which we have been attending. The sharp distinction between God and the idols, which is the fundamental note in the idea of God and of considerable secular significance, depends on conceiving him as radically independent of or other than the world and everything in it, so that he can be seen in sharp contrast with everything finite. If God were simply one feature of the world, or were an extension of the world, or were dependent on the world in some fundamental way, the contrast would be lessened and the whole point of the difference between God and the idols would be weakened. Conversely, however, the world and all that is in it must be seen as radically dependent on God, as coming from him, as his creation, if he is to function as the ultimate point of reference giving order and meaning to the multiplicities and pluralities of experience: if the world were independent of God (as he is of the world), then orientation on him would be of no significance for life here and now.

The claim that God is "Creator and Ruler of the Universe" is simply an expression of this order of priorities, which gives the word "God" its peculiar character and also its significance for our secular life. The personalistic and agential overtones of such words as "creator" and "ruler," far from detracting from the meaning here, in fact make it possible; for it is in such relations as creating and ruling that we see most clearly and vividly on the finite plane the sort of one-way dependence we are seeking to express in the notion of God. The kind of deliberate power that can be exercised by human wills and intelligence over material objects (as well as over other human beings) is so much more extensive and impressive than mere physical relations of force and dependence, or vital (but blind) organic relations of part to whole or life to life, that the human person or agent provides the most obvious—and perhaps the only viable—paradigm or image in terms of which to conceive God as radically independent and autonomous, free and creative.[4] It is only natural, therefore, that the notion of God should be shot through and undergirded at every point with anthropomorphic or personalistic overtones: it could hardly perform in any other way its function of giving us sufficient perspective on this world and its goods to make possible discerning the problem and danger of idolatry.

In this essay, noting that the word "God" has recognized meaning quite independently of its use by believers, and that we all, in learning English, have acquired the rudiments of

[4] See Chapters 3, 4, and 6, above.

that meaning, I have argued that the word has considerable secular utility because of the questions it poses. These can give us a critical distance and perspective, which are available in no other way, on the realities and values of life. The word "God" therefore, and with it appropriate secular theological analysis and criticism, should not be allowed to die in our culture—not merely for the sake of religion or faith, but for the sake of our secular existence itself.

Index

Index

Act, action, 125–128, 135–136, 181; master, 136–138
Agent, 126–127, 183. *See also* Act; Man, as agent
Aldrich, V., xvi n
Anselm, 90
Anthropomorphism, 80, 157–158, 222–223, 268–269
Aquinas, 129n
Aristotle, 77n
Atheism, *see* Naturalism; Secularism
Augustine, 80n, 111n
Auschwitz, 176, 178, 184n, 192, 200
Austin, J. L., 96n, 104n
Ayer, A. J., xvii n

Barth, K., 3, 5, 20, 21, 42n, 51n, 159n, 215
Beckett, S., 41
Belief, *see* Faith
Bellah, R., 161n, 258n
Berger, P., 30n, 90n
Bergson, H., 60
Bible, *see* God, biblical view of
Blackstone, W. T., 42n
Bogen, James, 181n
Bonhoeffer, D., 215
Braithwaite, R., 99n
Brown, N. O., 215n
Buber, Martin, 41, 258
Bultmann, R., 42

Calvin, John, 112n
Camus, A., 171n
Cavell, S., xvii n, 101n, 189n
Collingwood, R. G., 204, 230, 254n
Comte, A., 44n
Cook, John W., 189n

Dante, A. C., 181n
Death-of-God movement, 8, 24, 31, 124, 226
Dilthey, W., 208n, 210n, 214n, 219n
Dualism, 42–45, 47–48, 161–162, 230–233, 252–253

Edwards, Jonathan, 112n
Eschatology, 184–185, 193–194
Events, interconnection of, 129–133, 141–142
Evil: moral and natural, 190n; problem of, 171–176, 177n, 194–195

Faith, 68–70, 93–94, 98–100, 110n, 226–229, 250, 252–253; and unfaith, 67n, 199, 227n, 245–248, 254–256; grounds of, 226–256
Farrer, A., xii n, 80n, 158n
Ferré F., 42n
Feuerbach, L., 15, 81
Fitzgerald, P. J., 181n

Florovsky, G., 234n
Freud, S., 81
Fromm, E., 13

Geertz, C., 30n
Gilkey, L., 8n, 119
God: act of, 119–147, 181–184,
    198
  analogical doctrine of, 70n
  as agent, 15, 78, 119–120,
    124–125, 148–153, 180–
    184, 269
  as Creator, 90–91, 193–194,
    230–231, 252–253
  as Infinite, 67–68, 69n
  as Magician, 181–184
  as moral, 106, 111n, 113–
    114, 175
  as personal, 60–68, 93, 149–
    153, 157–160, 252, 268–
    269
  as presupposition (of action),
    105–113, 239–240, 254–
    256
  as symbol, 107, 109–114
  as transcendent reference
    point, 33–34, 265–269
  "available" and "real," 85–
    88, 92, 95–99, 150–151,
    169n
  biblical view of, 61–62, 113–
    114, 119–120, 128, 137,
    179–180, 182–183
  encounter with, 66–69, 160,
    239–240
  hiddenness of, 12–13, 80–81,
    85–86, 158–159
  Jesus as paradigm of, 147,
    165, 168, 241
  knowledge of, 66–67, 71, 78–
    81, 139, 149–153, 159–
    166, 237–242
  omnipotence of, 177–183
  proofs of, 86–87, 99–100,
    226–227, 243, 254–256
  revelation of, 66–67, 71, 78–
    79, 148–170, 221, 240–
    241; see also Revelation
  sovereignty of, 91, 146–147,
    196–198; see also

  Providence
  transcendence of, see
    Transcendence, God's
  See also Death-of-God
    movement; Faith;
    Idolatry; Providence;
    Theism; Theodicy;
    Theology
"God," meaning of, 7, 82–88,
    90–96, 230–232, 257–270
Goffman, E., 90n

Hamlyn, D. W., 181n
Hammarskjöld, D., 217
Hampshire, S., 64n
Hartmann, N., 265
Hartshorne, C., 129n
Harvey, V. A., 132n
Hegel, G. W. F., 15
Heidegger, M., 46, 79n, 217
Heilsgeschichte, see History,
    theistic view of
Heimbeck, R. S., 9n, 42n, 96n
Hepburn, R. W., 80n
Hick, John, 96n, 177n, 188n
History: modern view of, 123,
    131–133, 141–142; theistic
    view of, 137–140, 142–147,
    162–164, 167–168, 184–185,
    197–198
Hugh of St. Victor, 112n
Humanism, 162, 164, 165, 264.
    See also Naturalism;
    Secularism
Hume, David, 47n, 151n

Idolatry, 82, 266–268
Irenaeus, 188n

Jaspers, K., 51
Jesus, 23, 143, 145, 165, 168,
    241
Job, 12, 194
Jonas, H., 231n

Kant, I., 55n, 59n, 101n, 109n,
    114n, 122, 130, 134, 151n,
    203, 213n
Kierkegaard, S., 6, 13, 98n
Kuhn, T. S., 101n, 243n

Laing, R. D., 83n, 154n
Language, *see* Man, as symbol-user
Lee, A. R., 83n, 154n
Levi-Strauss, C., 90n
Limit, limitedness, 46–60, 64–67
Luckmann, T., 30n, 90n

McLain, M., xiii–xviii, 145n
Macmurray, J., 73n, 138n
Malcolm, N., 189n
Man: as agent, 33–34, 100–109; *see also* Agent; as historical, 186–192; *see also* Self, as historical; as symbol-user, 48, 89–90, 101–104, 154–155; finitude of, 46–60, 150–153, 158–159. *See also* Persons; Self
Mascall, E. L., 77n
Materialism, 59–60, 105n
Melden, A. I., 181n, 189n
Metaphysics: and faith, 60–61; purpose of, 102–104. *See also* World-views
Mill, J. S., 112n
Miracle, 121, 130n, 177–178, 183–184
Mythology, 42–44, 48–51, 70, 161–163

Naturalism, 162, 164, 176, 210–213, 251–252. *See also* Humanism; Secularism
Nature, natural order, 93, 120–123, 130, 132–133, 138–139, 141–142
Neo-orthodoxy, 3–5, 20–24, 26
Niebuhr, H. R., 5
Nietzsche, F., 41, 217, 265

O'Brien, G., 174n
Otherworld, *see* Dualism; Mythology
Otto, R., 68, 218

Paul, 111n
Peirce, C. S., 113n
Pepper, S., 99n, 206n

Persons: and things, xiv–xv, 73–74; knowledge of, xiv–xviii, 63–66, 73–75, 149–150, 152–156, 159. *See also* Man; Self
Phenomenology, *see* Religion, science of
Phillipson, H., 83n, 154n
Pike, N., 188n
Plotinus, 77n
Price, H. H., 94n, 107n
Providence, 146–147, 162–163, 193–194. *See also* God, sovereignty of

Relativism, *see* Self, as historical; World-views
Religion, 29–30, 90, 161, 209, 214–218; science of, 17–19, 32–34
Revelation, xiv–xviii, 73–75, 148–170. *See also* God, revelation of
Rieff, P., 215n
Right and true, 107–109
Rubenstein, R., 178n
Russell, B., 212

Sartre, J.-P., 41, 265
Schleiermacher, F., 8, 58n, 131n, 216, 218
Schutz, A., 90n
Science, *see* Naturalism; Nature; Religion, science of; World-views, secular
Secularism, 41–44, 122–124, 210–213. *See also* Humanism; Naturalism
Seeing-as, 96, 109n, 110n
Self: as historical, 186–189, 229, 235–236, 243–245, 249; finitude of, 46–60; inwardness of, xiii–xviii, 63–64, 73–75, 149–150, 159, 220. *See also* Man; Persons
Slater, P., 110n
Smart, J. J. C., 255n
Smart, N., 191n
Sociology of religion, *see* Religion
Strawson, P. F., xiii, xvi

Theism, 209, 214–215, 219–
   223, 252–253. *See also*
   Faith; History, theistic view of
Theodicy, 173–176, 194–199
Theology, 17–37, 87–88, 168,
   179n; as a perspective, 25–
   32; as practical not
   speculative, 100–113;
   method(s) of, 6–7, 20–35,
   78–81
Tillich, P., xii n, 5, 8, 22, 65n,
   77n, 81, 82, 215–217, 263
Transcendence, 72–81, 161–
   162; God's, 15, 64–67, 72,
   76–81, 158–159, 266–268;
   interpersonal, 63–67, 73–
   81; teleological, 75–81
Troeltsch, E., 132

Unamuno, M. de, vii
Unfaith, *see* Faith, and
   unfaith

Van Buren, Paul, 42n
Van der Leeuw, G., 218n
Virgin birth, 130n

White, A. R., 126n
Whitehead, A. N., 60, 129n,
   133n
Wisdom, J., 96n
Wittgenstein, L., xvi, 96n, 104n,
   109n, 189n
World, 203, 206–207
World-view(s), 203–208, 224–
   225; secular, 210–213, 251.
   See also Humanism;
   Naturalism; Secularism;
   religious, 209, 214–218; *see
   also* Religion; theistic, 209,
   214–215, 219–223, 252–253;
   see also Faith; History,
   theistic view of
Wright, G. E., 119n, 179n

Ziff, Paul, 84n, 92n, 102n